more praise for

infinite tuesday

"In his memoir, *Infinite Tuesday*, the highlights of [Nesmith's] career speak for themselves. . . . Jimi Hendrix, who supported the Monkees on their first tour, got the Monkees; John Lennon got the Monkees; Zappa did too. These countercultural icons understood the genius of its premise—simultaneously celebrating and satirizing popular culture, fabricating a faux-Beatlemania to rival Beatlemania itself—and recognized its brilliant execution."

—*Wall Street Journal*

"The Monkees were the beginning for me; the amazing thing is they were only the beginning for Mike Nesmith. This is the way a genius lives life right. Great stories of his buddies Hendrix, Timmy Leary, and Douglas Adams, adventures while inventing the music video and changing home video, yogis in California, VR, and why you should never complain about the air-conditioning on a private jet. Nez inspired me when I was thirteen and now with this book he continues to inspire me at sixty-one."

—Penn Jillette of Penn & Teller

"You know it's a good book when you quote lines and anecdotes from it, and claim them as your own. *Infinite Tuesday* is fascinating and funny! In a word, *Nezmerizing*."

—Jack Handey, author of
Deep Thoughts and *The Stench of Honolulu*

"Mike Nesmith is a pop culture spirit guide. Every creative person should take this revealing, hilarious, semi-hallucinogenic trip back in time through all the biggest cultural revolutions of the late twentieth century. Nesmith himself was a driving force in many of them. This book is honest, moving, and inspirational."

—Jay Roach, director of
Austin Powers and *Meet the Parents*

"Nesmith may be most remembered for his role as the stoic guitarist in the Monkees, but his brilliant, candid, and humorous new autobiographical musings give readers a much clearer picture of his originality and inventiveness. . . . Nesmith's entertaining memoir reveals his creative genius, his canny ability never to take himself too seriously, and his restless questions about the value of spirituality."

—*Publishers Weekly*

"*Infinite Tuesday* is a picnic in forward motion. The table is full of gems, big and small, and studded throughout with a full cast of characters. I am already looking for volume two and, please, let there be one."

—Ed Ruscha

"Nesmith is an artist, adventurer, and thinker whose nimble creativity soared far above the appellation he was given: 'the smart Monkee.' In *Infinite Tuesday*, he details the inner forces, from personal to spiritual, that kept him forging ahead—and that created stumbling blocks as well. Unsparing and revealing, this book is an unusual, unforgettable read."

—Ben Fong-Torres

"Nesmith is witty and ironic and has a fund of amazing and often absurd stories. *Infinite Tuesday* is unlike any other music or movie autobiography."

—Alex Cox, director of *Repo Man*

infinite tuesday

MICHAEL NESMITH

infinite tuesday

An Autobiographical Riff

CROWN
NEW YORK

Published in the United States by Crown, an imprint of Random House,
a division of Penguin Random House LLC, New York.
crownpublishing.com

Crown and its colophon are registered trademarks of
Penguin Random House LLC.

Originally published in hardcover in the United States by
Crown Archetype, an imprint of the Crown Publishing Group,
a division of Penguin Random House LLC, New York, in 2017.
Subsequently published in paperback in the United States by
Three Rivers Press, an imprint of Random House, a division of
Penguin Random House LLC, New York, in 2018.

Photography credits can be found on page 305.

Library of Congress Cataloging-in-Publication Data
Names: Nesmith, Michael.
Title: Infinite Tuesday / Michael Nesmith.
Description: First edition. | New York : Crown Archetype, [2017]
Identifiers: LCCN 2016058926 | ISBN 9781101907504 (hardcover) |
ISBN 9781101907511 (pbk.) | ISBN 9781101907528 (ebook)
Subjects: LCSH: Nesmith, Michael. | Rock musicians—United States—
Biography. | LCGFT: Autobiographies.
Classification: LCC ML420.N456 A3 2017 | DDC 782.42166092 [B]—dc23
LC record available at https://lccn.loc.gov/2016058926

ISBN 978-1-101-90751-1
Ebook ISBN 978-1-101-90752-8

Cover design by Christopher Brand
Cover photograph by Michael Putland / Hulton Archive / Getty Images

146122990

THIS BOOK IS AFFECTIONATELY DEDICATED TO:

Buttercup
Dielan
Sweetrib
Boomer
Frack
Spot
Isaiah
Abigail
Lilly
Fritz
Roy
&
Dale

. . . AND TO ALL THE OTHER FAITHFUL COMPANIONS OF THE WORLD—YOU KNOW WHO YOU ARE.

contents

infinite tuesday

preface

Amarcord is the title of my favorite film by my favorite filmmaker, Federico Fellini. It is an Italian word that, loosely translated, means "I remember." But that is not all there is to it.

The word describes something ineffable. I have not found a sentence that completely wraps around it. So it is with this book.

There are books that keep meticulous and well-researched timelines on their subject. This is not one of them. This is not to say there is fiction here. I am committed to the facts as I know them, but I am aware that I remember them only one way.

I accept that although my memories seem to come from the past, in reality they don't. They come from the present, remembered not as they were but as they are.

Each remembrance here marks a place where a *band* formed—a band of colleagues, a band of players, a band of thieves, a band of ideas—ephemeral, burning bright, then dispersing as unpredictably as it had formed. In these fleeting moments, lives changed, ideas were conceived, far horizons brought into view.

A band breaks up, but the gathering exists forever in its effect and becomes foundational. Seen through the altitude of mind, these bands, these gatherings, these bouquets are both the footprints and constellations of our lives.

Even though the spheres of remembrance tend to keep the meanings of these connections separate and distinct, they are not. One can see from a certain height the universe as a world of ideas that are interconnected in ways that are hard to explain directly.

My hope is that this book opens a door into the present and that you will laugh a lot—even though this is not meant primarily to be a funny book. From these threads, perhaps one may see how to weave their own fabric, to recollect and gaze at their own tapestry.

I

There is no principle of causality in a mere sequence. That one thing follows another accounts for nothing. Nothing follows from following except change.

—Marshall McLuhan, paraphrasing David Hume

"I keep thinking it's Tuesday."

I was having lunch with Timothy Leary in the late 1980s at a little sidewalk café near Sunset and Gower in Hollywood, California. Tim was famous for, among other things, encouraging everyone to take LSD and drop out of school in the 1960s. From there he took it on the lam from Harvard, where he had been a professor, and spent the next couple of decades running, in and out of prison, writing a book—*The Politics of Ecstasy*, published in 1968—lecturing, leading, explaining while waving his arms and balancing on the point of a spear. Maybe it was a spear he was wielding; maybe it was at his back. In any case he was always one step ahead.

I very much liked him, and we had become a bit more than

acquaintances. He was mature by then, trim and fit, with a big smile, and still handsome enough to turn the head of every third woman who passed by. He had an intellect like a switchblade, and he was ruthlessly direct, so I was always very careful around him: careful to be precise and clear, careful to think through my answers to his questions, and careful to listen. He once publicly chided me for using a cliché. The cliché was apt for the situation, but it was a cliché, and he was right to take me down for it.

During this lunch, we were talking about priorities and motivation. I asked how old he'd been when he started thinking about the order of importance of life's big questions.

Early high school, he said.

Next question: What was the hierarchy? What was your quest, the most important thing to you, then?

"The same thing that is most important to everyone in their teens," he said. "'What do other people think of me?'" That was at the top of his list. Number two was similar: "How do I look?"

Given that Leary had rearranged the priorities and aims of a generation, these were startling answers. I was delighted by them. Those had been exactly my priorities as a kid. Vanity, thy name is teenager. I laughed hard, and he did too, when he told me how worry defined interest and how widespread and idiotic was the dynamic that set so many of life's agendas.

Such a notion took a lot of courage to confess—the same kind of courage it took to tell everyone to take LSD and drop out. *Courage* is maybe not the exact word, but it is as close as I can get to describing the kind of propellant that guys like Leary burned.

Douglas Adams, the author of many radio and television shows, movies, and books, most notably *The Hitchhiker's Guide to the Galaxy*, was another friend I paid careful attention to. We were close, and I dearly loved the man. He careened around ideas with a kind of flat-out open speed that made him take the corners off things. He was very funny as a writer and even more hilarious in person, especially when describing an object right after having knocked the corner off it, like when he explained how hard it is to move a sofa up an apartment stair if it gets stuck between two dimensions.

Douglas and I became extremely close during the last ten years of his life, in the 1990s. I learned early to never get in a car he was driving. When I say "I learned," I mean to say I learned I should know better, but I did it anyway and it was terrifying every time. He had a very fast Mercedes and drove like a maniac, more interested in what was going on inside the car than out. In the same way that *courage* doesn't quite describe the governing impulse of Leary's powerful stances, *careen* doesn't quite describe Douglas's driving, or his astounding thought processes.

I mentioned Leary's hierarchy of teenage priorities to Douglas one afternoon, and he laughed too. He confessed he'd had the same set of pursuits.

At a dinner with some friends later, Douglas began one of his stories, which usually quieted any table—not only because they were fascinating but because they normally took at least an hour to tell. This one built slowly, and my attention built with it.

He was talking about his sense of humor and how it had developed. When he was kid, he said, he had these notions of what was funny but found no one to share them with. Then, one day, he saw a cartoon by Paul Crum that changed his life.

I didn't say anything then, but I sat up straight. I too had seen a cartoon by Paul Crum that changed my life.

With a mixture of glee and somber respect, Douglas described the cartoon as a turning point of sorts that had faced him in the direction his life would take. Two hippos are standing in the middle of a river, in the middle of nowhere, surrounded by an empty expanse of nature. One says to the other, "I keep thinking it's Tuesday."

It was the exact cartoon I'd seen, and I'd had the same reaction to it. At that dinner, Douglas made the same points about the same cartoon that I had made to myself. The cartoon was a window into a playground where other people thought as we did, and it had become the dead reckon for both of us. It showed me that someone else shared my sense of humor and my sense of absurdity. Douglas said the same thing, and for both of us it was a world changer.

The cartoon had been published on July 21, 1937, in the British magazine *Punch*. Neither Douglas nor I would have seen it then. It came to each of us at its own pace; we found it in our own way and time.

After dinner, I told Douglas of the connection, and he smiled almost knowingly. He said it was simply the nature of evolution for us to have a point of connection that spanned decades, and that it revealed a sodality of large and mystical proportions. Douglas was an avowed atheist and a hardline evolutionist, so he knocked the corners off this sodality the way he did most things, fitting it to his own worldview.

Throughout my life I have stumbled time and again upon these far-flung connections between me and others—always to my delight and surprise, always filling in another piece of life's puzzle. They trace a reticulation that is the stuff of dreams, outside the explanatory reach of anthropology, beyond fraternities or institutions or career paths. They are expressed most precisely by Tom Stoppard's definition of laughter: "the sound of comprehension."

At every conjunction of this colligation there is a resounding and deep laugh to be had. There is recognition. It's the laugh of the shared cosmic moment when we see it. Adams, like Leary, was immersed in playing the same game that I was, on the same pitch with the same goal.

In Douglas's slight smile that evening, there was the shared life of the secret society—of a satisfied and slightly smart-aleck family.

I grew up in Dallas, Texas, but I left for good when I was twenty. My girlfriend, Phyllis Barbour, was pregnant, my biological family would not have understood, and I wanted to write and sing songs and make my living in the arts. The relatives were lovely people—for the most part sweet and good, with an occasional thug among the cousins for spice and murder—but art seemed a low priority among them.

My mother, Bette, was a standout, strikingly beautiful with flaming red hair, but she had pulled herself away from the biological family to a small degree, mostly by the nature of her extreme financial success. She had invented Liquid Paper, a typewriter correction fluid, and would grow it into an international business worth millions. Eventually, she would sell it to another huge corporation for a great deal of money.

The relatives were proud but seemed a bit confused by her. She attributed all the success of her business and her great good fortune to her study and practice of Christian Science, which was a far cry from the Southern Christian theology of her upbringing.

I felt some of her connection to the religion—especially the teachings of the illusions of a mortal dream, the unreality of the senses' picture—but not like she did. I had been raised in the teachings, and I could see why she had given her all to Christian Science and could understand the great debt of gratitude she felt for it. But the ideas had come to my mother as a revelation and she was devoted, whereas I had been exposed to the ideas intellectually and did not share the moment of conversion with her.

I was nevertheless surprised to see how the teachings created such a distance between us and our biological relatives. We were not estranged exactly, just not good company. I think it was worse for me than it was for my mother. Having lived her whole life among the relatives, she was more comfortable in their company than I was; she was accustomed to feeling set apart from them. For me, the divide was more unsettling. As the artist Louise Nevelson once famously said, in her family "you could know Beethoven, but God forbid if you *were* Beethoven." That's how it was in our family; they labeled some aspirations as loony, and those labels were abrasions to my nascent sense of how one might pursue the arts.

My girlfriend being pregnant, and our being unmarried, exacerbated the problem of relations among relatives, so Phyllis and I quickly married and fled to California. The choice of location was more about the weather than the art scene. New York, the other possibility, just seemed too cold, so California it was. I was to learn that weather choices in life are some of the more profound.

Up until then I wasn't writing anything, but the pressure of my new circumstances—being on my own with a new wife and, soon, a child to support—threw me into a well of woe I did not understand as a young man. I wanted to make a living playing and singing. I had no idea such a life would be so strange and so painful. I started writing songs to explain the pain away. Those early songs were crude, but they provided a way for me to turn melancholy into relief.

I had a nice guitar, a gift from my mother and stepfather at the time, but the ring finger on my right hand was ankylosed, so I was not a very good player and likely never would be. Before the move I could neither read nor write music. I couldn't even write prose for that matter. Writing was a mystery. Phrases turned in my mind, but it had never occurred to me to write them down. I cared too much about what other people thought of me.

In the California sunshine, my first priority became finding food and shelter, but the idea that I would attempt to do that by pursuing this barely present skill didn't faze me. It seemed like a reachable goal. I started making stuff up to write songs about. I didn't realize at the time that in that act I was making up the rest of my life.

When Pygmalion created Galatea, he carved her from ivory, a substance of some permanence and inherent beauty, because she was his ideal, and because he wanted *her* to have permanence and beauty, to come to life. Under the governance of others' opinions, and our need for food, clothing, and money, I ignorantly started carving my ideal from sand. However hard she may have tried, Aphrodite could never have breathed life into that, and neither could I.

What could I do? Constrained by the impressions of my childhood surroundings and stuck inside a culture whose walls I could not see over or find a way through, I was locked in Leary's hierarchy of priorities: What do people think of me? How do I look? I didn't know I was locked in at the time, but so what—as Lord Buckley said, there I jolly well was.

I decided the easiest thing to do was to copy Bob Dylan. He may have been a copy himself, but in those times it was hard to tell and it didn't matter anyway. To my mind, the operative notion was find something to sing and play, even if I didn't have anything to say.

Dylan was a Greenwich Village folksinger with a harmonica on a neck brace and a way with words—the reference standard for folk singer-songwriters of the times. I admired his persona and the lilt of his lyrics, although I would often lose the drift of his thought. Still, I liked the way he sang, and it was an easy reach for me. I couldn't carry a tune, and his MO seemed like a good workaround for a singer of my limited ability.

I didn't sing Dylan's songs. I couldn't. But I started to learn simple old-time folk tunes that were easier to sing, and these would usually cause enough of a stir to get me a folksinging job. Songs like "Wreck of the Old 97" and "Banks of the Ohio" were low-hanging fruit and fit well with my simple guitar skills and Texas drawl. If needed, I could intensify the drawl to ludicrous levels to fit the origin of the tune; the more backwoods the sentiment, the stronger the twang. The songs themselves would finally redeem all that, since they were the legacy of real people who had lived a version of my times, however far removed it might have seemed. There was a connection of substance.

Then, in February 1964, Phyllis and I watched the Beatles on *Ed Sullivan*. It was shattering, an indescribable experience—not unique in the times of man, certainly, but unique in ours. The Beatles' appearance on *Sullivan* was media curiosity as tectonic shift. That first appearance had an audience of seventy-three million, and the change it wrought was profound. People's lives were altered forever. For me it not only revealed a new horizon; it marginalized the whole popular folk movement of the day and moved Dylan off to the side with it.

Phyllis and I, even though we had been on our way to becoming hardened folkies and traditionalists, had our sense of art and music rearranged at a basic level. This had already happened to me a bit when I replaced rock and roll, which I first heard in the late 1950s, with folk music. The pomp of Presley and the swagger of Jerry Lee had a tinge of the surreal, to my mind;

something in their presentation left the blues behind, something that left me out. Folk music was authentic and political, and the melancholy was true. Folk music had an emotional center that was deeper to me than the rock and roll of the 1950s.

The Beatles were something else again. Not only did they look spectacular, the public approbation of their music and personalities was overwhelming. What "other people thought" of them was akin to what people might have thought of benevolent extraterrestrials: awe, wonder, and unbridled delight. I was right in step with this, and I wondered silently at the music and design: How could anybody get that good?

It was almost as if the 1957 rise of rock and roll in the US had been a false dawn for 1964. It was not lost on me that Elvis and Ann-Margret made *Viva Las Vegas* in 1964 as well. *Viva Las Vegas* was an effort at having fun. The Beatles were pure joy.

What *was* lost on me was the fact that Davy Jones also appeared on that same episode of *The Ed Sullivan Show*, as part of the cast of the Broadway musical *Oliver!*, reprising his role as the Artful Dodger. Later, when he was in the Monkees with me, he remarked, utterly without irony, on watching the Beatles' performance from the wings of the theater and thinking to himself that he "might like to do that."

Davy had his highly developed abilities as a song-and-dance man to make him reasonably, if not plausibly, aspire to the same level of success as the Beatles. I had nothing. As the future unfolded, it would always seem wildly ironic to me that I was the one given credit in the press for being the "only musician" in the Monkees. Nothing was further from the truth.

Certainly I was playing folk songs, and I had a band I sometimes played with, and I wrote songs. But in all of it I was flying blind. I was thrilled that the songs I was singing and playing were working well enough to get me a little money to live on, but I was just as surprised as I was thrilled.

I fell in love with the Beatles that night in February, and I could see that a new standard had been set. But I also felt very far away from this artistry of the Beatles. It was all way out of reach for me. While they were speaking a language that captivated me, it was a language I did not understand and could not speak. I wasn't sure whether I was locked in or out, only that I had no key in either case.

Around adults I kept quiet about the Beatles, because most adults I knew did not particularly care for them. Most people over thirty mocked them and derided their playing and singing and songwriting. Unknowingly but methodically, they created the generation gap.

Other forces were at work during those times, too, far outside my own narrow sense of what was happening. Ken Kesey was building a bus for Neal Cassady to drive him and his friends across the country to meet Tim Leary and his friends. Andy Warhol was opening a can of Campbell's tomato soup in New York while Ed Ruscha was buying gas at a Standard Oil station in LA. Jimi Hendrix was playing guitar as a sideman to Little Richard on the chitlin circuit. John Lennon, when not playing or recording, was spending hours in front of his telly.

It was unthinkable to everyone who had just fought World War II that the music, the fashions, the designs, the whole cultural imperative of the victorious warriors would be torn down by their kids as if it were ugly curtains in the den. Armed with originality and invention, the youth of America would take off their clothes, tie them in knots, and toss them into vats of dye with all the colors of the rainbow, then go skinny-dipping and make love while high on grass and LSD. Put any four in a room and they would start bands like the Grateful Dead. The generation gap was deep enough that one could die from falling into it.

The early rock and roll of the 1950s was subsumed and

transformed by the rock and roll of the 1960s. How could this be? I asked a friend of mine at the time why he thought the Beatles had effected such a profound change. He answered in one word: *hair.* It was a flip remark but probably truer than either of us knew. It shows how little anyone understood what had taken over.

Many said it was the new music. Many said it was the new drugs. Many said it was the new art. Many said it was television. Most said it was all of the above. Certainly these forces all came together to create the Monkees.

The paradox was that in the very middle of innovation and invention, the Monkees were a transparent concoction, a copy carefully attached to the innovators of the time only by the homage of imitation, unoriginal by every account. There was no effort to hide this artificiality, because it was a feature, not a fault. It was meant to function as a parade flag, not the parade itself. The surprise came when something so obviously created from whole cloth became an existential fact, a reality unto itself, and then created a venomous and righteous backlash that tore the flag away from the parade marshal and set it on fire.

The creators of *The Monkees* may have thought they were creating a simple television property, a paean to the times, but what they were actually producing was Pinocchio. The show and all its parts and characters would come to life and begin to breathe and move and sing and play and write and think on their own. What had started as a copy of the 1960s became a fact of the 1960s. What had started as fanciful effect became causal fact.

Bert Schneider and Bob Rafelson were the producers of *The Monkees.* They had been given the keys to take Bert's dad's car for a spin. Bert's dad was Abe Schneider, and the car was Columbia Pictures, where Abe was president. The joyride turned out to be a script for a television show based loosely on *A Hard*

Day's Night. Paul Mazursky and Larry Tucker, who wrote the pilot, carefully watched all the new moves of youth and dutifully put them in that first script.

The show angered Beatles fans in America, the tie-dyed rock and rollers, sending them into fits of dismissive repulsion. It also created a sub-generation gap, an echo of the larger one. This one was between older and younger siblings. If the seventeen-to-twenty-year-old Beatles fan and serious music lover loathed the Monkees as a cheap copy, the nine-to-twelve-year-old television baby thought they were a matter of fact. Their television set was coming to life, just as they had thought it might. Older brothers and sisters might shout them down, but the preteens recognized their own reality, even if they couldn't explain it.

In LA I had landed a job as the MC of the Monday night hootenannies at a club called the Troubadour, just before the bottom completely fell out of the folk boom. These were gatherings of folksingers sharing songs with one another. The owner of the Troub paid me ten dollars for the night and let me play a song. As Hootmaster, I also got to pick the acts that went onstage. My playing kept improving and so did my rhymes. The twang would also get me through "Pick a Bale of Cotton," to the amusement of some.

In the meantime, I was watching a cultural revolution far from the mainstream, without any idea of how to get in—watching from a backwater shore the lights of a party boat as it passed. I felt sure it was leaving me behind.

Little did I know.

Shortly after I got the job as MC I replaced it with a job playing high school assemblies in all the tiny towns of Texas. I played Victoria. I played Falfurrias. I played Van Horn. All in all around forty cities, none of them large. Even though it was remote territory, I saw that television was rearranging this landscape as it was the entire country. There was reverence for this new medium but essentially no reverence for the past. Originality was the currency. The past was worthless.

I had gone out to do these small-town shows with a bass-player friend, John Kuehne (pronounced *Kee*-nee), whom I met at San Antonio College around the same time I met my wife, Phyllis. John started playing stand-up bass behind my solo guitar, and the two of us made a nice tight sound. He had moved to LA when Phyllis and I did and lived with us in a tiny two-bedroom apartment in North Hollywood. When I got the jobs in Texas, John and I hit the road together.

The traveling was hard enough. The tiny Texas towns we played were thirty to fifty miles apart, and we played three to five shows a day. The shows consisted of a set of old folk tunes and some children's songs, and one song I had written before I left Hollywood: "Pretty Little Princess." It was a simple ballad and not a very good song, and I can't remember it well, but the effect it had on the school assemblies was bewildering. After a verse or two, the girls in the school would start screaming like the girls who chased the Beatles, and the principal and teachers would start sweating and, more often than not, would panic, pull me off the stage, and shove me out the window of a teachers' lounge into a parking lot, where I would make a run for the car.

This happened a couple of times a week, and to this day I have no real idea what caused the stir, but it was pretty easy to see the Beatles' influence in the behavior of the kids around anyone with a guitar making music.

It had taken hold almost immediately. The *Ed Sullivan* Beatles appearance had been on a Sunday, back when I still lived in Texas, and the following Monday I was in line at the cafeteria at San Antonio College, about to say hello to one of the women who worked there. I didn't know her outside that school-lunch context, and it was usually a quick, pleasant exchange—a recognition and a friendly "Hi!" On that Monday she looked at me, her mouth dropped open, her eyes got wide, and she shouted, "Oh my God, you got a Beatles haircut!"

I had done nothing of the sort; I looked exactly the same as I had since I met her. Her reaction to me registered deep: she was caught in the throes of a perception fashioned by the lightning bolt that had blasted through her TV the night before.

Now, as I stood onstage in tiny public schools on the back roads of Texas, I saw a similar transformation in the minds of the audience. When I began to sing the one song in my repertoire they could not have known, the one I wrote, they saw me with new eyes. Beatlemania was upon them, although there was not a Beatle in sight.

In Corpus Christi, Texas, the local radio station began reporting sightings of me as I did some grocery shopping, and a slow buzz started over the airwaves. Kids in cars started to go where the last sighting was, and finally when I walked into a 7-Eleven, the girl at the cash register screamed and broke into tears. I was dumbfounded. She told me of the radio reports. I turned it on in the car and drove immediately to the radio station.

When I got there, the whole station crew came to a stop and stared. The station manager asked me if I was George Harrison. If the rock and roll of the 1950s was surreal, this was a psychosis of some kind. When I told the guy I was not George Harrison and wondered aloud why he would possibly think that, he threatened to call the police and have me arrested for fraud.

The axis of the earth shifted a little. I felt dizzy.

The whole tour was like that. The national atmosphere created by the advent of this new cultural dynamic was a miasma. I was in the thick of it and could barely find my way back home.

After six weeks I came back off the road in Texas a beaten

and confused man and returned to a worst-case Hollywood mugging. I found out that all the tour money I had been dutifully sending back to my "manager" had been stolen by her. The plan had been to send her the money so she could take her commission and give the rest to Phyllis. But she gave nothing to Phyllis, and when I got home Phyllis burst into tears and asked if I had some money for food. I had almost nothing, only enough to buy some baby food for Christian, our son, and a couple of bottles of beer for ourselves, the rationale being that beer was nourishing as well as a fine palliative.

A crack had opened between two dimensions, and I was caught in something I knew nothing about. On a tour to purvey early cheap-shot slave-labor and railroad folk tunes in the style of Dylan, I had encountered the hysterical praise of delusionals who thought I was George Harrison. The world had gone crazy. It was not what I had in mind when I came west, but it was what I got. I did not know where I fit, what I would do to make a living. It seemed I had chosen a trade I could not perform very well, and that I was now surrounded by thieves. I was truly frightened. I began a slow and devastating collapse, physically and mentally. As the descent steepened, I spiraled into a mixture of madness and physical illness that became a sickness of the soul, and soon became a spiritual crisis.

In the few days following my return from Texas, I wrote songs just to stay alive. Whatever the physical illness was, it did not keep me from playing, especially since I played the guitar like a drum, sort of banging on the strings and keeping time by slapping the top of the guitar. It made a lot of noise, but it wasn't what one would call musical. Nonetheless it served as a base for four new songs: I poured everything into them, all the pain and all the hope that stirred. They were the apotheosis of melancholy—pure, sweet, and simple, from a heart I did not know I had.

The spiritual illness slowly abated and with it the physical. When I was well and hearty enough, I went back to the Troubadour to see if I could get my old job back as Hootmaster. It was a Monday night and the Hootmaster who had taken over when I left for the Texas dates was none too happy to see me. At least he let me play.

I took the opportunity to play the four songs I had written, completely abandoning my goofy Dylan impressions and diving deep into the cool pools of my own soul—and then something entirely new in my life happened. After each song the applause increased, and by the end of the short set, the place went up in smoke: cheers and yells and stomping. Cries for more rang out repeatedly but were useless, because the only other songs I knew were the twenty-eight-verse folk tunes I sang in Texas, and I wasn't going to spoil this outpouring by singing an arcane train-wreck song.

The four songs I sang were "Different Drum," "Nine Times Blue," "Propinquity," and "Papa Gene's Blues." The audience's approval and acknowledgment were overwhelming. It was nothing like the screams of the confused adolescents in Texas. This was real understanding and encouragement from a crowd I knew to be authentic music lovers and connoisseurs. I discovered a reciprocity between performer and performee, the actor and the audience, that was a balance. The audience and I were in the same mental space; they listened and cheered while I poured out the songs, both from the same standpoint of understanding. Stoppard's comprehension was now Stoppard's cheer as well.

I smiled in deep gratitude, waved good night, and ambled off the stage. Randy Sparks, the owner and manager of a folk-singing show group called the New Christy Minstrels, came up to me as I walked off the stage and offered me a publishing deal on the spot. I asked if I could borrow twenty dollars until I signed the deal, and then I asked how much he would give me for the songs' publishing.

He said yes, and six hundred dollars.

It was all the money in the world to me then, and it was falling right into my pocket because of the songs I sang and the way I sang them. It would feed Phyllis and Christian. It would save me from drowning. Indeed, it would at that moment validate my entire existence.

The earth's axis squeaked into alignment.

It would not be until decades later, at the Leary lunch where we discussed priorities, that I would become aware of the range of forces at work on this wonderful night at the Troub, but I knew something was up, even if I didn't know what.

When I showed up that night I was broke, financially and emotionally. I cared nothing about how I looked or what anyone thought of me. I had gone out that night to sing for rescue, solace, to heal myself with my own songs and voice. To search for something real I could depend on. Anything would have worked, as long as it was genuine. I had come to the end of the rope of games. I had given up looking for anything, since I didn't know what to look for, and what I found was my own voice.

Randy gave me the twenty bucks; I shook his hand and agreed to show up the next morning at his offices. The New Christy Minstrels were a cash machine for him and his publishing company; he had seen the opportunity in arranging old public-domain songs and claiming a copyright. My new songs were part of his venture into original material as a publisher.

One of his employees at the publishing company, Barry Friedman, helped set me up with contracts and such and showed me an office where I could take my guitar and write.

It was only a few months later that Barry came in one morning and showed me an ad in *Variety*. It was a casting call for *The*

Monkees, a TV show. They were about to go into production on the pilot, and Barry encouraged me to go try out.

There is a moment during certain interactions when one notices a reaction to one's own action, a non-time moment, exponentially faster than the speed of light, which sets the stage for the future. It is an incidence and its unexpected coincidence, a strange lattice indeed, with no outline or any obvious organization. It is more like a neural net, or a star field, or the Internet. It is the moment of choice framed by the internal question "How do I react to a reaction?"

When Barry said, "You should go try out for this," I saw that latticework, that star field, and a distant star twinkling through the mind's eye. I didn't understand it or know where it would lead, but I felt I knew it now that I saw it.

Over the years I learned to listen to people like Barry Friedman, who were always around, looking in a different direction than I was, seeing things I didn't see, like the Monkees audition ad. Or when Harry Gittes gave me the screenplay for *Repo Man*. In that case, I felt I was in the presence of something unique. I was hooked after reading the first page of that script. It was something I would never have come across had it not been for Harry and his antennae. Same for Barry and his.

My mother raised me without my father. It was just the two of us. I spent a lot of time in the care of others and alone. At about the age of three I was left in a day-care school while my mother worked. In the school they had a record player. I loved the music every time they put it on and would rush to the record player and sit in front of it, close to the speaker, listening without moving. On one occasion something in the music captured me, and I stood up on the chair I had dragged in front of the record player and began to wave my arms as if I were a conductor. The conducting seemed natural to me, even though I had no understanding of what it meant.

I stood there seriously conducting the record player for a while and then became aware that the adults were all watching me. They were in a cluster gathered around a doorway, and I turned to look at them. They smiled. They waved. They looked at each other and nodded.

I remember the ideas that occurred to me at that moment. I could see how cute a three-year-old pretending to conduct an orchestra must have seemed to them. I also became aware that I had become aware of myself conducting, and in that instant the joy and rapture were gone. But even though my tiny mind was confused, I felt the presence of an influence apart from and above the amused stares of the adults. The reality of this influence felt solid and natural and dependable. It let me know that my conducting was real, from the soul, and that the self-consciousness was only the result of wondering what the little crowd of adult observers thought of me.

This force, this simple drift of thought, was, of course, the uncompromising muse, and it would be with me the rest of my life.

I did not know how much pain it would cause or just how toxic it could be to other people. I did not know it would surround me with a lifelong loneliness and render me blind in certain directions of thought. I did not feel it again for decades, until that Monday night at the Troubadour when the audience came alive and reached out with a genuine connection.

There, the audience was not amused or pleasantly diverted. Each and all of us were in the same place at the same time in the same state of mind. There, the muse was in control, bringing us all together around an idea, linking us in a lattice of coincidence, connecting us with a shared experience.

After that night at the Troubadour I was suffused with this exquisite muse, and her benevolent power lingered for days. It lingered when Barry Friedman suggested I answer the ad and perhaps try out for the Monkees. She smiled and nodded at this, so there was no hesitation from me.

It was another gift from this, my beautiful muse, beguiling and bewitching, erotic and seductive, sensitive and intelligent, powerful and gentle, who had shown me my voice and rekindled in the present the past fires of my toddler mind.

Had I also known what was about to happen I would have taken a longer look through the dream chiaroscuro, and I would have seen that this muse was not one of the nine of Greek mythology or even unique to me. This muse was wearing a clown wig and had a red rubber ball on the end of her nose.

2

The reason why our sentient, percipient, and thinking ego is met nowhere within our scientific world picture can easily be indicated in seven words: because it is itself that world picture.

—Erwin Schrödinger, *What Is Life?*

One day, while I was living in New Mexico, Douglas Adams called, as he did from time to time, to ask if he and a friend might come stay for the weekend. These calls surprised me at first, but I didn't mind them. I had come to learn that the British friends I had all shared a certain skill that made them delightful houseguests: they were all possessed of an uncanny ability to disappear a few seconds before I needed privacy and to appear the instant I wanted company.

On this particular occasion, Douglas told me he had Terry Jones, one of the Pythons, in tow. I had been an ardent Python fan ever since Phyllis introduced their show to me, and the idea of a weekend with Douglas and Terry Jones sounded like a good time. I didn't know whether to expect an evening discourse on a sofa stuck between parallel universes or a parlor game of the Summarize Proust Competition, but either one was fine with me. I told Douglas to come at once.

By this time, 1994, I was with my third wife, Victoria, and we lived on a small ranch halfway between Los Alamos and Santa Fe. It was a textbook adobe building with a set of little structures around it that served nicely as guest rooms.

The guest room I had in mind for Terry had inadvertently turned into something of a storage room for pillows and pictures and other things. Just before he and Douglas arrived, I straightened it up quickly by setting out all the stray pillows—there were a lot of them, at least twelve—in a row on the bed, sort of decorator style. They stacked more than halfway down the bed and it looked a little silly, but so did the designer style of the times, and I couldn't do much about it since I had nowhere else to put them.

Once they arrived, we had a good dinner and great conversation. It was all I had expected: Terry was a delight, we were all silly and relaxed, none of us talked of our respective professional spheres, and the conversation drifted around stars and physics and Hollywood and London society, mostly rummaging around for a good funny story, a joke, or at least a play on words. It was the model of casual, comfortable dinner conversations I have had over the years, usually with Brits in Britain.

Soon after dinner Douglas and Terry and I were off to our rooms for the night. I showed Terry to his room first, and Douglas was with us. Terry walked in, and I asked if there was anything he needed. He took a few seconds to survey the room. Finally he said, "I might like an extra pillow."

For a nanosecond I panicked. All the pillows I had were in the room. I said I would go look around, but Terry reached out and touched my arm and I saw the twinkle in his eyes. Douglas laughed, and then I did too.

I learned this was a particularly British skill: to be so believable in the delivery that when the irony dawns it is twice as funny. Over the years, many of my British friends have remarked that England is the only nation that offers a college degree in sarcasm. I knew many Brits over the years who could have had such a degree, and that characteristic was one of the main reasons I became an ardent Anglophile.

I wasn't always so attuned to the scene in England. It was Phyllis who had first made me aware of the Beatles and their influence in 1963, months before their first Sullivan appearance. She was an avid reader who not only digested classic novels regularly but also kept up with the news. She told me the Beatles were going to be on TV and that we should watch it. She had followed their career for some time at that point through the world's papers, which were treating the fans' reaction to the Beatles as big news.

At the time I lived in a little garage apartment in back of a large house within walking distance of San Antonio College, where I was taking classes, and I didn't have a TV. I had only a bed, a chest of drawers, and a desk next to a bathroom. I made money for college by reading to my landlady's son, George Paschal, who lived in the large house with his mother. He was blind and working on his PhD in history, and he needed to get through a stack of books for his degree. So I read to him for a dollar an hour and rent on the apartment.

The Paschals did have a television and I had taken to having cocktails with George and his mother while we all watched the evening news. Chet Huntley and David Brinkley would be reporting, and as George listened to their commentary I'd describe for him the pictures that accompanied the sound.

With the Beatles' *Ed Sullivan* appearance approaching, I decided to ask George's mother if Phyllis and I could watch it on their TV, and she said sure, if it wouldn't bother George. George said he would like to see the Beatles as well, which meant he wanted me to call the play-by-play.

By this time, the Beatles were starting to show up on American magazine covers. The excitement of the *Sullivan* appearance was building daily.

As Beatlemania broke out across the US over that weekend, the Beatles were on more than just *Sullivan*. We got to watch the band's arrival at the TWA terminal in New York, hear Chet Huntley say sardonically, "Someone asked what the fuss was about and we found we had no answer," and see the Beatles' line of limos snaking through the crowds out in front of the Plaza Hotel and the Ed Sullivan Theater.

Finally the Beatles appeared onstage. During their performance, I tried to describe to George what was happening, but I was dumbfounded. I kept saying the same thing over and over: "This is amazing."

George didn't think much of the Beatles' music, as far as I remember, but he couldn't see them. Seeing them was a large part of understanding what they were about, but even that wasn't it. There was more than music there, more than four guys playing and singing, and more than new haircuts. When I rewatch that performance now, much of what inspired and thrilled me that first time has faded. The recordings of the show don't do it justice, because the recordings don't convey the tenor of the times.

The performance pointed the needle of the world's design compass toward London. I knew that these guys and their music, and this new direction of the arts, would rearrange the social order and be in my life for a long time.

✣ ✣ ✣

After the *Monkees* TV show was on the air, the first thing I did when I got enough money was get on a plane with Phyllis and head to London. London was to the 1960s what Paris was to the 1920s, except with a much farther reach, driven by TV. I wanted to try to understand what was stimulating the arts coming from the city, from Not New York and from Not LA. I wanted to get a look at the force at work there, if there was one; I wanted to see who was steering it, if anyone was, and what it meant, if it meant anything at all.

When I got to London I expected a dazzling scene with the sizzle and flash of artistic exploration and advanced ideas, but that didn't happen. The center of a hurricane is calm, and London was right in the eye.

No one in the center seemed to know much about what was going on in the outlying reaches—the spirals of flying furniture or the twisting of cultural latticework. I made the club rounds, met the Beatles and many of their friends, examined the galleries and architecture, the studios and the theaters, the boutiques and department stores, and I noticed it all was marked with what I have come to call "easy speed." Easy speed is when massive motion, like the motion of a planet, is somehow summoned and big ideas manifest in spectacular yet elegant displays of alacrity, ingenuity, and beauty without the slightest visible effort from anyone involved.

Before I arrived in London I had not met John Lennon—I didn't even know how to contact him—but I thought if I could meet him and spend some time talking, it would be a great addition to the trip. Alf Weaver, a Londoner, was helping me out as a guide and driver and providing me with some security. I asked him if he knew how to contact John, and he said he might be able to get an address. He also suggested it would not be a good idea to show up unannounced at the door. I decided to send John a letter, but I made it a telegram, so it would arrive separate from the other fan mail. I wasn't sure what to say, so I just wrote something like, "Hi, I would like to meet you if you have time. I am at the Grosvenor House in London." But I needed to feel sure that he would know it was really from me—I needed to come up with some kind of structured signal like semaphore, except without me waving any flags. I signed the letter "God is Love. Mike Nesmith."

I don't know what part of the message worked, but he called a few hours after I sent it and invited me and Phyllis to stay with him and his wife, Cynthia, at his house. He sent his big black Rolls-Royce to pick us up. This was the first I learned of the grand English tradition of having houseguests.

Up until my visit with John, my main window into England and its culture had been listening repeatedly to the LP of *Beyond the Fringe*, a London stage presentation of the comedy troupe that included Peter Cook and Dudley Moore. I thought they were off-the-wall hilarious, with routines comparing the heat death of the universe to four hundred cerulean trousers left at the London transport lost and found, and that sort of thing. But that did not adequately prepare me for John's subtle humor or his appreciation of sly irony.

When we arrived, John was in a kind of breakfast den next to the kitchen, examining the cover of the *Safe as Milk* LP from Captain Beefheart and His Magic Band. I was surprised and happy to see the album because I had been at those sessions in LA and made a friend of Beefheart, an artist of extraordinary scope who wore a smock and a perfect diamond soul patch, and whose real name was Don Van Vliet. One of the producers of the album, Bob Krasnow, had been a close friend as well, as well as my manager and record producer before I got the job on the *Monkees* TV show. So for a moment at John and Cynthia's house, it was as if John, Beef, Kras, and I were all friends in the same room. I was sure Bob and Don would be very happy to know John was aware of the record—and was maybe even a fan of it. Maybe he could even be part of our band of avant-garde LA artists. Don had played an electric flour sifter on the record: possibly the next big rock-and-roll instrument.

I asked John if he liked the album, and he said he hadn't heard it. He had just received it unsolicited in the mail, was wondering what it was, and curious about why it was there. I was a little deflated. It was the fastest breakup of any band I had been in.

John then asked if I wanted a drink, and without thinking I said I would love a glass of milk. There was the breath of a pause as he looked at Cynthia and said, "Well, *we're* in for a good time, aren't we?"

At first I was embarrassed, because I thought he thought I had refused to drink with him. Then I made the connection between the offer and the *Safe as Milk* LP he was holding and it dawned on me that he thought I had been cleverly ironic. I laughed and said, "I'd love a drink of something in a moment. I really *would* like a glass of milk now to settle my stomach from the ride out." John smiled, and Cynthia got me a glass of milk.

I had missed John's first cue, but we each knew that at least we had the same sense of humor.

My times with John and Cynthia were pleasant nights out at clubs to watch someone perform, a good meal to talk things over, after-dinner drinks, and lying on the floor of cabs to get back into my hotel through the paparazzi.

After a few visits, John and I found a shared sandbox of wordplay where we could waltz among the verbs and nouns, puns abounding and riffs a-popping. Convivial as it was, it became apparent that he and I had only momentarily and superficially connected, caught for several delightful extra whirls circling the roundabout intersection of two orthogonal streets.

I was happy to meet John and ready to dive into conversation. I imagined talking about creativity, arts, and pop culture—maybe even the minutiae of instruments and favorite songs and singers. But this was not to be. In fact it was off-limits, more or less. The manic scene of producing a TV show and the ambition-choked streets of LA had not prepared me for a laid-back "have dinner, socialize, make wisecracks" atmosphere. That was the way it was in Lennon's home.

Life in London then was life lived in service to the arts and to the simplicity of doing, an almost impossible-to-grasp feeling of being in harmony with harmony itself—or as John put it in "Tomorrow Never Knows," floating downstream. It was easy going—sort of. In the center, there was no one in charge, no visible agenda. Everyone seemed to be under the control of a force of nature. So, "nothing to get hung about."

I was nonpolitical mostly because of my naïveté. I embraced a social order that I had cobbled together in the Dallas public schools and among kids in my neighborhood—a kind of civics lesson of the streets. It was a shallow knowledge that engendered the belief that anyone could be president of the United States if they just worked hard enough and were well behaved. I loved ideas of fairness and justice for all, the comic-book-hero motivations. But I was clueless as to real politics, even though I lived in the United States, under the long shadow of a war machine, in a conservative bastion of a city, a city where a president had been assassinated.

John and I never discussed politics explicitly, but as far as I could tell his politics were focused on his concept of peace and love as political acts. I did not think of love as a political engine. I thought of peace and love as self-sustaining and providential, healing and comforting in a world of apparent heartbreak and suffering. It was a subtle yet distinct difference to me.

John was playful and funny, a true artist of the highest type, but over time I lost touch with him. Among the existential realities that governed my life I could not find what I needed to fully understand his rules of behavior, so I could not share them. We ended up talking past each other some of the time. This made for no conflict between us. We were good playmates for the little time we spent together. The communication was collegial and smart, but for me it was incomplete. I loved the music, the arts, the spiritual awakenings of love and politics, but I was outside of the social system, outside the culture and even apart from the crowd.

This incompleteness came to mark my disconnect from the entire eye of the London hurricane. The artists there had the approbation of the world; they heard the roar of the swirling winds of the era's cultural storms as cheers of encouragement. But such validation was no part of my life. By the time I was in London I was nearly a pariah in the US, pummeled by opprobrium and ridicule and reviled among my peers.

My natural bent was toward peace and love; my natural life was harmony and tolerance; my proclivities were kindness and loyalty, mercy and forgiveness. But in the eyes of the rock cognoscenti and the arbiters of hip, the Monkees were a fraud, created to an evil purpose of greed, and I was assumed to be a perpetrator. As near as I could tell, John did not hold that opinion of the *Monkees* TV show, but we never talked about it. Indeed, John was one of the few points of connection to the London arts scene for me and had brought me far inside his world and among his friends.

When I was in LA society, I was politically repugnant to the people I most respected and with whom I mostly agreed.

London was familiar and friendly, and revealed how far from the center I was and how little I understood of the process by which that center had been created.

What did become apparent and finally undeniable was the fact that the Beatles and the whole British Invasion were not the Visitation.

The Visitation had not yet come, although it was about to. In all my travels through London-at-altitude it was categorically the most astounding and important thing that happened to me.

One night, in the spring of 1967, John and Cynthia and Phyllis and I were to meet at a restaurant for dinner, and John was late. He came in breathless with apologies and explained he had gotten caught up in a club where he was listening to a band. He produced a portable cassette player the size of a small loaf of bread, laid it in the center of the table, and played what he had recorded.

It was Jimi Hendrix playing "Hey Joe."

Everyone at the table was silent, and it dawned on me that we were all speechless. We all stared at the recorder as if it were some type of alien egg, something from far outside the limits of our normal waking state.

When the song was over, someone said, "How can anybody be that good?" Whatever Hendrix had plugged into—whatever Visitation he brought upon us—was, first of all, good. It came with the instant recognition of a real thing, a true thing, an innovation.

When I got back to the hotel after that dinner, I ran into Micky Dolenz. He told me he had seen Hendrix and asked him if he would be the opening act for the next leg of the Monkees tour, and Jimi had agreed. I was thrilled and confused.

This conjunction of Hendrix and the Monkees was staggeringly weird in my eyes, but the idea that I would get to see him playing live night after night was electrifying. It would prove the most lasting and substantial aspect of all my trips to London.

If London was the still center of a storm that was changing the artistic, social, and political landscape of the world, Jimi was a maelstrom, both the center and the circumference, with his own gravitational force. He was music as mass, and all that revolved around that music changed the landscape of the mind. Hendrix moved through aural boundaries the way Duchamp moved through retinal ones. From the Purple Haze came *Nude Descending a Staircase* as "Little Wing."

The British bands' rearrangements of the US rock-and-roll legacy had generated a storm, but Hendrix opened a world where a whole new type of music was born. The world that he discovered, the sonic possibilities of instruments in a rock-and-roll band, shaped the bands that came in his wake. From the way he used the amp—turning the volume all the way up and using his guitar volume as overdrive, sending the sound into a sweet and mellifluous distortion—to the wah-wah pedal that shifted the tonality, what he unveiled changed even the Beatles and the Stones. The range of nuance—especially the extremely loud—and his melodic structure and lyric content all had some history, some foreshadowing, but Hendrix revealed a performative aspect of music that was life, that brought the best of all the musical worlds together. When Hendrix played, something came into existence as a fact that had not been there before he played.

That being an opening act on a Monkees tour would bring Hendrix into a world of popular awareness was curious and oddly poetic. That it would galvanize the Monkees' assassins for their final push was no surprise.

Jimi came onto the Monkees US tour that started up in Jacksonville, Florida, in July 1967, and that was the first time

I met him. He had hair out to here and was wearing exotically lavish psychedelic clothing. I found him to be a gentle and kind soul, soft-spoken and a bit shy. There were times watching Jimi play that I felt the company of Wagner or Beethoven, other times Bo Diddley or Buddy Holly, and other times Gershwin or Max Steiner. We became friends of a sort during that tour and stayed in touch in the years that followed.

The first night he played I went incognito to the sound check at the stadium and stood at the foot of the stage a few feet away from him and Mitch and Noel, the other two members of his band. When Jimi started playing, I stopped breathing for a second and found myself standing about three feet farther back from the stage than I had been, but with no idea how I got there. It was the first time I ever saw a Marshall stack, a five-foot-tall amplifier with enormous power. Jimi played through two of them, as did Noel, the bass player.

The music was unlike anything I had ever heard, but it was almost beside the point. The Beatles' TV appearance and their subsequent records were the best played, the most artfully written and harmoniously sung, but they didn't come close to what Hendrix was doing performatively.

I listen to Jimi's records now, even his live recordings, and they have very little of what I heard that night at sound check. No kind of recording could contain it. I watched him every night after that for about ten days, until Jimi gave the finger to everybody in the Monkees' audience at Forest Hills Stadium in New York and walked offstage. He moved out of the miasma of the Monkees tour into his own hundred-thousand-seat stadiums and played for reverential crowds that did not shout "We want Davy!" while he played and sang "Foxy Lady."

I was not close friends with Jimi, and our subsequent contacts were infrequent and usually hurried. But I saw him one last time, and he did a good deed that defined him for me as a person.

I was back in London to kick off a tour of the First National Band, a group I had put together and written new music for. This was my first time to play and sing songs I had stored up during the *Monkees* TV show. I was at the height of pariah-hood with the press and the pop critics, and the reviews of my new album, *Magnetic South*, were excoriating. Even other contemporary bands were suspicious, and we were mocked by bands on the same concert bill with us.

RCA had called a press conference for me, and I knew I was in trouble by the way the promotion man who set it up was acting. He kept reassuring me that everything would be fine in a way that only made me sure he knew that no one was coming.

However, when we got to the conference center at the hotel, the place was jammed with reporters. The promo man was clearly relieved—and surprised. A few minutes after the press reception started, I looked up and saw Jimi coming in the door. He walked straight to me and gave me a hug, and we exchanged glad hellos. I asked why he was there, and he told me he had gotten a call saying that the responses to the invitation for my press conference were not going well and asking if he would come and lend his support. He said yes, he would be there, and had allowed that to be announced to the trades.

His presence at the conference made a huge difference to me that day. It was one of the most generous acts of support I had experienced from a fellow artist, and was especially welcome given my state of mind, which was mightily confused, artistically and personally. Hendrix was curious about the music I was making, and we talked. I gave him a record but felt shy the moment I handed it to him.

That wasn't all of it. A few minutes after Hendrix arrived,

Ringo Starr came in with the same story. He was just as warm and supportive as Jimi had been. We were talking when a reporter came up to Ringo and me, interrupted, and started talking to him, asking questions about the Beatles. Ringo would have none of it. "Oh, no," he said, "this is his press conference," and shooed the guy away.

I suppose there are pictures of Jimi and Ringo and me somewhere in the archives of some music-press paper, but I have never seen them. What I have from that time is my memory of it, and the forever gratitude I feel for what they did for me.

Two days later Jimi was dead.

It is hard to overstate Jimi's importance in music, just as hard as it is to explain it. Hendrix rose to a level that was available only to those who were there in real time. What's left in his recordings is like remnant light, like echoes of the big bang. Nothing one can hear now fully captures what he did in conjunction with the spirit of the times. It's the same with symphonies and big bands, where the music was designed to be played live and recording was confined to paper, allowing other players to only approximate the sound.

The music of the 1960s, born as it was from the American blues legacy, has a staying power, but its impact lessens over time. *Nude Descending a Staircase* still exists, but its effect is softened now, as it occupies the space it created for itself. The thrust of some new idea that opens a new door is always most exciting when first encountered. Then it slowly turns. We begin to live with art's legacy almost immediately after it is created.

John Cleese, one of the Pythons, said to me once as we were riding on a bus together that all comedy gets less and less funny over time. I think he is right. Although the Pythons have endured for me, they were never again as funny as when I first saw them. It may be that comedy is particularly susceptible because it is best when absurd and irreverent, and time covers comedy routines with a patina that's toxic to that spirit.

When I got home from London the second time I went, in 1967, after the "Day in the Life" sessions and another weekend at John's house, I wrote a song about him and the Beatles and Fred Astaire and Ginger Rogers that I titled "I'll Remember You." John and I had sat at the upright piano he was painting in his garden room, and I started playing the chords to "I Remember You," a Johnny Mercer–Victor Schertzinger song that had been a big-band hit and was more recently a hit for Frank Ifield. John remarked on the first chord change, from C major to B-flat minor, and he played along a bit. The original circus poster for Mr. Kite was on the wall in back of us. I made a mental note of the moment and set it aside until I wrote "I'll Remember You." I didn't use that chord change in my song, but John did in his.

I was going to record the new song and send him a home cassette of it as homage and a thank-you. Harry Nilsson had made a close friend of John and told me he would send John cassettes regularly, which he said John loved to get. I kept meaning to get the song recorded for him, but time passed and I didn't get around to it.

The Beatles broke up; John moved to New York with Yoko Ono and became a peace activist and performer on his own; and almost before I knew it the 1970s had come and gone as well.

My memories of London served me well as a touchstone for art's potential. During that time I was exploring new avenues of thought, trying to find a safe and sheltered landing spot after *The Monkees* had gone off the air in 1969. I kept writing and making albums, kept hanging on to the music I loved and trying to explore more possibilities. In the 1970s, I had set my sails for video and television, and the music took on a visual component.

Finally, in the late 1970s, I got around to recording the song I had written for John. I was working with a good band during a session for a record, and I took time out to record and even do some polishing of "I'll Remember You." I packaged it up in a cassette but left it in a desk drawer, always meaning to send it, but I kept forgetting.

Then one night I heard that John had been shot to death on the streets of New York by a crazy man. It was horrible.

Years later I made a video of "I'll Remember You" for an NBC show I had called *Television Parts.* I put it in one of the episodes as a farewell.

I have returned to London many times since the 1960s on many different errands and enterprises. The heritage of that time is still a large part of the identity of the town and is forever imprinted on my mind, but it is dimmed a bit, atrophied, and in some degree lost, by the veneration of the ages that followed. In a city that is mostly swallowed by its own history, I found it curious that the thing that defined London to me, and what defined the sixties, never came to know itself.

The day Jimi came to my press conference, he came up to my room afterward and we had a drink and a smoke and got to talk quietly a bit. Jimi said that he was thinking of branching out into R&B and putting together an R&B band. I was surprised and I suppose it showed. His early work was still resonating down the halls, and I could not imagine how an R&B band would work in comparison. He said he had also been taking singing lessons.

I blurted out, "Why? You have one of the greatest voices in rock and roll, if not the greatest. You sing the way all rock singers want to sing." He said he felt like he sang flat. It occurred to me that he had no idea how good he was. He was too close to it. He had no idea of the magnitude of his work or that he had made history with his songs and his playing. It also occurred to me that Jimi had never seen Hendrix live, like I had.

I had the same sort of exchange with John one weekend. He brought home some acetates from the *Sgt. Pepper* sessions and played them. We listened together, and I was thrilled to get to hear them. After one song, I can't remember which one, he said he thought the bass was a bit loud and might need to play a different part. He then asked me what I thought. What I thought, of course, was that my musical realities were slowly being altered. All I could think was how amazing it all was. I told John that, and I think it may have embarrassed him a little as well. I realized that he had no clue about who he was in the context of the Beatles. He had never seen the Beatles play. I had. Jimi had never seen the Jimi Hendrix Experience; John Lennon had never seen the Beatles. They were forever barred from knowing them.

3

Look at the thing. It's so imposing. Imagine a man at the turn of the century coming to a small Southwestern town and seeing a building like this. What stability and civic pride. It's an optimistic architecture. It expects the future to make as much sense as the past.

—Don DeLillo, *Libra*

My father essentially disappeared when I was four, after he and my mother divorced, although I came to find out later that he was kept away as much as he stayed away. In his absence, my childless great-uncle Chick occupied the space as the primary male for me while I was growing up.

Chick wasn't around too often either, but when he was, it was a pretty good time. He was my great-uncle by marriage; his wife, Aida, was my great-aunt, the sister of my grandmother. So it was Chick-and-Aida. In my toddling years I called them Unca Chick and Aint-eye-eeh-doh, and when I was in my forties I named a recipe after them: Chicken Aida, made with tomatoes, hot peppers, onions, garlic, butter, and chicken.

I learned to love them both a lot. It took some doing, because as hard as I tried, I never quite understood where they were coming from intellectually, politically, socially, or even anthropologically. Chick was a political paradox, a mixture of hard reactionary racism and dedicated support of Democrats and the liberal cause, except as it applied to civil rights. The conflict made political discussion with him entirely off-limits. But I didn't see it as a problem; I had developed no interest in politics. What I finally accepted was that they were good people at their emotional core but sometimes got a little too close to the fire for my taste.

Chick was a never-ending source of fascination for me. He had been a drill sergeant in the Marines during World War II. He was a big guy, six-foot-four, 275 pounds, with a loud and broad Texas accent, and he loved a good time, which included gambling, booze, and golf. He hunted, fished, watched football on TV, and poured a little bourbon in his coffee in the morning: Old Crow, as I recall. He laughed a lot and loved to laugh.

Chick did not have a wide vocabulary, so the laughter served him well as a punctuator, and he had a winsome smile and a few opening lines to gain attention from women or a crowd. After that, he did not have a lot to say. His ordinary communication consisted of colloquial phrases made up of words of less than two syllables and was peppered with epithets for cadence.

This is why I found it so strange that one of his rituals on Sunday mornings was working the giant crossword puzzle in the paper. It may have been the local paper or the *New York Times*, but whichever paper it was, the crossword filled up most of the bottom half of one page of the Sunday Amusement section. He would get his coffee, hit it with a shot of bourbon, sit down with a ballpoint pen, and work the puzzle in ten or fifteen minutes flat, completely filled it out, top to bottom, side to side. Then he would get up, go outside, and start in on one of his projects—carving pictures of flying ducks out of plywood, using a burn stylus to make little signs for his garage wall, or working on his boat's motor—or head to the golf course to gamble.

Part of the enigma that was Uncle Chick came into a degree of focus one Sunday after he had finished the crossword puzzle and left for the golf course. It didn't make sense to me, this extraordinary word skill, and Chick didn't really discuss anything with me that gave any hint about his thought processes. So on this Sunday I pulled the paper out of the trash, where he had thrown it, and looked at the puzzle, searching for clues.

When I first looked at the filled-in puzzle, it seemed normal. Words like *moon* and *igloo* and *kayak* were in their proper place. Then I started to notice words like *fonqi* and *nmfberhng* and *qplltrkller.* Then I finally saw that most of the words were unrecognizable, and weren't words at all. As this sank in, I was glad I was alone in the house. I carefully folded the paper up, put it back in the trash, and backed away.

Chick made a lot of things up, I think, but I never knew which was which, who he knew and who he didn't, who he admired and who he dismissed, or what he did or didn't do for a living, so I never asked too many questions for fear of excavating another nonword. Aida loved and tolerated him, and that was a big endorsement, because she was the epitome of the patient and loving caregiver. By reason of that example, I gave Uncle Chick a lot of room and a lot of patience, too. Curiously, Chick supported my efforts at music and the arts. His encouragement counted for a lot and I was grateful for it, though I was unclear what he thought he was encouraging.

In all this, one thing emerged that would become a staple of my own thought and development: Chick taught me quantum theory.

Well, sort of. What he taught me was how an internal combustion engine worked, and it was the first time I thought about quantum theory, in essence if not in fact.

I asked Chick if he knew how an engine worked. He said yes, and drew a picture of one for me in his nice artistic hand. The drawing was clear, a half section of one cylinder with all the constituent parts. As Chick talked, pointing out and explaining various parts of the engine, I began to see that an engine was a system of ideas. Each part of this simple system revealed more of the operating principle that governed the whole, and each part was in a ready state in that definite system.

As Chick explained the intricacies of the little one-cylinder engine, he shifted from his usual mix of opinions and revolving aphorisms into the elegant simplicity of explaining from direct experience. He clearly understood what he was teaching, so I was able to understand it when he explained how the parts worked. In addition to basic quantum theory, from this I also learned that only teachers who understood what they were teaching could do that, and with that realization, my world opened a little.

Chick was, unawares, teaching me how to learn. At that moment, I stopped reaching for knowledge and started searching for understanding. The difference at the time was drawn a bit crudely in my mind, but the distinction between knowing what one understands and understanding what one knows seemed clear. While not the finest point on the compass of critical thought, it was a general direction toward the light of intelligence. I learned then to distinguish teachers by whether they taught from opinion or by exemplification.

Chick's twang was indescribable, but the closest comparison is to Lyndon Johnson's. The *r*'s were curled, then stretched out; the *a*'s were mashed diphthongs—*great* was pronounced "grite." I have found nothing in the pronunciation guides I've consulted that could represent the way Uncle Chick pronounced *Mike*, except to say the *i* is not a diphthong. The *ike* in the Texas drawl is sui generis, as near as I can tell. Actors fail at it the same way they fail at the Bostonian *ar*.

The accent, however, was not the focus of Texan phonology for me. Instead, the cadence was my focus. Chick taught me, again by example, the power of rhythm in language, spoken or written, and this idea uncovered one of the cornerstones of my aesthetic foundation, although I did not know it at the time: captivating rhythm.

What fascinated me as much as anything about Uncle Chick was his careful and precise way of cursing. He used only a few different cusswords—not really curses, evil in intent, but more like a sailor's cussing, more of a backyard business-and-barbecue cusser. He was filling spaces in speech with meaning that otherwise would remain unrecognized or, worse, misunderstood.

Cussing for Chick had less to do with the meaning of the cussword and more with the lilt of it when set in a sentence. He might as well have said "budda da BUH" instead of "son of a bitch," because the rhythm was the thing that counted. No one minded the presence of "son of a bitch" in Chick's speech, because it didn't literally mean son of a bitch. It wasn't even an imprecation; it was a dance step.

When he would take me to his deer camp, the cussing among him and his hunting buddies would commence in a rush, in an almost florid, poetically nuanced way. "How the hell are you?" was not the same as "How in the hell are you." His greetings and appellations were all carefully shaded. "Hey, Earl" meant something different than "Earl!" And the "How are you?" that followed was carefully, even if unconsciously, timed to fit the meter of the word or sentence that would come after it. "Hey, bub" was affectionate. "Hey there, shotgun" was affectionate and respectful. "Hey there, shotgun. What in the hell is going on?!" was the supreme greeting; it carried respect, affection, and endearment. *Shotgun* was for his closest male friends and was an endorsement of the highest order.

I would later learn that most of these rhythmic quirks have been studied and understood to a degree by linguists, but for me they were a revelation.

I would eventually write and record a song called "Roll with the Flow," but I sang it for Uncle Chick long before I recorded it, and when I did, it resonated more deeply than almost any other moment I had with him. He made me recite the words slowly, and he wrote them down and memorized them. From that day forward, whenever we met he would recite them back to me and laugh and say, "How in the hell are you doin', shotgun? I've missed you, son of a bitch."

"Budda da BUH / da buh dada, / DAH DAH? BuDAHda, / budda bu DAH."

It wasn't the melody or the meaning of the words of "Roll with the Flow" that affected him. It was the rhythm of them. Within this we communicated harmoniously and spiritually, beyond politics, society, or philosophy.

So it was that Uncle Chick was the first member of my first band.

One continuously positive idea I've carried from my early years is an ever-expanding notion that the past does not create the present—that what seems set in perpetuity can be instantly changed. This was never an argument for randomness, but more of a sense of an eternal present that was constantly updating, revealing more and more of the moments that comprised infinite Life.

The notion was first set and made as clear as pain by the assassination of President Kennedy. There was a choice I had to make when JFK died so easily and the world changed so drastically. The choice was between being afraid forever of the day an asteroid would strike the earth and eliminate existence as I knew it, or being calmed by a faint yet certain sense of a permanent ever-present Life that persisted in any event—the life that "goes on." I chose the latter, and in that choice the idea of omnipresence increased from meaning only "everywhere present" to including "always now."

Texas was a strange place to me, so I never understood it as community. Being among Bette, my mother's sister Yvonne, Aida, and Chick was all I knew of Dallas. They talked about much I didn't understand. I had a few places I could connect, and those places were oases, but the politics and society felt distant. I was unable to grasp the ideology that was the basis of the conservative politics there; all I saw was its murderous hatred of any ideology set against it. As I got older, Dallas was not a city I felt like I belonged in, and certainly not in the 1960s.

My mother's life story deserves a book of its own, and I can do only slight justice to it here. She was a remarkable woman, in everyone's estimation, and was a tremendous influence in my life. That influence was not always welcome, but I have no doubt it was always lovingly offered with the best intentions. Mother had her usual mother problems with her son, and I had mine with her, but all of them paled in the light of what she contributed to my life and her steadfast commitment to her highest sense of right.

I was born when Bette was eighteen, on December 30, 1942, in Houston, Texas. She and my father divorced in 1946 and she remained single. My mother's family lived in Dallas, so we moved there to be near them.

Throughout Bette's life I was as close to her as you might think a young single mother and son could be. Even after I left home at eighteen, we talked almost every day, several times a day. Every time we talked, some portion of that time was spent discussing metaphysics and Christian Science.

Bette was a good mother and we were very close, but it was clear that her most important pursuit was her study and practice of Science. I was not neglected or abused in any way, but often

I felt like I was a nuisance who was along for the ride with a single woman.

The story of how she came to Science from the religion of her youth—which may have been Baptist; I was never sure—was told to me many times. It was about an astounding healing she underwent shortly after I was born. I can report it only as hearsay, but I believe it to be mostly true. I was too young to delve into the story when it happened, and when I got older I never thought to probe. I heard it from several family members, including Bette herself, and it was fairly consistent across them all.

Somewhere around 1943–1945, when I was two or three, my mother was diagnosed as having uremic poisoning. This was perhaps due to some type of kidney failure, but in any case there was no known certain cure at the time. Her health declined, and finally she was told that she could not live much longer. She slipped into a coma and was given roughly twenty-four hours to live in her last examination by a medical doctor, who said one evening that she would be dead by morning.

My father, Warren, had been raised in Christian Science, and his maternal aunt was a practitioner. The aunt was called, came to Bette's bedside, and overnight Bette returned to normal. She awoke with all symptoms abated and was healthy and about her usual activities in a few days. The disease never returned.

After this, a Christian Science church in Dallas, which was respected and well established at the time, became the center of Bette's life and consequently of mine. I distanced myself from the church organization, but I was deeply interested in the teaching.

Bette was no one to cross and no one to question, much less scold. Being somewhat vague and not terribly articulate in her communications, even though she was very smart and very talented, she had a limited ability to explain her ideologies or her thought processes surrounding them, and she was highly reactive to any criticism of either. Christian Science was one of the worst subjects to bring up to her for a critical discussion; politics was another. Civil discourse was not a part of my childhood home.

No other family members discussed ideas around me. They were all playful after a fashion, but when it came to the complex things of life and serious consideration of philosophical or scientific questions, there was no interest expressed and no discussion to be had, except with Bette.

This was not always a good thing, because her arguments were oftentimes circular and her bases for logic biased. Ritual and doctrine are not part of the teaching of Christian Science—spiritualism and supernatural mysticism are specifically denounced—so when she would stray into supporting her beliefs and understandings with these methods I would get confused and withdraw. Any conversation that started along those lines would come to a swift and certain end in silence.

Bette loved the arts and loved to paint and sculpt, but she was the only one in the family who did. She was not terribly good at painting or sculpting, but she had an almost perfect eye for both and could find the finest examples in galleries and in her general comings and goings. As she became more successful, she brought more and more beautiful art into her life. Days before she died, she bought a small and lovely painting by Georgia O'Keeffe, a landscape called *Taos, New Mexico*. When it was delivered I hung it for her on the wall next to the bed in the room she died in. It lifted her spirit.

Her love of the arts nourished me as well, and even though there were few intellectual discussions about them, I could watch her choices and learn greatly from her spiritual understanding of what made them good and true. When she built the building that housed the final Liquid Paper Corporation, she insisted on and got a large budget for art. The building was notable for its architecture, and the art inside it made it look as much like a gallery of modern art as an office building.

Around 1948, a few years after she and I moved to Dallas, she bought a small five-room house with an inheritance from her father. I don't know what the finances were, never understood much about the overarching financial picture, but I knew that my mother was concerned about making ends meet. She would often burst into tears of panic that would panic me in return as a child.

She was held back in the ordinary job market because she was a woman, and she was always looking for an opportunity to rise out of this economic prison. She made her living by keeping two active jobs, one as a secretary and the other as a commercial artist. These two skill sets would combine in her invention of Liquid Paper, and her single-minded love for the true and beautiful would serve as a guide to great success in the business.

When she invented Liquid Paper, I was about twelve, and I was a willing helper and supporter for several years, although I had little interest in the business and wasn't motivated to learn. I was more interested in cars and women, which is how Leary's priorities—"what other people thought of me" and "how I looked"—translated for me at the time.

This love of cars and women, however, created an ever-widening gap between Bette and me. From my first sexual awakenings I sensed a change in her feeling toward me, and she became more and more estranged from me as I grew older. As usual, we did not talk much about this specifically. Her feelings toward me started to cycle between attraction and repulsion—as did mine for her. When we were in sync—when we loved and admired each other at the same time—things were good between us, and when we were out of sync—one loving and the other distanced—things were uncomfortable. In the rare times when we both were far apart, we became terribly angry.

This distance was a double bind for me, because I loved her dearly and did not understand why she had stopped loving me. Such are the tensions between a single mother and her only child.

To our benefit, we both had an ability to completely forgive. It was a type of forgiveness she had learned from Christian Science teachings and taught me. It was a saving grace we both could lean on.

There was only one notable time when we talked our way calmly through a potentially life-altering misunderstanding—a watershed moment when I was in my thirties.

Women's liberation was a big consideration and topic of discussion for Bette. Once she demonstrated her success, she felt the sting of being denied her due respect because of being a woman. She raised the subject with me only once. She asked me, "What do you think of women's liberation?"

I did not hesitate, since I had very strong feelings that were clear in my mind. I said, "I think it is the most advanced social idea since racial equality." There may have been a smile from her, but it was so slight I couldn't tell for sure. There was certainly an almost palpable feeling of relief, and from that time forward she opened up to me in a way she hadn't since I was prepubescent.

My answer was guileless and sincere, which is one reason it was so quick. It never dawned on me until I saw her reaction that she thought I might hold women in an inferior place in my thinking. With a mother like her, misogyny could not have been further from me. She daily demonstrated courage and fortitude and wisdom and strength, which I admired and emulated. She taught me how to be a man's man. In the same way, she showed me the value of my own femininity.

Even in writing all this, it is not possible for me to give a complete picture of Bette McMurray. She was my mother, and I was her son. In the end she knew me no better than I knew her, but the love we shared was pure and real.

My family didn't have a television until sometime in the mid-1950s. The first one I saw was at a neighbor's house up the street. I was not allowed inside the neighbor's house, because they already had too many children of their own all gathered around the set, but I could sort of see the set through the screen door, so I stood on the porch and watched, and like the rest of the world I was hypnotized by it, regardless of what it was playing.

Eventually a friend of my mother's gave us an old TV they had, but of course "old TV" at that time meant only a few years old. By 1957, I was well acquainted with most of its offerings, and in August of that year I saw *American Bandstand.* It was the first time I saw my generation on TV, and it was the first time I was engulfed by media fog.

I could watch *American Bandstand* and see myself and my goals among the girls dancing before my eyes. *Bandstand* was mirror-media for me. Musically, I thought it was a little strange. Bobby Rydell, Frankie Avalon, Fabian, and the other Philly kids were singing in some musical language I had never heard and didn't really enjoy. Nevertheless, the dances and the dresses, the tight pants, skinny ties, and slick stacked hair looked like I wanted to look, and if I needed to, I was confident I could figure out a dance to do there in front of Dick Clark.

That same year, because of a still-unaccounted-for aesthetic reason, Harley Earl put fins on the new Chevrolet and most of the GM cars. I thought the 1957 Bel Air convertible was a great-looking car that I would look great in, and that the girls on *American Bandstand* would think I was really terrific if they saw me that way.

One of my school friends had a new 1957 turquoise Chevrolet convertible, and when I saw it I nearly swooned. The top was down, it looked miles long, and my friend's mother offered to let me drive it. Behind the wheel of that car was Nirvana. My friend, his family, and the car all moved to California a few months later. The natural inclination, entirely reasonable to me then, was to follow them.

I decided to run away from home.

Of course, I would not be the first bird to trash a piece of the nest by jumping out before I could fly.

First, I wrote a letter to one of the girls on *American Bandstand* so I knew I had someplace to go. She didn't answer, but that was no reason to stop me. I reasoned, somewhat circuitously, that a trip to California in the family car, a 1957 Triumph sedan, would cost fifteen dollars, which I could steal from my mother. I reasoned that I could steal the car as well. I had all the justifications in place I needed for stealing from my mother, because I thought she was mean to me. I could take the family car, because it was sort of mine anyway, and besides, I really needed it.

I didn't think much about whether stealing was a good idea, what grief it might cause my mother, or how heading to California would get me to *American Bandstand,* which was in Philadelphia. I planned my escape and decided that, indeed, the best way to get to *American Bandstand* was by way of California, since that would allow me to follow my friend's convertible.

I have to report that some shards of this lunatic reasoning remained even as I got older. Later, when I was starving in LA with Phyllis and our son Christian, and Randy Sparks gave me a $600 advance for my songs' publishing, the first thing I did was convince Phyllis we needed to race out and buy four chrome wheels for our 1963 Chevrolet wagon before we bought food.

They were Keystone "mags," but not real magnesium; rather, they were made out of chromed steel. We didn't have any income, not too much to wear, nor a stable place to live, but we had chrome wheels, so almost all was right in the world. We looked cool. People liked us. We had shiny objects. Was there more?

I had no idea at the time that these tiny slivers of insanity were the tent stakes for what would become the infrastructure of a full-blown Celebrity Psychosis.

But we will get to that.

When I ran away from home, I actually made it to California, visited my friend with the Chevy, borrowed some money from his dad because the Triumph broke down, abandoned the impossible trip to Philly, and came back to Dallas. I rehearsed an apology for my mother that I had designed for dramatic effect and then delivered it to her on the doorstep of the little house in an awful and insincere moment of the worst sort.

So came the end of the first extra-nest excursion. But I wasn't back where I started. I had blown that up. I needed more ideas. It would be hard to top the last set, for sure, but I could take some time. Maybe I could join the Air Force. I actually could join the Air Force.

I have no idea what was motivating me or why I did any of it—not a shred of self-awareness about it, then or now. No self-justification, nor a second of remorse or regret—only a vacant wonder. I can report that I have learned almost nothing from my younger weird doings except that learning by experience is an awful way to learn.

4

You cain't judge a apple by lookin' at the tree
You cain't judge honey by lookin' at the bee
You cain't judge a daughter by lookin' at the mother
You cain't judge a book by lookin' at the cover

—Ellas Otha Bates, a.k.a. Ellas McDaniel, a.k.a. Bo Diddley

The little house in Dallas where we lived during the 1950s was only a few blocks from an intersection that marked a line between white and black neighborhoods. There was a convenience store there where I could walk to get a drink or pick up some groceries for my mother. The small five-room frame houses in our neighborhood were all aligned behind little lawns along paved streets with a curb, but just beyond the market, all that changed. The streets there were a tar-and-gravel mix with no curbs and no driveways and ramshackle, two- and three-room tarpaper shacks strewn among scruffy trees.

The difference was stark. Even as I had matured with this difference, it was hard to understand. Beyond an unseen line behind the market was a neighborhood of all poor black people; on my side of the line it was all poor white. We all knew we were poor and we knew we were black and we knew we were white but my child mind could not construct any reason why some people lived one way and not the other.

When the little kids in my all-white elementary school started using racial epithets and saying that some races were better than others, I recoiled. While it was only talk among children, it seemed to me as if the talk had leaked onto the playground from a broken sewer pipe, even as the children merrily splashed about in the effluence. I jumped away because it smelled bad and repulsed me. I could not understand subtleties then, but I could spiritually sense that something was terribly wrong and was disturbed by it. I was surprised that my refusal to swim in that pool cast me out of the kid society, away from the cool and cute. It hurt my feelings, but it did not change them.

Around the corner from the market there was a laundromat where my mother would do washing, and next to it a tiny bar with a big, loud jukebox. This was a place of curious wonder for me. I would stand at the door of the bar and listen to the music. I now know that it was mostly blues by Jimmy Reed and Bobby Bland, Lightnin' Hopkins and other Texas bluesmen, but back then it was just music to me. I loved it from the first note I heard.

Another constant source of music was the piano and organ at a music store in the sprawling Inwood shopping center. In the plate-glass front of this music store, a man would sit and play a great monolithic organ, and the sound would be piped out into the parking lot through large speakers that hung outside the glass just under the eaves of the building. I would stand in this small sheltered spot, sometimes for hours, watching and listening to him while my mother shopped or did other errands. I thought it was the greatest music I had ever heard. He played "Tico Tico" and "Perfidia" and other kinds of movie and 1950s pop schmaltz, all of which sounded like angels singing to me.

It went unnoticed by me for several years that the man sitting at the desk-like organ playing "Tico Tico" had elicited the same response from me as Ike and Tina Turner singing "A Fool in Love." In my youth this mixture was independent of context; it was all just music and all just perfect. To my delight it was never-ending. It was music in every direction of thought.

When I was fourteen, I applied for a job at the music store where the organist played in the window, and I was refused. Obviously I was too young, but I just started working there anyway, on my own. I came in one day, hung around, saw a broom leaning in a corner, grabbed it, and started sweeping up and organizing the storeroom. There was just enough of a bureaucracy that no one knew whether I had been hired or who I worked for or what I was actually doing there. I came in the next day, and the next, and they all got used to me. No one told me to stop, so I kept coming in, even though I wasn't getting paid. There was music playing all day long, and that was plenty for me.

After a while I started selling records, interacting with the customers, and arranging the stock like a real employee. The staff finally figured out I was there of my own volition and not getting paid anything, and one day out of pity, the manager offered to let me take home some records as recompense—the new 45 rpm big-hole records. I could take home three a day. That was the only pay I ever got, but it was more music, so it was ample and I was grateful for it. My mother's friends and even my mother were proud of me, because they thought I had a job. No one asked how much I made, not even Mom.

This established a pattern that would repeat over the years. I would just hang out where I wanted to, lend a hand where I could, and not worry about getting paid as long as I was where

I wanted to be. This seemed right to me at the time and offered plenty of return for what it was.

I used the same MO in high school. Even though I was told that if I failed seventh-grade algebra I wouldn't be able to move on, I somehow slipped through the bureaucratic cracks. As an invisible walking wounded, I stood in line at the new high school on enrollment day, filled out forms, enrolled in classes, handed in paperwork, and moved along.

When the time came, no one seemed to notice that I wasn't going to the classes I had enrolled in—like algebra. I went only to classes that interested me, whether I'd enrolled or not. As long as I made it to a seat before the tardy bell rang, I was ignored, although I did find myself mysteriously "enrolled" in some of the classes I attended out of interest—at least the teacher would call my name to see if I was present. But apparently no one checked to see if I actually belonged there.

My self-designed school day consisted of three lunch periods, three choir periods, two speech and drama periods, and a homeroom. I also tried out for the school play, got the part (Andrew Carnes in *Oklahoma!*), and went to rehearsals. No one seemed to know that I was outside the system, askew on the rolls, getting no credits, and causing who knows what kind of havoc in the tax-revenue-per-student accounting.

My mother knew I left for school and came home from school at the right times, and that seemed good enough for her. She was working hard at two jobs just to keep the lights on and food on the table. She was distressed by my not having homework, but unless someone called from school about my behavior, which was almost never, she ignored my schooling, just as she never asked to see my paycheck from the music store.

It was fine with me. I loved the music and singing in the choir, loved the school play, and three sessions of lunch meant I got to socialize with people I liked. After a time, though, this was all wearying, as I saw distant graduation days and parties looming and knew I would have to bail or get busted. The far-off sound of a school band playing "Pomp and Circumstance" rang in my head, but with these words:

You're ignomiously failing
You are really a jerk
You're so far outside the system
You will never get work
You're ignomiously fail-ing
You will never get wooork!

(repeat over and over until everyone gets their diploma but you)

I didn't know what *ignomiously* meant and found out only later that it wasn't a word at all, just a make-believe cousin of *ignominy*, but that worked for me because it fit the rhythm of the song. *Ignomiously* was legitimately pejorative; that much is certain.

I started rolling back my school attendance, and the music store quickly took over as the center of my world. I stayed longer and longer hours and took home all the hits, the R&B records, blues records, country records. I listened each night to one record after another.

My record collection grew and so did my circle of friends, including some great-looking girls and popular guys. They liked me and I liked them. I could get a date for the seasonal proms, which I went to, with the prettiest and most popular girls in school. How I looked and what they thought of me seemed in fine shape, even though my own sense of self was floating untethered in the mist.

I hung out with nerds and athletes alike, enjoyed the football games and the choir classes and rehearsals, all the time incongruously outside the system. But my public education was going nowhere, and I could easily see that the path I was on would lead to nothing down the line: no higher education, no college or technical school, or in the words of the surrounding adults, "no future." I was not happy about this, but on the other hand I didn't know what I was missing, so I didn't feel sad about it either.

I had no doubt that music was the most important thing in my life, and I was getting an education in that. Every day, when I brought home the newest records, I learned a bit more, and my awareness of music and its reach began to expand. I was becoming more and more confident at telling the good from the bad. I stopped appreciating all music equally and realized there was a distinct type of sound and singing I liked, although I had no name for it. I was certain Fats Domino was a real thing—so was Chuck Berry and so was Little Richard—but I couldn't tell anyone why. All of these men were outrageous on some level—far beyond the social norms of Dallas. They were heroic, unafraid of expression, and willing to go where music led them, so they became leaders for me. They were unofficially in charge of an artistic and cultural revolution. *Normal* and *rock and roll* were counterirritants.

Having these records from the top rock and rollers of the times was a type of intervention in my life. When Fats Domino came out with "Ain't That a Shame," I heard and felt the New Orleans sound of his piano in a way that let me recognize it anytime it was played. His singing-through-a-smile style, where the words rolled around the resident Creole in his voice, was a joy, and even with a line like "my tears fell like rain," the whole tone and tenor of the record was uplifting. Fats was the real deal, and I knew it.

The lovely young girls from high school started to sort themselves in my life according to how they regarded the music I was listening to. Such distinctions then were not much different from how it is now in the world of pop music. There were recognitions of what one thought of as good music that served as passwords between friends, that meant entry into or exit out of social circles. I had my own personal inside source of music—the record store—that helped me curate friendships and figure out who to pursue and who not to bother.

This was the only real education I was getting, and it was deeply interesting to me. I started refining my ideas and came up with some concepts that remained useful for the rest of my life—so far.

I remember a date with a particularly attractive girl who I loved being with. She was so pretty, and I thought that was really enough. Being with pretty people made me feel pretty; I wasn't trying to think much deeper than that.

On this date, however, a new dynamic popped up. I asked if she had heard "Ain't That a Shame" and she said excitedly, "Yes! I have. I love it! Do you?" I said, "Yes, very much!" It felt as if I had just completed a marriage ceremony, like I was floating in some deep pool with her, mermaid and merman together in our own private lagoon.

She went on to say that she had the record, which surprised me, since I knew it had just come out. Then she asked, "Did you know that Pat Boone attended North Texas State University?"

I sat confused by this apparent non sequitur for a nanosecond, and then it dawned on me that Pat Boone had recorded Fats's song and was getting a lot of airplay. But I hadn't heard it. I didn't listen to the radio stations that played artists like Pat Boone. When I explained that I was talking about Fats Domino's recording, our lagoon split along two sides of a sandbar. Her side disappeared into the weeds, and my side felt very lonely.

I explained that Fats wrote the song and had recorded it first, with a great band out of New Orleans. She had not heard the Fats Domino version but promised she would listen, and a few days later I brought my record over to her house.

I assumed she would love the Fats Domino version and that

it would be a new light for her. I was so wrong it hurt. As the record played, she listened in near horror. She sat dead still and stared at the player.

I explained that this record was part of the new music coming out of the South, out of New Orleans and the Delta, and it was changing everything. It was rock and roll, and the great rock and rollers were players like Chuck Berry and Fats Domino and Little Richard. She drew a line at Little Richard as if I had thrown a bolt into the fruit pie she was eating. She allowed that she liked Elvis a little but thought he was "animalistic and crude" and that he didn't really need to do all those hip gyrations since he really was handsome enough "on his own." Little Richard was a mutant in her eyes. "What is *wrong* with his hair?" she asked.

I withdrew, and as her front door closed behind me I had the impression that her perception of Fats had created a barrier to her appreciation of his own version of his own song. Then it slowly dawned on me that maybe it had little to do with Fats or Pat. Perhaps her dislike of the Fats record came from, among other things, the fact that she heard Pat's record first. I realized that her initial impression of "Ain't That a Shame," as sung by Pat Boone, probably created a barrier between us as well. I named this "first impression" hypothesis "Boone-ing": when a person can't get past their first impression of a thing, perceiving it as the standard for all other versions simply because they experienced it first. This became a lesson to myself. First, to be aware of Boone-ing when it happened in my own thinking, and second, to beware of it.

Of all the records that came through the record store door, one in particular stood out. It was a seminal record for me, in part because of an extraordinary connection I made as I listened to it for the first time.

The record was "Bo Diddley," sung by Bo Diddley. When I first heard this one song, I was impelled to buy the LP, with twelve songs on it. That record revealed many of the intricacies of the aesthetic foundation I had been forming, and they would be a special part of my musical life from then forward.

There was poetry in the way the music of Bo Diddley came about. One remarkable element was the way the band was arranged. There was the usual bass and drums, an occasional piano, but the core of this band was Bo on guitar and vocals; Jerome Green, who played maracas; and Peggy Jones, who sang and played rhythm guitar along with Bo. They were inspired players whose playing might be uneven but was always powerful and to the point.

Bo and Peggy—later nicknamed Lady Bo by an adoring audience—crafted a rhythm style between them that was infectious and irresistible to me. It had a pulse that was like a cantilever between the first beat of a bar and the last—a skip—that has to be carefully parsed in order to be analyzed but is dead easy to feel. Once one feels the bones of this rhythm, it becomes commanding and contains everything from metabolism to metaphysics.

I instantly recognized it as being from the same kit bag that Uncle Chick used for cussing. The cadence of Chick's speech had the same infectious pulse that Bo Diddley's and Peggy Jones's guitar playing did. I don't think Uncle Chick and Bo Diddley's band would have stayed alive in the same room with each other for very long, but for me, my own *bud / buda dudda / buda dudda / du-du* was complete now with the unlikely and unforeseen connection of this basic rhythmic element. The confluence of the phonology of Chick's swearing and the musicality of Bo's playing shaped a landscape of musical thought I would build on for years, even when I wanted to play songs like "Beyond the Blue Horizon."

I could never have played in Bo's band, but oh how I wished I could.

There was a club in the late 1950s in Dallas called Louann's that was a hangout for dancing and drinking and carousing. It was mostly for the throwaway evenings of drunken college kids, but the musical acts that played there would become the stuff of legend, some of the most famous players in rock and roll history. Chuck Berry, Little Richard, Fats Domino, Ike and Tina Turner all played there, and these were the secondary acts.

The club's headliners were the big country acts of the time, like Ray Price. Strangely, the biggest act in Louann's history was Lawrence Welk's polka orchestra, which drew over six thousand people—not that the club could seat them.

When the acts that appealed to me came through Louann's, I would go if I could. One night I went to see Bo Diddley.

Bo Diddley's record was my first impression of Bo Diddley, so Bo was Booned for me. Now I wanted to watch him and Peggy and Jerome doing live what I had only heard them doing on record—to see if it was real.

When they took the stage I could see that this was a band of the strangest and highest order. Bo created an astounding presence, with his low-slung homemade guitar, his white sport coat and bow tie, and his band all in red plaid jackets with bow ties—except for Peggy. She was in a skintight one-piece gold lamé suit and stiletto heels. She was attached to a low-slung electric guitar similar to Bo's. They were playing through Fender Reverb amplifiers. Before they played a note, their presence made the whole room crackle with electricity.

When they played, something started up like a powerful engine, different than with any other players I had heard. There was something fundamental in their beat heard live; it was as if

Bo pulled everyone up, and the audience changed physiologically. I remember a feeling in my chest, like I was about to break into laughter. They were their own constellation in their own space. The cantilever that Bo and Peggy created in their rhythms made space for itself, just like the art of Marcel Duchamp and Richard Hamilton, Hendrix and Lennon.

The maracas mixed in the legacy touch of Latin claves and a drop of Southern hambone, so when Peggy and Bo added the thunder from their guitars, the result was a pulse that made everyone move, that made me want to sing, that sat me straight up and held me there. When the thunderclaps started pausing in tight syncopation with the drums, the rhythm roared like a wind-driven rainstorm on water. Floating. And when Bo sang "I look like a farmer, but I'm a lover!" I knew exactly what he was singing about, what he was saying. Bo and Peggy and Jerome were the first iteration of the Jimi Hendrix Experience in my life, the first time I kissed the sky.

When Bo played live that night, I heard music for the first time that matched what I heard in my head. Up till then, I heard lots of music that came close but wasn't ever really complete. This was not only complete; it was infinite, and it was real.

The twelve songs on that first Bo Diddley record from 1958 became my foundation in rock and roll. When I played my solo section on the first Monkees tour, it was Jerome Green holding eight maracas at Louann's that I would emulate in homage.

By the time I started going to Louann's, school had passed on, which is to say it had died for me. I had to get out of town and away from all my friends' graduations and parties and what to me was my high school's funeral. So I chose the Air Force. I thought I would sign up and fly silver jets, and be removed from the cadaver of school, taken out of a mysterious city and led to a glamorous life where surly bonds were surely slipped.

I went into basic training at Lackland Air Force Base in San Antonio, and to my curious fortune, Aida and Chick had just moved nearby. However, basic training allowed me no time for leaving the base and I knew early on I had made a mistake in joining. It would not go well for me or the Air Force unless I fixed this.

My notions of the military had been shaped by the movies, but in the actual Air Force the men who succeeded at military life were cut from much different cloth than I was. They were leaders, some were real heroes, and they were focused on the discipline and regimens of a fighting machine. I knew nothing of this kind of life. My battles were all in my head.

The leader of my troop (I'll call him Ray) pulled a few of us together one morning at 2:00 and asked us to go with him as his attendants to a fight he was going to have with a guy who had tried to bully him earlier. Ray was military top to bottom, a big guy, and he seemed very comfortable inside the military life. He looked sharp, and he was a natural leader. He and I had become friendly, so I agreed to go, with the idea that I would only watch. We walked side by side toward the parade grounds with the other men. I asked Ray how big the guy he was fighting was, and he said he was big.

Ray took the guy out with a couple of swift hits, and after the monster crumpled, Ray gave him a cookie and put him on a leash. The guy agreed to be Ray's bodyguard, and Ray took another giant step up the military ladder in the eyes of all of us. This was who I wanted keeping America safe.

A few weeks later I went to my CO and said I should probably go before anything bad happened. I explained that the longer I stayed, the worse it was going to get for both me and the Air Force.

He was a young captain and said that he would not want me to go under a cloud. So he offered me a general discharge under honorable conditions, but not before offering me a job that almost made me stay. My scores on the various aptitude tests I had taken while joining the Air Force were impressively high—which probably said a lot more about the tests than it said about me—so the CO offered me an assignment to an intelligence unit, a small team that traveled around the world in its own plane. It was a sweet deal, but I passed. I knew it was not to be.

The Air Force would be better off without me.

Buh dahdah / be buh da duh da / ba da da.

Not exactly Bo Diddley, but close enough.

Dallas was not the place to show up with an early general discharge from the military so soon after World War II. I hunted around for a place to hide, and Aida suggested I might like to try San Antonio College, a community college close to her and Chick, where she could provide some support. While in the military I had gotten my GED, so at least I would qualify for admission. My mother thought this was a great idea; Chick, not so much.

Chick's drill-sergeant days made me an object of derision for him. The fact that I didn't hunt and watched the halftime show instead of the football game made him pretty certain I was a sociopath—and probably gay, which to his mind was the worst of all afflictions.

College still seemed like a much better idea than the military, if I could get in. More significantly, I had gone to see Hoyt Axton, a popular folksinger, play at a folk club in Oklahoma City while I was in the Air Force, and watching him, I started to think I might be able to do that—to sing and play folk songs.

What did it matter that I couldn't play the guitar, couldn't sing very well, and didn't know any folk songs? I would be going to college and hanging out at the student union with pretty girls and singing folk songs. They would like me. I might even figure out a way to get a cool car.

That Christmas, in 1961, my mother and stepdad gave me a guitar that I took to San Antonio College with me. Ten days later, I played my first concert, a paid gig for a group of young, attractive graduating nurses, all female. I'm glad I wasn't in the audience, because I would have been embarrassed for me.

It sounds prodigious, teaching myself guitar and giving a concert in ten days, but it wasn't. I simply stayed in my little college apartment and hacked away twelve hours a day. Ten days later I had been playing for 120 hours, more or less. My colleagues at school who played guitar showed me some folk songs, and I tried my hand at making up a few. The music was so much fun to play that I became totally immersed in the practice and lost all track of time.

By the time the opportunity to play for the nurses came around, I was ready, with about twenty minutes of folk songs and no reasonable fear. The nurses loved it. I made a joke about the banquet food that got a laugh, my first from an audience. That put me and the audience at ease, so I pressed on, ignorant of any standard of entertainment other than my own. I did fine, got paid, and decided to do more. I wanted to learn to play better and learn more songs, but even the folk songs I heard and wanted to play were out of reach for my level, so I started making songs up.

The lyrics came first—or I should say, nonsense syllables came first while I banged on the guitar. And I mean literally banged, like a drum. I had to make up the melody according to what I could actually play on the guitar, but the lyrics would flow from rhythm and sound. The nonsense syllables would spontaneously form words, and even a rhyme sometimes. From there, a meaning would start to come into focus, and the song would more or less sing itself to me. Then I would quickly record what I had on a tape recorder, write the lyrics down, and commit the song to memory, where it would live as an actual thing.

The lyrics, rhyme, and melody came easy this way—not to say they were any good, but only to say they were easy for me to cobble together. What was hard was playing. I was not a very good player and was pretty sure I would never be, so I learned to lean more on the writing and develop it.

I was just writing whatever popped into my head. This was valid, but I realized later that it was not the same as writing from a point of view or developing an idea with a specific purpose in mind. It was a cross between singing and spewing, and while it made for some pretty good tunes and simple love songs, it was not really the same as framing an idea with music to express it.

But in the early going, none of that mattered. What mattered was the same thing that had mattered for years: How do I look and what do people think of me? Cars and women.

A great piano player said to me once in a rehearsal, after a spectacular rendition of a difficult song, "Man, we can get lots of chicks with this." I wasn't sure whether it was a joke or not.

I came up with some good ideas about how to make money playing music, and I even managed to get myself a very cool car: a 1959 white Bugeye Sprite. It was just the car I wanted and would be perfect for bopping around. And it was the car, the guitar, and the songs I was writing that attracted my future wife, Phyllis.

Phyllis was literate, and her literacy saved me from illiteracy. Suddenly there were real and meaningful words to the Bo Diddley beat of my life. She had blasted through high school and enrolled in San Antonio College when she was sixteen. I knew almost nothing about her except that I was drawn to her intelligence and grace. She was a petite brunette with lovely features that made her photogenic as well as attractive in person. Most important, though, she was a terrific girlfriend and a better wife.

We shared the clumsy moments of getting to know each other, but we found each other's shortfalls funny—actually, she had none I could see, but I still found her amusing, and I had plenty of shortfalls for both of us, so she was laughing all the time. She sang and knew something about folk music but not the singers. When she introduced me to the songs of Bob Dylan, she pronounced his name *Die*-lan. Later, when we got a dog, she named the dog Dielan as a recognition of her naïveté.

I had no sense of poetry or literature, but since Phyllis had enough for both of us she lifted me up. She was the first one who told me I was a good songwriter. It had never occurred to me.

I had no idea of poetry as an academic pursuit, but I knew Bo Diddley backward and forward, and I wanted to go at least that far with rhythm. Every rhythmic intricacy was embedded in that pulse, and I could transfer that to every sonnet and phrase with a little twist here and there to make it fit. I learned early to keep all that to myself. I listened dutifully to discourse on prosody, but none of its lessons played finer, louder, or more sublimely than Bo.

This is not to say poetry was worse than Bo. Phyllis would open a door onto the whole world of literature and music and art; these would come alive for me as I got hold of the deeper spiritual sense available through education and study. Unfortunately, that door was opened when I was in my twenties, in Los Angeles—where I would learn that Hollywood is a no more suitable environment for an autodidact than the cockpit of a space shuttle.

5

> And then it's ultimately of course not even actors we're espying, not even people: it's EM-propelled analog waves and ion streams and rear-screen chemical reactions throwing off phosphenes in grids of dots not much more lifelike than Seurat's own Impressionist commentaries on perceptual illusion. Good Lord and the dots are coming out of our *furniture*.
>
> —David Foster Wallace, "E Unibus Pluram"

One afternoon before he was a movie star, Jack Nicholson was up at my 1960s-modern house, high on a hill overlooking the San Fernando Valley. We were out by the kidney-shaped pool. The small part of the kidney was indoors, and around this decking inside was a large faux-log fireplace with a hood that came down from the ceiling, a dinner table for twelve, and a full bar with bottles of booze on glass shelves lit from underneath by fluorescent lights. Jack and I would sit at the bar, look out at the view, and tell each other stories. He was the better storyteller between us by several orders of magnitude.

Easy Rider had just been finished and was waiting in the wings for release. Jack was speculating about the scenes he was in—one where his character gets a helmet and another where his character smokes dope for the first time—and was sanguine. He felt sure this was going to be a big break for him. So did I, but not because I had seen it. I just had so much confidence in Jack's take on matters like that. He had an intuitive sense of things.

I met Jack through Bob Rafelson and Bert Schneider, the producers of *The Monkees.* He was introduced to me as part of a team that was coalescing around Raybert, their production company. We became friends and steady companions right away. Jack was still bombing around the streets of LA in his yellow VW convertible looking for work as an actor-writer-director, and he was good company.

As we sat by the pool talking about career and next steps and the arts, he said that he had made a personal rule that he would never appear on television. I was up to my knees in television, so I wanted to know more.

He said, "Theater is life. Cinema is art. Television is furniture."

I laughed. It was the first time I had heard that, and it may have been original to him. No one had distinguished the forms like that for me before. Marshall McLuhan was writing then, and his book *Understanding Media* was causing a stir. One of his ideas was that television was a "cool" medium because it took effort from the viewer to get the content from it, requiring the viewer to engage in a way that film and print did not. The television viewer had to create the image they were seeing.

Though movies were popular entertainment, they were considered art by popular opinion, and the people in the movies were considered artists. Television actors, by movie standards, were merely bits and pieces of the furniture. If it weren't for the money that it made, television would have been swept away by the studios along with 3-D and CinemaScope. But it did make money. It was the most popular medium in the 1960s and was much more powerful than anyone then knew.

Jack's point was that television would not help someone become a movie star. If he wanted to become a movie star, he needed to avoid TV entirely, and he was right.

Avoiding television was something I never thought of, and I could not have chosen one way or the other. The circumstances that had thrown me into TV were now circumstances that were keeping me there. Phyllis and I had fled Dallas to keep from getting caught in the disparaging dismissal of being unwed and pregnant, and now, in LA, our little family was sprouting and setting out roots, one of which had wrapped itself around a television show.

Jack did part of the writing for the Monkees movie, *Head*. He and the other guys in the Monkees, plus Bert and Bob and I, all headed out for a weekend in Ojai, north of LA. We played around and smoked dope and raced golf carts and talked into a microphone and tape recorder, telling jokes and stories. Jack took all that dialogue and helped put together a film script that I thought was terrific. It was highly psychedelic, since everyone was high on grass, and it was surreal, since we all lived in Movieland, but it shook the base of media in a way nothing I had seen before had done.

Pop culture was burgeoning, but nothing was growing like television in the 1950s and '60s. In the US it had started developing in the late 1940s, and as early as 1956, Richard Hamilton named his Pop Art piece showing a large television console in a living room *Just What Is It That Makes Today's Homes So Different, So Appealing?*

Something was going on with TV besides being furniture.

Head was a child of that culture. The *Monkees* TV show fit into the pop-culture world like a soup can in a Warhol painting.

The design content the soup-can label might have on its own was irrelevant. A label was just a sign, but as art it had become significant, as far as pop culture went. The medium was distinct from its content. I felt confident that what was physically real about television—the dancing dots of light and their ability to conjure or reflect a moving image—would stick, but the content, the series sitcoms and dramas of television, would change, mutate over time, and fade into shadows in the arc-light glow of LA.

Jack's sense of television as furniture represented a point of view that marked the limit of the Monkees for me in more ways than one. When he made the remark, I was well into the second season of the show; the response from the creative team there to my efforts to contribute had been essentially "Shut up." Since I never had an opportunity in the show to do much more than jump around, I thought I would let the whole phenomenon wind down until I could gracefully jump off.

The show and its environs had gotten weird in the extreme in its last days. To my eyes Bert and Bob had transformed from the New York hipsters-in-suits they had been at the beginning to full-on hippies in tie-dye and beads.

Shooting days for the show were an anything-goes kind of madhouse. The Monkees had become palpable to a whole class of prepubescent TV watchers who saw much more in the show than was put there, and it had become excruciatingly important to them. The fan letters spoke of lives saved and changed because of the existence of the Monkees.

While I was glad that others had found meaning in the show, I had made no real connections through it. My writing and music had not developed and remained where they were two years before. They were amateurish and in need of care and nourishment. I had gained some experience in music and film production and was a minor celebrity, but I was in the same place artistically as when I started, except I had a lot of people angry at me. At the beginning of the show, my suggestions were swatted away like gadflies, but by the beginning of the second season, when the show had become a success and the actors were no longer expendable, I had the Queen's veto and was considered dangerous.

The Monkees was filmed at the corner of Sunset and Gower, on a soundstage built in the 1930s. Part of the time we were filming, Cary Grant was next door making one of his last films. Sally Field was doing *The Flying Nun* on another stage.

The *Monkees* stage and set contained mostly hand-me-down equipment from the Golden Age of Hollywood, the 1930s, '40s, and '50s—huge Mitchell 35mm film cameras with bulbous noise-suppressing blimps surrounding their mechanism, 25-foot-long boom microphones, and lights the size of home refrigerators. The clumsiness of the gear made shooting a tedious, old-time process.

The show was regularly directed by James Frawley, but from time to time the producers would invite directors to come and guest-direct a segment of the show. They had some famous names come through the doors to check it out, but none of them ever directed. I found out later that many of them thought the show was "lame-o," a phrase that worked its way into the *Monkees* cast and crew lexicon over time.

The show had fallen together much the way the band had. I think there was an effort to copy the work of Richard Lester and his direction of *A Hard Day's Night*, but I never could tell if anyone knew how to direct like that.

What happened between the time we filmed and the time the show was cut together and aired was a complete mystery to me. While we were filming, there seemed to be little interest in sticking to the script, and there was the constant presence of a belief that everything would work out all right after a free-association editing session where everything would be tossed into the show at random—guest appearances out of nowhere (I had Frank Zappa as my guest), cuts between non sequiturs, abandonment of all but the slenderest story line, and running around doing "romps" that were cut in over the top of the music tracks.

All throughout the filming of the show I was an unaware and unhelpful participant. I wasn't angry or spiteful in any way; I simply had almost no idea what to do.

I arrived on this set as a student poet and singer, kind of a traditional troubadour with roots in the Middle Ages. I would write a poem and set it to music, mostly so I could remember it and perform it for an audience live. When I took the job on *The Monkees*, I thought this was what I had been hired to do, or at least some version of it. I was under the impression it would require me to write, act, sing, and play as one of the main cast members of a TV show about an out-of-work rock band. I learned in the very first days that I was somewhat right but mostly wrong.

When I asked Bob Rafelson when we were going to record the music, he said we didn't need to, that it was part of the production process that would be handled by other people. This method was a part of the usual approach for adding music to motion pictures. I said I thought we were going to play as a band, but Bob said we wouldn't have the time to do that and perform in the TV series.

I was confused. I was not clear from the first meeting with Micky, Davy, and Peter how it was all going to work as a band. Peter I knew as a solo folksinger who sang Pete Seeger–type folk protest songs and played the banjo. Davy I knew was the Broadway star of *Oliver!* who could dance and belt a song from a stage, and Micky I knew as a TV star from his days in *Circus Boy*, an early TV series. Being from the South, and being drawn to blues and country music, I felt like a misfit from the beginning, but it seemed that the differences were going to have to be managed somehow if we were going to be a band.

Who would play what and who would sing and who would write and who would produce the records was of keen interest to me—what would be my part and contribution?—so I was unprepared for the idea that the four of us would have nothing to do with any of that. It seemed as odd as it was disappointing. I had seen the opportunity arise to make music in a band, but now it was quickly slipping away.

Then it occurred to me that perhaps we might be able to become a band of actors who played the part of musicians who were struggling to make a living together as a band. I started to make adjustments to this. In high school I had made choir buddies in the school choir—very close, mutually supportive friends who socialized and played and sang together, in school and out, around the music we all were learning. It was the music that created the camaraderie, but here in the world of TV it was the show and the acting that seemed to be the basis of relations, though it was not social; it was a job, and the whole enterprise was compartmentalized. Maybe this would be something I could learn over time, but it would take some adjustment. It was becoming clear that I had not been hired to play music or to write it, which was OK with me, except at this moment of insight I didn't know exactly what I had been hired to do.

Bob Rafelson was curly-haired and physically big but presented himself as approachable, and had an infectious laugh and what seemed to be a genuine interest in people, so I told him of my confusion. He asked what kind of music I liked and would like to play if it were up to me. I had no specific idea of what kind of music would fit, but I told him I would get some records for him to listen to. He gave me thirty or forty dollars and said I could go across the street to a record store called Wallichs Music City and pick out records I liked.

I knew Bob was very familiar with Beatles records and other pop tunes, so I bought Bo Diddley, Ike and Tina Turner, Jimmy Reed, and Chuck Berry. Bob said he loved all that kind of music, but that it wouldn't work in the show because it was too bluesy and too far in the margins to appeal to mainstream television watchers. Still, he said, if I wanted to be involved in the music and help produce some, he would see what he could do about including me in it.

Bob sent me to Bert Schneider, his partner in Raybert. Bert's control of the business side of things appeared to be total, but I was not sure what else he did. All production decisions more or less flowed through him, because he was making the deals. I suppose my questions about the music must have fallen under the heading of employee negotiations.

I respected Bert and was impressed by him. He was a tall blond in his thirties with a lanky grace to him, quite handsome according to the ladies, and sat with his feet on his desk every time I saw him. He had a slow-going demeanor and a quick bright laugh that shone as intelligence. I didn't know it at the time, but his father, Abe, was the head of Columbia Pictures, the owner of Screen Gems, which was the entity that was producing *The Monkees*. During the time we shot the pilot for the show, I took the opportunity to get acquainted with everyone, and Bert stood out as the most complex character to me. He was obviously smart, cultured, highly educated, and had an edge that became sharper over the time I knew him. As far as I could tell, this edge was anchored deeply in the advancing anti-war sentiment of the American public, along with the rapidly developing counterculture and civil rights movement.

Bert told me that all the areas I thought I was going to participate in were more or less fully staffed, and all I was required to do was be an actor. Bert, like Bob, told me I was welcome to poke around and look at how the music would be made and how the show would be written and produced, but he made it clear that my duties were limited to showing up on the set and delivering the lines in the teleplay. I was disappointed, but I didn't let on. It was a good job and I understood the limits, so that was enough.

Live performance was still my guiding light. I cherished and protected the flame from the night at the Troubadour that had introduced me to a real audience and opened the mystery of what it was like to perform, singing my own songs. It was inspiring stuff—and nowhere present in the conceit of the show. I did not expect that being a cast member of a TV show would provide that kind of a ride; nevertheless, I felt confident I could render a fetching facsimile of a musical performance as an actor on the show, and that seemed to be all anybody wanted. The bottom line for me at that time was that I was grateful for the work, whatever it might have been.

Still, I happily accepted Bert's offer to poke around, and I even went to the first writers' meeting for the series, after the pilot had been shot and sold to NBC. I was in that meeting only about a half hour before I realized how little I knew about writing for television and how much of an irritant I would be if I stayed. The only thing I remember was the decision to use the real names of the actors as the names of the characters on the show.

I think this happened because the pilot did not sell right away. I understood it did not test well, so the series was initially rejected by the networks. Bert and Bob, as young New Yorkers, had a streak of hip that traded on being avant-garde and adroitly subversive. That covert subversion was becoming the lingua franca of the 1960s counterculture, but Bob and Bert were going to have to tone it down if they were going to sell the *Monkees* pilot as a series to a national network.

The test audiences found the characters on the original pilot derisive and sarcastic, and they were very much disliked. The characters came across as arrogant and ignorant kids getting underfoot, not as hapless hopeful musicians doing madcap silly pratfalls. It wasn't funny. I can't remember the name of the character I played in the first pilot, but it was not Mike Nesmith.

It seemed to me that the decision to change the names of the characters to our real names and to include our actual screen tests as part of the pilot was intended to humanize the show. Over the years, everyone connected with the production of the show in a senior capacity told me that this was their idea, because after the real names were included, the show sold. The screen tests, basically question-and-answer interview films of us on a set from another show, made the pilot scenario seem more real, and the characters were now closer to the four of us as people.

As the years passed, I could see that this name change was where a reckoning point was fixed. I knew nothing of McLuhan at the time, but going over his footprints later I saw that making our real names the names of the characters infused the show with enough Pinocchio-itis to push it far into uncharted territory.

In 1965, after *The Monkees* was sold but before we were in production, I went to visit one of the people who were making music for the show. I came away in shock—both at what I heard and at the process by which it was made. The best description I can come up with is that the music was thin—like jingles for cigarettes and soap. I wanted to quit and told Bert so, but he calmed me down by asking me what I would do if I were in complete charge of the music. I had no idea, other than a sense that the music I had heard for the show was not it.

For me, the Beatles were writing the songs of my life. The bar they had set for pop music was in the stratosphere. They were singing about subjects that required sophistication and had a clear point of view that required high artistry to express. Dylan was a mutant on the pop-music scene. No one was sure whether he was a folksinger or a rock and roller. He was innovative and sui generis, arguably the reference standard of the singer-songwriter for the times.

In fact, popular music in general was starting to take on a tattered image in the shadow of such titans. Once, a pop song could be fatuous and banal and still very popular, but that was changing. Popular music was coming from the hymnal of a new church. These new popular artists like Dylan and the Beatles were delivering their own point of view, uninfluenced by what the masses might think.

But those Beatles and Dylan songs were getting fainter behind every door that was closing on the soundstage. The music the show's producers wanted to make was music for the masses—just as the pop standard was shifting to music that artists were making for themselves. That was the single distinction between outgoing and incoming popular music.

Television compounded the problem of delivering high-quality, dense material—art, music, and poetry—because the medium was so little understood. Once an idea was loaded into television, no one was quite sure how it would be received and interpreted. I would love to have been in a music ensemble that could have tackled the form of American blues like the Rolling Stones had, but a band conceived and written for television was not that band, and I knew it.

I appreciated Bert's offer to let me produce, or perhaps curate, the music for the show, but it was clearly out of my reach, and I told him so. I wanted to help, but this was like the Air Force all over again. This was not a group of players who needed or wanted what I had to give, especially since I had no idea at the time what that might be. I just wanted out.

Bert's offer was an effort to make me stay. To this day, I have no idea why he felt compelled to keep me on the show. In television, as in movies, troublesome actors were usually dismissed unceremoniously and the next willing actor put in their place. I declined the offer but said I would stay. He said he hoped I would continue to submit songs and encouraged me to get to know Tommy Boyce and Bobby Hart.

Tommy and Bobby typified the friendliest and best of the LA pop-music scene. I was not an immediate fan of their music, but I was happy to get to know them and happy that Bert had facilitated that. I had no way to collaborate or write with them, though. I thought the first record they made for the show, "Last Train to Clarksville," was first-rate pop music, but then what did I know about such things? T&B seemed to be capable hands, and I was more or less satisfied that I could perform their songs, if they asked me to play guitar or sing, and enjoy it.

Before *The Monkees* aired, "Last Train to Clarksville" was released and quickly became a hit. But the record was not uniformly well received. The music junkies, hippies, and flower children, the followers of Leary's *Politics of Ecstasy*, regarded the music as if it were the police arriving at a frat party. They called it bubblegum music and banished it as illegitimate and, furthermore, as dangerous, disrupting their new-music taxonomy. So the word went out.

Then Tommy and Bobby told me they were competing against another musical effort coming from the East Coast. A group of writers in the Brill Building who worked for Screen Gems, which was under the control of Don Kirshner, had started writing songs for the show, and the rumor was they were going to provide more and more music. *Provide* may be too generous a word. Tommy said that he and Bobby had been promised the job of writing music for the show, and now it was being parceled out—some to Kirshner, possibly some to me—so he wasn't sure exactly what to do or how to think about any of it. He wondered if I did.

I was amazed. I had no intention of writing songs for the show. Bert had said I should submit some songs, but I had no idea how to write a pop song any more than I knew how to levitate. I told Tommy and Bobby that. They seemed relieved.

But I was now distressed for a different reason. I thought Bert and Bob had final control of the music. Could it be that in fact they had no control and the music was going to be shipped in from a remote office of the publishing company owned by the studio?

I could not find any comfort in this—not that my comfort mattered much to anyone, least of all Don Kirshner and the Brill Building writers. The music was in such a nonconcentric orbit with respect to the show's basic situations and narratives that it appeared to be an afterthought. I retreated all the way back to my job as an actor, but now with a certain detachment. I assumed no one would notice.

Bert, however, did notice and would not leave it alone. He offered to give me full control of four tracks on each album. I think he knew the importance and value of the new rock and roll, and that the music for the show needed to clear this bar. Nonetheless, I refused again. Selection of the music for the show was starting to look like a battlefield, with each side arraying itself against the other in grotesque displays of costumes and weapons. I said I would submit some songs through the channels, but I didn't want to get into a fight with anyone.

I made song demos at the Screen Gems publishing offices and submitted them through those channels, but the submissions came back to me summarily rejected. I didn't know at the time that the rejection was coming from the Brill Building—from

Kirshner and his minions, who wanted all the show's music to come from their shop of tunesmiths and land on their balance sheets.

The critique, if I can call it that, was clear: My songs were not pop songs. They did not have a hook. They did not have the title in the lyrics. They sounded more like country songs and weren't very good for even that. If I had been a skeptic, I would have thought Kirshner had a hidden agenda concerning the control of the music, but I was not a skeptic and the criticism seemed accurate to me in the context of the needs of the show. But the rebuff did not lessen my confidence in the songs as songs.

One of them was one I had sung at my personal-best Troubadour night. But the inspiration from that night was disappearing into the morass of television production, which was typified by the confusion of a girl who threw herself on the hood of my car.

I was driving to work early one morning—I left around 6:00 to get in wardrobe and makeup before the show started filming at 7:30—so there was very little traffic. I was stopped at a light at the corner of Beverly and Santa Monica, and no one was around but a pretty young girl. She was walking across the street in front of my car—my brand-new, first-money-purchased Buick Riviera—when she glanced at me and recognized me. Then she screamed and threw herself across the hood, pounding on the windshield and yelling, "Mike!"

I was flabbergasted. I stared in wonder and shock. It was shades of George Harrison and the Corpus Christi 7-Eleven all over again. After a minute or two she seemed to shift to some other state of mind and got control of herself. She got up off the hood, straightened her clothes, and walked away, obviously embarrassed. She was gone as quickly as she had appeared, as if nothing had happened.

But something *had* happened, and it felt profoundly abnormal to me. The girl had no notion of who I was other than being a real live person who resembled the one she had seen on television. I had no way to connect with her except through my windshield wipers.

I didn't know whether this sort of thing was happening everywhere. I knew something like it could happen in Corpus Christi. I knew it had happened around the Beatles' performances. Now I knew it could happen in LA, sitting at a traffic light early in the morning. The light turned green, and I sat there in my car, bewildered, not moving until another car appeared behind me and honked.

In this general pall, I pressed forward and, again with Bert's encouragement—almost insistence—recorded some music for the show: "Papa Gene's Blues" and "The Kind of Girl I Could Love." Bert told me he was going to put them in the show and on the first album and urged me to keep recording as I wished. He threw open a great door for me, and I was grateful and happy, but I was also wary and disconcerted. Put simply, I had no idea how to do what I was being asked to do.

My songwriting process did not take into any consideration whether the song would be popular or accepted. I wrote poems about things that interested me, that were part of my everyday life and my musings as an artist. The music itself tended to have a twang and a country/blues sensibility and the odd touch of lounge and big-band organ music. I never thought of them as pop songs, only as songs that would be a message of my own to a live audience.

The recording session for those first songs had not gone well. I didn't know any of the members of the band hired for me except guitarist James Burton, whom I had specifically requested. I was aware of James because he played on Ricky Nelson's record "Hello Mary Lou," a song I liked.

At the first big studio session in RCA Studio A in downtown Hollywood, the session players sort of took over for me and to my great relief pulled everything together into a record. I was thrilled to see a studio at work, pleased to get the opportunity to record my songs, but these were not the sort of records I had intended or thought I would make. I heard the songs in my head differently from the way the session guys played them, but since I had no idea how to convey my musical ideas to them, the arrangements just drifted into what the session guys intuitively knew. The session players all said "head arrangement" to each other as we got under way, and that seemed to suffice.

I was disappointed at the way the records came out, but I did nothing to change any of it. The session players themselves were astonishingly good, supportive, and willing to do anything I asked of them. Sadly, I didn't know what to ask. I was being pushed along by the huge celebrity sail that had unfurled on my tiny and seriously under-equipped boat, and ignorance was acting as wind. I said it sounded great and thanked everyone, and then breathed a sigh of relief along with the disappointment and confusion inside.

After the first Monkees album was released, it earned a gold record, and Ward Sylvester, one of the producers, made a quick and simple announcement about this after the day's shooting at the soundstage to the cast and crew. I asked how many sales a gold record indicated, and was told it was 500,000 in the United States. The first thing that popped into my mind was, *What happened to all the other 149,500,000 people?* Foolishly, I said this out loud, and the set went silent in revulsion.

At that moment I became a contrarian, perverse and ungrateful. How could I ask such a question? It was innocent and sincere, half an irony on my part, and it wasn't until I got the reaction that I gave it any thought. When I saw the recoil of my workmates, my desire to be well thought of took over, and I began to think how I might try to better fit in.

It was too late, of course; the damage had been done. Bert and Bob had put two of my songs into the show. I was seen as a full-fledged music provider, and I was expected to uphold their constitution and to defend the enterprise. Instead I was seen as acting like an ingrate and potential traitor just as they were going to war with Kirshner.

My weekly paycheck from *The Monkees* was $480, with a special bonus of $100 negotiated by my agent. I have to this day no idea what Davy, Micky, and Peter got paid. We never spoke of it. I was thrilled. It was a good income for me and those times, and it put food on the table and gas in the car.

I assumed that was going to be about the extent of my Monkees riches, but I had not counted on record sales, record royalties, copyrights, and other fees relating to songwriting in general. The salary paled in comparison, and I can't really say how much the music alone paid me because I don't remember, but it was more money than I had ever seen in my lifetime or in one place. Every day more came from the hidden recesses of the world of the songwriter and publisher and record sales.

Phyllis and I built a big house on a hill, with panoramic views and a rambling floor plan, in a fancy-houses neighborhood on Mulholland. I had never built a house, had never decorated a house, had never bought furniture from furniture makers, and neither had Phyllis. My ideas flowed from comic books and the popular press and the last thing I'd heard. My idea of furniture came from television ads for furniture warehouses. My idea of comfort was a recliner. LA décor was a pastiche, shifting with the sands of ticket sales and the latest knee-jerk of the populace. I had no clue how to avoid doing the same thing, so I did do the same thing.

Bert and his wife, Judy, were cut from a different cloth altogether. They were sophisticated, New York–fashionable, and artsy. On one of the maybe two times they came over for dinner, Judy remarked on how lovely a piece of our furniture was, a chest I never took much notice of before. The decorator had bought it, and I thought it might not be so good because it looked a little beat-up to me. Wasn't new furniture supposed to be new? When Judy was out of earshot, Phyllis said, "Well, I guess we're keeping the chest." That pretty well summed up our taste.

We weren't the Beverly Hillbillies by any stripe, but I was naïve and uneducated. Because she read a lot, Phyllis knew how to use and pronounce words, and on more than one occasion she gave me credit for being clever where none was due. Once, I used the phrase "cast dispersions upon" and she thought I was saying *dispersions* instead of *aspersions* as a sort of high-level pun. I wasn't. I really thought that was how the phrase went. Like Uncle Chick, I had just filled in the boxes with whatever would get me over a linguistic hump.

I was in the fast lane going really slow and getting the finger a lot and didn't know it. Whenever Phyllis found out an idiot wind was blowing, she would shield me from it and gently correct me. She was a good woman, so naturally I did her wrong.

By "wrong" I mean terribly wrong. I told her on the way out to LA that I was not going to be a good husband, that I did not want to be married, and that I felt forced into the whole thing because of a mistake we made. She responded by saying, "Let me take the child. I'll raise it alone and never look back." And I responded, "No, no, please don't leave me." That kind of wrong.

It's not easy being stupid, even though in ways it is unavoidable. But stupid is one thing. Mean-spirited and loutish is another. I was gaining very rapidly in the department of awful. I am grateful to this day that I was a man of peace—I didn't hit people or get in physical altercations. I also did not get hit by anyone except my mother and Phyllis, who on occasion could not contain herself at my awfulness and would slap me.

Davy and Micky and Peter all fought—verbally and physically. They broke into halfhearted meaningless fistfights at the drop of an insult. The set would turn into a playground of entitled eight-year-olds at a private school. I was always for stepping back and letting them fight it out, but it was not my choice to make. By the time the show was in full production, we were prime meat, and the producers and directors and others didn't want us to get injured, so they would jump in and stop the slapping.

The rage of impotence, feeling like a marionette on the end of a string that disappeared into a nowhere above me, began to increase daily and weirdly with every royalty check and every new girl throwing herself on the hood of the car, and I couldn't shake it. On the set and in life in general I began to feel somehow entitled to lose my temper anytime I chose. I was on TV. I was a media star. I was recognizable. I had a gold record on my wall. My run-away-from-home-and-join-the-air-force logic was taking an exponentially stronger hold of me.

I would like to report that there were moments of quiet and solace and inner peace, but that would be false. My days in LA passed in a nonstop terror ride of missed steps and missed cues, of social disgrace and ineptitude. The richer and more famous I got, the worse it got. I had a pretty good teacher in one of Andy Griffith's characters, Lonesome Rhodes.

I have no idea why, but one of the first tasks I was given when I started coming to the lot at Columbia was to watch old movies, and the first movie Bert showed me was *A Face in the Crowd*, in which Griffith starred as Rhodes, a dopey drunken drifter who gets put on the air and becomes an influential radio and television host. I saw it in a screening room alone and wondered why I was sent to watch that film. It was so far from what I thought we were doing, and I could not imagine why Bert wanted me to see it. It took decades for it to dawn on me.

There is a moment in the film when Rhodes is talking to the studio publicist just after *The Lonesome Rhodes Show* is canceled. Rhodes asks for some help, and the publicist says, "Don't you know that I hate you?"

This happened to me too.

I stopped by to visit an assistant recording engineer at his home unannounced, just to say hello. He had bought a new house and told everyone about it at a recording session, and I thought I would celebrate it and take a little tour. When he opened the door and found me there he wouldn't let me in and said, standing in the doorway, "Don't you know that I hate you?"

No, I didn't. But I still didn't make the connection with *A Face in the Crowd*.

Into this scene of 1960s LA, there came into view for me an awful and enormous force besides television and its internecine dramas. It is thick, rank, and overwhelming, and it comes in the most beautiful shapes and sizes, and yet it is not a physical force. It is not gender specific or age specific. It passes through the gates of economics and social scenes unchallenged, its only credential being the necessary pulchritude. I have come to call it Celebrity Psychosis.

This force is not an effect but a cause of behavior. It is most like a pathogen, and it has many symptoms. There are those who are sometimes able to resist the malady, but if one is not inoculated by the art of being human, it is almost impossible to avoid.

Whatever character flaws may exist in an otherwise simple, sincere person, Celebrity Psychosis amplifies them by almost inconceivable orders of magnitude. Whatever beneficial or admirable qualities of thought one may have, CP hides them behind arrogance, willful pride, and a Stygian night. It is not a demon, but if it were, no fairy tale could describe its destructive power.

Still, I will tell you my tale of it, and you can laugh with me through the tears—or vice versa—as it came like a monstrous gladiator of unimaginable power into the arenas where the Monkees were performing.

When the second Monkees LP came out, I recoiled in defense and anger. Don Kirshner seemed comfortable setting the Monkees up as a scam, especially if he controlled the music, and he positioned the four of us, under our own names, as a "phenomenon" who had created the record and were on a parallel track with all the other fantastic bands of the time. We had, of course, done nothing of the sort.

I had not even heard the record. A couple of my songs were on it, but that was little comfort. It felt wrong to me—and not like in a play or a movie where something non-diegetic can be seen as "wrong," as in "not of the world of the play." This false-band album crossed a line somewhere. At the time I wasn't sure where, so faint had the line become on television.

I went to Bert and asked what the intent of all this was, and he said he felt it was part of the bigger picture of the show—that the show was coming to life, and we had an opportunity to set the Monkees up as a real enterprise and make music and television all under that rubric. He positioned it as all very legitimate inside the world of make-believe.

I couldn't really argue with him, because I didn't really know precisely what he was talking about. His was the magic of the Hollywood Mind.

The Hollywood Mind sits hidden and protected behind the curtains, wearing camouflage. The main metric for this mind's understanding of value is popularity, as gauged through things like ticket sales that are disguised as a public mandate. In the beginning, I felt that Bert was a sincere producer, wanting his creation to explore all aspects of expression. I got the feeling he wanted the music to pour forth from the four of us just as the show poured forth from the writers, in a creative effort. I assumed he recognized that such effort might provide the public mandate. But I misunderstood, since this was before I had come to know the intricacies of the Hollywood Mind.

A public mandate is only a stone's throw from mob rule, but the Hollywood Mind understands enough not to get in front of an angry mob. There is usually enough of a signal for the Hollywood Mind to know when to take the money and run. The Monkees and Kirshner had not quite gotten there, but Bert's Hollywood Mind was already gathering justification from a benign public's willingness to receive what the Monkees had to give even before it paid for it.

The Monkees were coming off several No. 1 records, but I don't think anyone knew how many units were really being sold. The only thing sure was the power of the desire that Monkees fans had to see us live.

That the show's creators had never thought we would actually perform live concerts went unnoticed and unremarked upon. When the opportunity arose, all the powers that were acted as if it had been part of the plan all along, but there was no preparation for it, no planning for it, and felt to me like a desperate cash grab by the execs.

No one knew whether the four of us could play as a band, but it seemed pretty simple to me. The show was about a struggling band, so if we were to actually play, we wouldn't need to be all that good, just sincere. Playing like a garage band would suffice, and I had the notion we could pull that off easily enough. We were already structured like a band kids would put together. A couple of us could play stringed instruments, a couple of us could sing, and somehow it would come together well enough to fit with the sentiments of the show.

Still, the four of us were suddenly on the front lines, and we knew it. We knew that whatever effort we made needed to be sincere and focused.

Micky tackled learning to play the drums like an actor learning lines, and it worked out enough to seem plausible. I could bang away on the guitar like a folksinger, playing block chords. Davy would be in front wiggling, which he did well, and Peter played bass mainly because nobody else could.

We started wailing away in rehearsal, trying to get a decent rendition of the songs on the records. It never sounded great, but it didn't sound all that bad. It was very much a garage band of kids who couldn't really make it. It was charming. It would have made a good television show.

We went out on our first tour, and that was the darkest part for me of everything that had happened to that moment. Fortunately the fans did not notice this.

The live shows were fun and they had their own legitimacy—Pinocchio was coming to life and fulfilling the wish of not only Geppetto but everyone else. As usual, though, the Pinocchio metaphor wouldn't completely map. Little wooden boys don't really come to life, and guys like Geppetto—who pray to fairies that they will—are not sane.

We didn't play well, and we couldn't actually play like the recordings, so what was happening live was something besides meeting those expectations, but it was something the fans loved even more.

I had to learn this. I had experienced nothing like it in my life before. The approbation was nearly hysterical, and the sound of the crowd was deafening in its happiness and exuberance. They were getting exactly what they came for—a life-changing, enriching, enchanting, and thrilling experience. The joy of those crowds was transforming for me, and playing for them, such as we could, created moments genuine and heartfelt from both sides of the footlights.

The Monkees had no critical cachet and were barred from most legitimate entertainment circles, but it was clear that Monkees fans did not accept this view. The din at the Monkees concerts moved me back two feet the way Hendrix would later move me back three—but not for the same reason. What was real about the Monkees' live shows was the fans' enjoyment and happiness, and that redeemed the effort for me, the effort of the practicing and touring and recording. For me there was little satisfaction in the performance itself, but I was happy because they were happy.

In putting together the show, we decided that we should each take a solo turn in the concerts to give the fans a good look at who we were as individuals. In a quirk I decided I would use my segment to do a Bo Diddley tune.

Though the organ player at my local music store growing up was as much a touchstone for me as Bo Diddley, as were Henry Mancini's theme for *Peter Gunn*, Mantovani, and anybody playing "Tico Tico," clearly Bo Diddley was the only one from that assortment who would be invited to this party. Jerome Green had inspired me with his handful of maracas, so I got four, two in each hand, and sang "You Can't Judge a Book by the Cover."

I had a great time performing it, but it was peculiar. *Peculiar* may be another wrong word. As I strutted and bounced across the stage in front of the backing band that played during our solo sections, I could only think of the power of BD with Lady Bo, driving that rhythm all the way into the base of my spine, and what a caricature of that moment what I was doing must be.

After the success of that Monkees tour, another one was planned for the following year. I don't know how much money the first tour made, but it must have served as justification for all that was to follow. If I had learned nothing else, I was learning the power of money to validate the Hollywood Mind and cement a Celebrity Psychosis.

I started to think that maybe there would be some further progress in recording an album of us playing and singing our own songs. I mentioned this to Davy, Micky, and Peter. I didn't get the feeling they liked the idea very much, but they didn't say no.

When I talked to Bert about it, he thought it a wonderful notion and began to help make it all happen. Bob seemed to fall in line as well, although he waved it off somewhat since he had his hands full with the TV show itself.

Making our own record was the only idea I ever had for the TV show, and it would prove to be fatal to the whole enterprise. When word got out that we were contemplating such a thing, the corporate factions exploded into war. Kirshner unleashed his hounds and swore he would never let us record and never let us get a hit record if we did. He did not aim that fusillade at the four of us. We were inconsequential in these matters. He aimed it at Bob and Bert, and I think that was his biggest and most foolish mistake.

We went in and recorded *Headquarters* over Kirshner's loud objections, and we also presented a recording of "The Girl I Knew Somewhere" that we thought should be our single. It was not a great record by the standards that were being set by the rock-and-roll community, but it was good enough. That it was the four of us playing on the album didn't really count for a lot in terms of musicianship, but Micky and Davy did a good job of singing, and the songs had a bounce to them that the fans accepted as our own. All of it appeared to enrage Kirshner.

At one point, Kirshner flew out to LA to present each of us with a large check, saying these checks represented what was in store for us if we would behave and go along with him and his musical plan. I had no idea what that plan was, but Kirshner scheduled a meeting for us to discuss it all.

So the following day, Davy, Micky, Peter, and I met with him and one of his lieutenants at the Beverly Hills Hotel. Kirshner was the immaculate executive as usual, cordial and friendly, nails, hair, collar, and tie all meticulously groomed. He was affable and open. Kirshner said he wanted us to give him our loyalty and go along with the musical program he was putting together using material from his Brill Building writers. I simply and, I thought, courteously refused, saying that my loyalties were to Bert and Bob because they had hired me and gave me day-to-day instructions on what they wanted me to do. I said I worked for them, not Kirshner. Bert had supported and encouraged the four of us to play and record together, and I had committed to that, so that was final for me. To my way of thinking, Kirshner was asking me to betray Bert and Bob.

Kirshner's lieutenant made the sad mistake of waving the contract in front of the four of us, saying it required us to do as we were told by the corporation and threatening that if we didn't go along with Kirshner, who was the corporate officer in charge of the music, we would be in breach of that contract and liable for all the damage we were causing; we would be sued for violating terms and acting in bad faith. I lost my temper and rammed my fist through the wall, as much for effect as anything, and said words to the effect that he should be careful about questioning my integrity.

It was an absurd moment in so many ways. My integrity was in tatters quite independently of the Monkees contract, although not when it came to any of the issues before us in the meeting. I was right, they were wrong—I felt solid about that.

Unfortunately, by this time Celebrity Psychosis was in full charge of my decision-making processes. The Hollywood Mind was outside my comprehension still, but the Psychosis was driving me further into delusions about what was possible and why. I had started to believe in the validation of fame and in methods of acquiring it that were cut loose from any sense of art, much less morals, ethics, or simple human kindness.

Headquarters was the only album the four of us ever made as the Monkees.

6

I met Jack Nicholson because Peter Fonda was a motorcycle-riding buddy of mine. Peter and I met at a local Topanga Canyon music gathering put on every so often by the musicians and artists who lived in the Canyon; everyone would hang out, play music, and socialize. Band potential teetered there like a boulder on the edge of a Southwestern mesa, since everyone played something or other and we all played together at these gatherings, listening and learning.

Peter and I hit it off because of our motorcycles. I had a Triumph Bonneville and he had a Harley, and we started riding around the canyons soon after he had his Harley chopped but before he got the Captain America helmet. Dennis Hopper came into those circles as a friend of Peter's, and Jack was a part of an even bigger concentric circle that slowly drew us all together by various means.

When Jack joined up with Bert and Bob to help make movies, I thought he was a perfect bandmate for them, and Bert,

Bob, and Jack seemed like they would be a great band for me to be in (after Uncle Chick and after Bo, Peggy, and Jerome).

By the time Jack showed up, the Monkees were nearing the end of the second season and were pretty much worn out. No one said so to me, but I think Bert and Bob were fed up. Kirshner had filed suit against them, they were suing him, and everyone around me was unhappy with the way things were going.

Bert and Bob said they were close to a decision to not do another season of *The Monkees*, and I was glad to hear it. They wanted to make movies, starting with a Monkees movie. Because I was friendly with Peter and Dennis, I also knew about *Easy Rider*. Peter would tell me the story of the movie nearly every time he came to the house or we were out together for dinner, and rumors were drifting around that Bert might give them the money to make it.

The story of the movie changed a bit each time Peter told it to me, so I couldn't get my head around it completely. It seemed to me that a movie with Fonda riding a motorcycle was a good commercial idea in any case. A Monkees movie did not sound like a good idea to me, because I assumed it would be an extension of one of the television episodes. But I was not thinking too much about either movie in depth.

As it turned out, working on the Monkees movie, *Head*, would be the best time I had with the Monkees and also the time I started regularly hanging with Jack, Bert, and Bob.

When Jack came on the scene of the *Monkees* TV production, he was not yet famous and was one of the few people I met who seemed self-aware and grounded. At the same time, his demeanor and sense of humor were exceptional and like catnip for me. I thought he was the coolest guy, and since this was long before the term *bromance* entered the US lexicon, some people in my crowd of friends thought my fascination with him was beyond the pale.

They also thought there was something abnormal in my preoccupation with Bert and Bob. It was true that my attraction to those three men was not usual for me. It wasn't in any sense sexual or even emotional, but I felt an affection for them that I imagine one feels as a member of a great sports team or, as I was to learn, a great band. Bands naturally coalesce, but the coalescence is not usually or easily seen. It is a close kind of affection that revolves around a love for a project or shared pride in work. At its root is an appreciation for another player. It is a feeling that can make for great times together socially, over meals and on adventures. It is a very strong attraction and can create a tight bond over time.

My discovery of the talent of these men started, as many such discoveries do, in Paris. Even though I had known Bob Rafelson for a while by then, it was only in the context of his duties on *The Monkees*. I finally got a good close look at Rafe (as I called him; Jack and Bert called him Curly) one crazy grass-and-acid-spiked night as we crawled the streets of Paris together looking for food.

No adventure seems to have quite the same spectrum of subtleties as trying to find some place to have dinner. Rafe and I started out around 4:00 p.m. with a little smoke and some cognac, and by the time we got through all the psychotropic substances we had with us, traded discourse about all the addled ideas we had on our minds, and walked miles through the ever-increasing shine of the wet streets of the city, we floated into the light of a Hungarian restaurant around 4:30 a.m. I thought it was the most beautiful restaurant in the best city in the world. I thought it was the best Hungarian goulash I ever had. I thought I was with one of the greatest guys I had ever met.

Since I was loaded to the earlobes with psychedelics, this seemed like a reasonable assessment. As the years passed, and as I now see the evening through *amarcord*—the lens of the present applied to the past—I realize that it was not only reasonable but also accurate. For me it was a nearly perfect night. We got back to the hotel just after dawn.

In that time I also got to know and understand Bob better, but not well. I realized I was probably locked out of his society and sophistication the same way I was locked out of many things. I didn't understand them; I didn't *get* them.

This had not mattered much when the only band I was playing in consisted of my Uncle Chick, but as I began to wish for more, being locked *out* of places started to feel more like being locked *in* somewhere I didn't want to be.

Bert, Bob, and Jack were heavy players: smart, educated, classy in their own way, and weird beyond all measures. I had no chance of keeping up with them, but I could and did enjoy them from afar, so I was happy to take whatever opportunity arose to walk the streets of beautiful cities with any or all of them, searching for food.

This wasn't a band I could ask to audition for, so I just had to wait it out to see if circumstances ever got to the point where I would be able to sit in with them and play a little. Right at the time I was suited up and waiting on that band bench, Dennis Hopper and I talked about the possibility of me doing the music for *Easy Rider.* Dennis was another of the movie types, as I called them, and I instantly connected with him through his nourishing visual sense. He would point out paintings and works around him, and just his acknowledgment would identify something as a work of art, define it as fine, and my eyes could see through his, to my great benefit. His moods were jagged and I never knew which way he might bounce, so he was not a dance partner, but as a player he had my attention and respect and he always brought something unique with him. So when he asked me if I was interested in supplying the music for *Easy Rider,* I was astonished and nearly speechless. I said yes and came up quickly with the notion of using a brass big band. I was thinking Memphis horns meets Harry James, but it was a bit like saying yes to someone who asks if you know how to drive an aircraft carrier.

The terrible truth was I didn't have any idea for the music, but I was so surprised that he even considered me I just said something offbeat, something I thought Dennis might like to hear. Dennis, because he had the sight of a master artist, looked at me for just a second to see if I might be kidding. But then he was courteous and let the subject drop. I was heartsick and not a little embarrassed that when Hopper threw me a chance to play with this band, I came up with amalgamated riffs of "Hold On, I'm Coming" and "Cherry Pink and Apple Blossom White." Really, what could I have said that was more natural to me? But it was the wrong riff at the wrong time.

Thus I sat alone on the side of the *Easy Rider* highway as they all rode off on their choppers. Later Bert and the rest came up with the master stroke of using popular music of the times—starting with Hendrix.

Rafe was very friendly but very competitive, and he seemed like an older brother, at least as far as I understood that role from movies. Bert was more severe and seemed wicked in a convivial and appealing way. Jack was another type of player altogether—carrying a deflation spear that he used on windbags, along with a drug-sharpened flair for hilarity that neither Bert nor Bob displayed. Jack and I could crack each other up and laugh until we both ran out of breath and collapsed, coughing.

Jack also had a deep understanding and appreciation of fine art, which he unintentionally conveyed to me during the times we were together. His house was full of paintings by unknown local artists, and as Jack got more money, the art got better and better. The then-unknown artists he selected, like Ed Ruscha, would become part of the pantheon, and the well-known artists he curated were selected by the Jack-knack, as I called it. For spotting authenticity across any room and under any makeup or any attire, Jack was unequaled in my experience.

I trusted Jack more than I trusted Bob and Bert, but that didn't mean he was more trustworthy. He may have been, but the truth was I liked him better. He was easier for me to be around, and that translated into trust. It may have been misplaced, but when a band starts forming out of cosmic dust, a lot of mistakes are made in terms of who does what, whom one may or may not trust, and who should or should not be part of the band in the first place.

With the Monkees movie, Bert and Bob had decided to kill the monster they thought they had created, and Bob asked Jack to help. They also asked the four principal cast players—Davy, Micky, Peter, and me—to participate.

At first I thought the suggestion was simply for the four Monkees to join in on a trip to Ojai to smoke dope, hang out with Bert and Bob and Jack, and race golf carts around the hotel. But no, they were serious about the four of us actually contributing to the screenplay. The idea was that we would all talk as a tape recorder was running—tell jokes and make up stories—and in that way come up with an idea for the movie. This produced about six or seven reels of recorded tape, as I recall, but there was not enough goodwill among us, so it was not a script by any definition. All the points of view were scattered in a way that revealed nothing except an occasional funny joke. We were not drawn together. The initial hopes for the Monkees had become the detritus of a collective dream we were all waking from, each in our own room, and each afflicted with our own case of Celebrity Psychosis informing us about the furniture in that room.

In my room, the CP was a full-blown raging pathology that

my meager efforts were failing to control. CP was starting to make me believe that things that had never happened had happened, to think about myself in ways I never had before, and to say things I never ordinarily would have—mostly insults I meant ironically but that were taken as offense, given what and who I had become within the Monkees enterprise.

Instead of coming across as teases, my feints and irony revealed the fissures in the uneasy collection of people around the Monkees, who were getting angrier by the day. Jack and Bob took the tapes and went to work on the script. I had not contributed as much as I would have liked during the Ojai riffs, but what came to light was a clear revelation that under any circumstances, I could not have helped them create the script that they ultimately made and named *Head*.

When the script was finished but before I read it, I was discussing it with Bert, trying to get a sense of what kind of movie it would be. He described it to me as a wild gamble. He said he thought it would be either recognized and revered, or reviled and unsung. There would be no in-between, no ambivalence. Love it or hate it were the only options. Millions would attend or no one would attend. He was right.

Even as we were filming it, I did not see that the focus of the script, as well as the intent of the movie, was the assisted suicide of the Monkees; *Head* was the coffin Bert and Bob had created for the whole endeavor. Everything was expected to drown in the revelations and surreality of the movie. The entire Monkees project, from the first TV show to the recordings to the live concerts, including the slightest artifacts—all were sacrificed in the opening shot of the movie, where the four of us jump off a bridge described as the "largest man-made object in the world." Either because of or in spite of the fact that Pinocchio had started to come to life, Geppetto threw the marionette off that bridge.

That the Monkees did not, in fact, die or disappear is another story. For in the end, Jack and the remarkable insight he embedded in the script provided an existential truth to the original fantasy of the show and revealed what happened in the minds of Bert and Bob; the writers, directors, and producers that surrounded them; and Davy, Micky, Peter, and Mike. Drug-addled, bizarre, obtuse, and ignored as it was, the movie still became an actual driving force. Instead of destroying all things Monkees, it emblazoned them on pop culture permanently.

Bob, who realized the script and brought out all the subtle elements that careful writing and good psychotropic drugs could place there, was clearly on record as wanting to be a film director and had chosen this as his first, and maybe only, film. He said the whole project fit on the canvas he was stretching for himself and his future works. It was an opportunity to show who he was as a director, and according to Bob, if *Head* was the only movie he ever got to do, then at least he would have had a chance to include all his favorite genres, from Westerns to David Lean–type epics to the "darkest thing on the planet."

At one point, Bob recounted that in a writing session he once told Jack that he was distracted because he was thinking about "the darkest thing on the planet." When Jack asked what that would be, Bob said, "that would be Victor Mature's hair." Mature was a good-looking stage and screen actor who had earned the nickname "Beautiful Hunk of Man" based on a line from the Broadway musical *Lady in the Dark*, in which he'd starred. By then he had for years been dyeing his still-fulsome head of hair an inky black, giving it remarkable opacity.

Jack, in a psychedelic flash of the first order, seized the moment. "That's it!" he said. "The whole movie takes place in Victor Mature's hair."

Had I been in the room, I would have laughed for hours at the darkness of Victor Mature's hair—such was Nicholson's grip on my drug-induced sense of humor. As drug riffs go, it is one of the greats, and it would serve as the magic carpet for the film, the serene fantasy behind the panicked psychedelia. Victor Mature's hair would be *Head*'s diegesis. The film would have no fourth wall to break. It would have five walls, all of which would be broken to start with.

Getting Victor Mature's actual hair in the movie was a problem I unwittingly provided a solution for. It was to be my only acceptable riff in this band of Bob, Bert, and Jack, but it was a flourish that I was and am proud of—a flourish with, as Dylan sang, "one hand waving free."

I was in the production offices at the close of a day, and Bob and Bert were discussing the right way to get Victor Mature to consider doing the picture. I asked why they didn't simply call him up, and Bob said, "Why don't *you* just call him up, Mike?" It was a challenge that came from an assumption that such an act was impossibly brave. "I will if you have his number," I said nonchalantly.

Bert said he did have it, in fact, so I called it, and Victor Mature answered the phone. I said something like "Is this Mr. Mature?" and he said "Yes." "My name is Mike Nesmith," I said, "and I am one of the Monkees on television."

He said, "I know who you are," and told me he liked the show. I thanked him and explained that I was calling because we were about to make a movie and would very much like it if he would be in it.

At this point Bert and Bob started saying, very loudly, "Yeah, right. Sure, Nishwash [my nickname from the TV show], like you're really talking to Victor Mature. Bullshit, baby! You are so full of shit! There's nobody on the phone!" The jabs were mean-spirited, but they were also funny.

I assumed that Mature heard all this, but I kept going. "I'm here with the producers now, and if you have a second, maybe they could describe the film to you."

Bert and Bob were now laughing as hard as I ever heard them laugh, certain that I was pulling an uproarious prank. I handed the phone to Bob.

When he said hello into the phone and heard Mature's voice, his laughter instantly stopped and his face registered the shock. Bert looked at him quizzically, and Bob silently nodded yes to Bert as he handed the phone to him.

All I remember after that is the satisfaction that comes from hitting the perfect riff, right at the moment when someone in the band says, "Take it!"

In my own way, I loved those guys. I even said to Bert one time at a dinner with just the two of us, "I love you, man," and I meant it as sincerely as I could, given the substance that had caused me to say it. But drugs or no, there was depth to my desire to hang out and play with Bert, Bob, and Jack. After *Head* was finished they kept me at a distance, so I never had too much to say to them. Jack told me to always call him before I came over, a real change in our usual MO.

Celebrity Psychosis had so entered my mind-stream that there was no possibility of anything happening like a band. Had I been of clearer vision, I would have seen the seeds of sorrow that Bert and Bob had already planted in the Raybert enterprise that would become BBS Productions, and I would have known to be grateful that I never got any closer to it than I did. I was almost desperate to land my little plane in their field and play whatever games they were thinking up, but some grace flagged me off, and I flew away into my own countryside.

Bert told me I should seriously think about suing him as part of the suits between Columbia and Screen Gems and Kirshner and Raybert Productions. He felt I personally had valid, actionable claims somewhere in all that, but I refused and told him I could never sue him. I told him I was grateful for what he did for me, giving me the job in the first place, and letting me share in the things I did. Overall, I thought of the experience as a gift, an odd gift to be sure but with a deep message for me that I am still parsing and for which I am never less than thankful.

Some time later, in the early 1980s, I asked Bob if he would direct a music video I was producing for Lionel Richie's "All Night Long." He agreed, but during that shoot, Bob told me that I had no chance as an actor and no real place in the movie business. It was in a misplaced and out-of-step conversation that was part of the sputtering of an engine that has lost its power because it has lost its fuel. I didn't pay much attention to the remark except to feel that Bob was reinforcing the fact that he was in a different league. To him, I was ping-pong and he was lacrosse.

The band of Bert, Bob, Jack, and Nez never realized itself. By the time the second season of *The Monkees* was over, the idea of it had been reduced to nothing but my own fantasy.

I was once in a major city listening to a large symphony orchestra play Mahler, and it sounded horrible to me. I was familiar with Mahler and knew that I liked the compositions, but not being a trained musician, I didn't really know why it sounded so bad, and not understanding the intricacies of classical music, I kept my mouth shut about it afterward. But I was really surprised at how little I enjoyed it.

As I became a better musician and my ear became more attuned to what made music good, it dawned on me why: the musicians couldn't play well. It was a bad band playing Mahler. The composing was first rate, but the orchestra was stumbling through the performance of it. The conductor looked wrong to me as well, but what did I know? That was only my opinion. The music, however, clearly sounded like a car wreck, with both of the cars playing Mahler on their radios.

Then I went to see the LA Phil—I can't remember the conductor—and heard what I thought was some of the best music ever. It was Mahler again, but the orchestra sounded great this time. After a short while I realized that the LA Phil is one of the great symphony orchestras in the world because many of the players in it are session cats. They play daily on cinema scores and commercial scores and theme songs, so when they get onstage at the Hollywood Bowl, they are razor sharp. They sounded celestial, the way an orchestra should sound, where all one hears is the music.

In mid-1968, just after filming *Head*, it came to me that I had the opportunity as never before to work with some great session players like this. The LA guys were superb, and I knew there were outstanding players in New York and London, but there was a very strong pull in my own notions of music toward Nashville.

The Nashville cats were becoming legendary as far as country music was concerned, but I couldn't just fly off to Nashville and record country songs in direct opposition to the stated needs of the show. It was still their money and their show.

But I could see that the Monkees project was entering its final phase. Many who were connected with the show were starting to look down other avenues and in different directions for activity. I thought if I could round up some session players in Nashville to record the music that Kirshner and the Brill Building had rejected, songs that were not hardcore country, I might be able to demonstrate their appeal to the masses. I didn't have much confidence that I would succeed at that, but at least it would be a legitimate effort, I could avoid hardcore country music, and by this reasoning I could do Monkees sessions in Nashville under the protection of Bert and Bob's production umbrella and with Screen Gems' approval.

I had never recorded my songs the way I wanted, and it

looked like now would be the time. I was not disgruntled, but I did have the notion that this was my last chance at a session like this, and if I was going to complete my Monkees obligations unrequited musically, then at least I would come home with my own recordings.

I asked Lester Sill at Screen Gems if he could set me up with a producer who could put together a band for me in Nashville. Felton Jarvis was his choice, so Felton called his best guys together and I headed east to record, with sessions set up between RCA Studios A and B. The two studios were different-size versions of each other and didn't sound that different to me, and while this was a time when the sound of a studio was supposed to matter, the sound I was looking for was still unclear to me.

I was more pointedly looking for a band—a group of players. The idea of sitting with a group of first-call Nashville musicians and playing my songs was thrilling, enough for me to go to Nashville even if we just sat in somebody's yard and played. That there would be a recording of the sessions was icing on the cake. What I didn't know was that Felton had hired players from all around the Nashville area, including the members of Muscle Shoals Sound Studio, who were soon to become legendary in their own right. What I didn't know was that I was about to fall into a tub of butter.

Just as we started the sessions, I got delayed and was extraordinarily late for one of the dates. While the guys were waiting, David Briggs, the pianist, started playing "Lady Madonna," which was the resonant Beatles piano lick in the world of music at the time, and the band there joined in to jam with him. Norbert Putnam was on bass, Jerry Carrigan on drums, Buddy Spicher on fiddle, Charlie McCoy on harmonica, Wayne Moss on guitar, and Lloyd Green on pedal steel.

The groove got so deep they couldn't see out of it, and Briggs started singing funny scatological lyrics to the tune, at which point the song picked up even more life and the groove hovered just above the core of the Earth.

The recording engineer had the good sense to hit Record while they were down in this canyon groove, and that was about the time I walked in. The studio that day was RCA Studio B on Sixteenth Avenue, in an area that's known as Music Row for good reason.

When I walked in, the place was full of virtual smoke and fire. It was full of the wisdom of sailors stuck in a landing craft singing about the girl they left behind—or maybe had in the boat with them. It was one of the best-sounding things I had heard in a while. The lyrics were ribald and crazy-funny in a hillbilly-porn sort of way, and I knew I was in for a good time with this band. I'm not a fan of the scatological, but I loved "Lady Madonna," and I loved what they were laying down musically. Briggs sang it "Lady Medushka," though he had no idea what that meant. It rocked. It was funny. It was solid gone.

We listened to "Lady Medushka" a few dozen times. After a while the band understood that I didn't care too much about the producing constraints prevalent at the time in Nashville, which was to get fifteen songs cut in three hours. I was where I wanted to be and doing what I wanted to do: hanging and playing with great players and cutting the grooves as deep as they would go just to see what was down there. I was thrilled to learn that everything I'd heard about the Nashville cats was true.

When I started playing them the songs I wanted to record, they listened and made little notes. It was markedly different from cutting a demo on my own in the Screen Gems Publishing demo studio and shipping it off to the Brill Building to see if it would be approved. Here, there was no competitive rush for control of a TV show score and no jockeying for fame or money. These players were immediately responsive and inspired by the music alone—most of the time.

If there was just a single nod and a "Yeah, man" or two, with no eye contact between the players, then I knew I had missed the mark. But if I got "Cool!" with nods and smiles among them, then the moment was a wonderful boost and my confidence soared. Even discounting the fact that I had hired them, which is roughly a 99.9 percent discount, the opinions they expressed still had the shimmer of sincerity, and I was encouraged. I had roughly twelve songs in different stages of completion, and nine of them made the cut.

Even with some songs biting the dust, I still had a buzz of satisfaction from the validation of my songwriting. This was unprecedented. The Wrecking Crew, the top LA session guys who played on many of the Monkees records, had been careful not to make too many comments about the songs because of the overwhelming political dynamics in the studio, but these guys from Muscle Shoals and Nashville homed in on the music and stayed there, and if they liked it, then they said so, and if they didn't, they said nothing. The whole session vibes started from this point of departure, and it was as real and as solid as anything had been in my musical life to that point.

Coming off the "Lady Medushka" jam session, these players wanted music they could get into and get down with and build tone palaces out of. When they said "Cool, man," they were looking me in the eyes and speaking my language. Thankfully, by then I knew enough to leave them alone and let them play my songs the way they wanted—to drop the reins, point across a new open field toward the distant horizon, whisper "Go there" in their ear, and hang on.

We recorded several songs over about five days, and during those days, the signature song that emerged—that almost stopped the whole session—was "Listen to the Band." After we recorded it and got it as we wanted, we started listening to it over and over and over again. When a recording is born, everyone wants to stop playing and just listen, especially if they are getting paid for it. It is a great moment, up one tier from Booneing: we knew that this recording would become the reference standard. We were not only hearing something *for* the first time, but something *at* the first time it could be heard. We were present at a birth, and while no one had a clue about the future of the song—whether it was great or lame-o, a hit or a miss—it was alive, and it was ours. I recall that we sat in the control booth listening to "Listen to the Band" one entire afternoon and evening.

Pretty soon other Nashville cats, friends of friends, were stopping by the studio during listening breaks as word got out that the sessions were easygoing and more or less open. People started showing up with weed, wine, and very, very good vibes. I could tell that news had spread that the music coming out of the sessions was exciting and new and worth stopping by to hear.

Even though I assumed the music would not get far in the pop world's burgeoning Monkees disaffection, it was still an exquisite and high moment for me. I was ecstatic.

After that, David Briggs and Norbert Putnam and a few others from that band of players kept playing together, recorded their own material, and went on the road for a while. The seminal Muscle Shoals records they did marched into the pantheon of truly great, culture-altering records. To my mind, when musicologists try to find the date and players and songs to pin to the start of the country-rock genre, I think of those sessions and those times and those players. They invented country rock, if anybody did.

After those sessions, the end of the TV show, and the unsuccessful release of *Head*, I was left to fly on my own, and things of the most mundane type took horrifying turns. I descended into the strange world of the incomplete, wandering through a personal closed-system entropy and heat death without the cerulean trousers.

The IRS, which I had ignored for several years, showed up with a huge bill for unpaid taxes and started seizing property. I ran away from the few assets I had, left money at Screen Gems in return for being let out of my contract there, and explored the land of turpitude with friends and foes alike. I did not think of myself as evil and mean, but I have little doubt that other people did. I don't know for sure because I didn't bother to explore. I was lost in a wilderness and desperate to find any path.

The one I uncovered was densely overgrown, choked by television, celebrity, and money. It was hardly a path—more of a depression in the natural grasses that grow untended in woods and by streams. The trails here were barely distinguishable from the undulations of the land itself, but as I stared into the distance I saw a little light.

The moment I perceived this faint path, I could see it was a tendril leading ultimately to a forest of beautiful trees and exotic birds. This slender vestige was just visible through the open door of the Palomino Club, a country-western bar and restaurant in the San Fernando Valley.

The house band there consisted of some players who were not yet famous but one day would be. Leon Russell was playing piano, and the bandleader, Orville J. "Red" Rhodes, was playing pedal steel.

I started going to the Pal, as it was called, just to listen to the band and drink alcohol. I never drank much; I was a happy drunk, but alcohol, like all drugs, did not really pull me in.

I only mention alcohol here because of its presence in the country-western ethos of the time. An evening out for me would consist of a meal and a couple of cocktails at the Pal and then listening to the band as they played the country hits of the day. Late nights on weekends, a country star like Merle Haggard or Waylon Jennings would perform a show.

Because of the politics of the times, country music was seen as a voice for the conservative right wing, and under that wing were racism, bias, fear, hatred, and the intolerance that marked the conservatives of the time.

I was appalled, but I could at least tolerate, and at most ignore, the shabby politics, because the music, especially the old country-western standards and artists like Johnny Cash and Hank Williams and Jimmie Rodgers, touched something deep within me, very much like the blues had done.

In the same way that Louann's in Dallas had exposed me to the great bluesmen and early rock pioneers like Chuck Berry and Bo Diddley, so the Pal revealed to me not only a house band of inspired players but also the best of the traditional and new country performers and singers. I loved seeing the great players who came to perform at their peak: Willie Nelson, Waylon Jennings, Buck Owens, Merle Haggard, and Jerry Lee Lewis, among others.

The night Jerry Lee played, I talked Nicholson into going with me to the Pal. This was still before Jack was a movie star, and he was unrecognizable to the general public as an actor, so he could travel freely and go to clubs without causing a stir. Jack made it clear that the society and politics of C&W music were very far from his nature, but I assured him he could set all that aside once he heard the music.

I was right. The minute Jerry Lee took the stage, the whole place went electric, and Jack's eyes never left him. At one point Jerry Lee began to introduce me from the stage, having no idea who I was or what I looked like. He had been told only that "one of the Monkees" was in the audience.

I had a table right in front of the bandstand, and the party with me was about eight people, including Jack. Jerry Lee started the intro, looking directly at Jack, finally pointing at him with a flourish and saying to the crowd, "Ladies and gentlemen, one of the Monkees! Please stand up and take a bow."

He waved for Jack to stand up. Jack waved him off, as Ringo had waved the reporter off in London, and pointed to me sitting across from him. Jerry Lee looked embarrassed, and then looked at me, then back to Jack with curiosity. I did a hunched-over, aw-gosh stand-up, looked around, waved, and sat down. There were a few pops of applause, faint praise indeed.

Later, on the way home from that performance, Jack told me he thought it was the greatest live show he had ever seen. I don't know what shows Jack saw, but I sort of agreed with him, leaving Bo Diddley and Jimi Hendrix aside. Jerry Lee was a fireball and lots of fun. Jack mentioned it to me over the years after that, still talking about the power of that evening.

What I saw that night was different, and Jerry Lee was only a part of it. Foremost to me was the power of Nicholson, even in a crowd. Jerry Lee Lewis had been certain that Jack was the famous one in the audience and introduced him as such. Nicholson's light was shining so bright even then, even when he was unknown, that Lewis pegged him for a standout.

Second was the playing of Red Rhodes in the house band before Jerry Lee came on. I had watched Red play many evenings before and would watch him many more. There was something about the construction, tone, and touch of the way he played that surpassed all the other pedal steel players I knew of.

The pedal steel guitar is an unusual instrument. It sits like a card table in front of the player, who also sits and stares down at the strings. There is almost no detectable external movement from the player, but all the limbs are at work as well as the musical mind. The notes are mixed between percussive bell-like tones and a swirling, continuous sound much like strings in an orchestra but very different sonically. There are sustained tones, in harmony with others, that soar over the top, creating a rich and soft bed of sonority, ghost notes, and phantom chords. The player can manipulate the sound with a steel bar in one hand resting on the strings, steel finger picks on the other hand, and both feet on eight or ten pedals that can change the length and pitch of the strings. The whole thing is electrified and put through an amplifier, where the player can choose the echo or delay, creating a stunning wall of continuous tones and harmonies. The pedal steel is the signature instrument of many country songs, and very recognizable once you know what to listen for.

Few people can play the instrument well, and Red Rhodes was an undisputed master of it. Red was a string section and a brass section and a Mars section all in one. The lines and fills he played inside the regular country tunes were like smoke and magic, wafting in and out of the soundscape like surreptitious sprites.

A band won't really work unless it creates its own complete ecosystem. As with any ecosystem, there must be a foundation. In the case of music, this is a tonal center, a design key, which sets the focus and direction of the whole system in its larger environment.

Red was the foundation of the Palomino house band's ecosystem, and while there were other notable players who came and went in that band, Red's pedal steel playing was its nexus. His playing consisted mostly of the phrases of traditional country-western music of the 1950s, from Patsy Cline to George Jones, rendered with his exquisite touch. It was music I honored and respected but didn't like as much as blues—or, for that matter, blues-and-organ music in a lounge. For, despite its country-western ranch overlay, the Palomino was a lounge, full of strange folk, blue-collar workers, and women with big hair reflecting the lights from the beer signs and polished, practical nails clicking and clacking on Formica bar tables to the rhythms from the stage. A lounge with a look and feel that united the randomly strewn wagon wheels into an oasis of music—that is, if one was thirsty for alcohol, adultery, and intermittent mayhem in a desert of sobriety, rectitude, and civility.

When I had first started playing in San Antonio and connected with John Kuehne, he only played bass and did not sing, but his bass playing filled out my playing, rounding out the sound of the solo guitar enough so that it would fill a nightclub or an auditorium as needed. He was easygoing and patient with me, a good friend, and came to LA shortly after Phyllis and I did. He was part of my early efforts there, including my night at the Troubadour.

That night, when Randy Sparks offered me a deal, he also offered me the chance to play in a group he was creating that was to be like the New Christy Minstrels, which was a very big enterprise for him. I accepted under the condition that John be offered the same opportunity, and fortunately for both John and me, the new band Randy was assembling needed a bass player.

The pattern of my including John in all opportunities that came my way was interrupted when I was hired for the Monkees, but I was at least able to get him a job as my stand-in. I was worried this would insult him, but it was quite the opposite. The pay was good, and the job seemed to fit John perfectly. He was there for all the shows, came on the road as part of the crew when the Monkees did concerts, and was an active part of my social life.

He was not in any sense a professional friend or a hanger-on, even when we were not making too much music together.

He was still foremost a bass player and very much his own man. He worked in various ensembles playing bass, always trying to get in a group that might go somewhere in the world of popular music, but it was not to be. He befriended John Ware, a drummer, and Kuehne and Ware became a rhythm section for various bands, including some I produced here and there, and part of my professional and social circles in general.

As such, the two of them were familiar with most of the proceedings of my life and were there to witness the steep descent I made after the show was off the air, when the air was let out of the tires on the Monkeemobile.

It was John Ware who suggested that he and John would make a good backup for me and my new songwriting efforts, but I was wary. I didn't want to try going out as a singer-songwriter, since that was not precisely what I was aiming at, but I knew I would need another player or two whatever I did.

I had asked Harry Jenkins, the head of RCA Victor, the Monkees' record company, if they were interested in me as a solo artist, and he asked me what kind of music I wanted to record. I didn't know exactly. I said I had been steadily writing and had songs ready to record, but in my head they were a kind of country music that was a cross between cafeteria-organ-Latin blues music and Hank Williams.

To my delight, he indicated that RCA might be interested if I would let the Nashville arm of RCA be my home for recording, and I quickly agreed. RCA Nashville was run by legendary country star Chet Atkins, and I thought he might even understand what I was hearing in my head. In any case, it would be a long way from the Screen Gems music factory.

I hoped I might even get to use the Nashville cats I had already recorded with. Ware wisely pointed out that if he and John were my band, we could not only record but could tour in support of the records we made, something the Nashville first-call session guys seldom did for a new band. We would be a real band rather than a pure studio effort.

Ware's idea had a solid feel to it, but I couldn't think who might join with us besides him and John Kuehne. I had become expert in alienating helpful friends and betraying loyal coworkers, and in the recent past I'd seen the dim light of torches coming up the road, carried by angry villagers who sought to kill me and my monster. In short, I didn't think I could get anyone to work with me.

Ware suggested otherwise and asked me to allow him to try to find other players. He wondered who I might like to approach, and my first choice was Red Rhodes. I had no hope of his accepting, but he was my first choice. A pedal steel guitar player—especially a magical-reality player like Red—was critical-path for the music in my head.

I thought I would also need a piano player to realize that certain sound, but Leon Russell was long gone from the Pal by this time. Red was still in place, however, and John said he could start by asking Red if he was interested in joining with us. I agreed to let him ask, but not gratefully. I still had much to learn about gratitude, and worse, was enmeshed in entitlement, one of the more repulsive elements of Celebrity Psychosis. One of the first casualties CP exacts, one of the first limbs it atrophies, is gratitude in the bearer.

To my good fortune, Ware pressed on, even without my proper and well-deserved gratitude and acknowledgment, or even much encouragement. He went to Red and asked him to join our band. To my great surprise, and everlasting good fortune, Red agreed.

Thus was born my next band, which I called the First National Band.

7

I was up on the roof of my garage with Johnny Cash, looking out over the city of LA. The house was the one I had built high in the hills near Mulholland during the days of *The Monkees.* I had made the flat roof of the garage into a kind of deck, and even though I seldom used it, this particular evening I took John up there to show him the view. From there one could see down the coast of Southern California—almost into Long Beach on a clear day. Just before that was Santa Monica, and just at the foot of the hills the house stood on, Beverly Hills spread out.

This was in late 1969 or early 1970. John had come for a gathering that was sort of my return hospitality for his gracious hosting of me and Davy and Micky at a breakfast at his lake house in Tennessee when the three of us went to Nashville to perform on his TV show after *The Monkees* was off the air.

I made something of a friend of John then, and we had some nice moments together. If I was in Nashville I might call him, and I heard from him sometimes when he came to LA. For the most part we touched each other's lives lightly and infrequently, but when we did, it was usually marked by a memorable occurrence. There was a connection between us that was atypical for me, and he said the same for him. Odd twists happened when we were together and persisted when we were apart, shared events that were unexpected for both of us. These events were few and slight, but they made for good dinnertime stories.

For instance, a year or so after this garage-top summit, I was working at my office in LA and had gone out on some business errands with my assistant, Esther. As we were coming back to the office, I told her I wanted to stop and grab a bite of lunch. I was used to eating at a few regular places around, but we weren't near any of those. I spotted a small Italian restaurant not too far from the office and said, "Let's just hop in here." I had never been there before, nor had Esther.

Esther and I went in, ordered, and were going over a few things when the maître d' came over with a portable phone. He said, "Johnny Cash is on the phone for you."

I looked quizzically at Esther, who shrugged as I took the phone. "Hello?" I said.

It was Cash all right, and I was flummoxed. How had he known where I was? I hadn't called the office, and neither had Esther, as far as I knew. I was in a restaurant I had never been in before, chosen at random as we drove along. How could he possibly have known where I was?

Before I could ask the question, John said something like, "Mike, I need to get your OK. I'm writing a book and just turned it in to my publisher. You're in it, and I want to make sure that what I said was OK with you. I wrote about the conversation we had on the roof of your garage, and I want to read it to you. I need to do it now, because they're waiting for me to get the approval right away. Can I read it to you? Have you got a minute?"

Things were spinning, but I said OK, sure. Happy to.

John read the few sentences that recounted the conversation we'd had on the roof overlooking Beverly Hills. It was in essence correct, and I said that was pretty much how I remembered it. He asked if it was OK for him to put it in the book, and I agreed. He said he wanted to talk more, but the publisher was waiting for his answer with my answer, so he rang off.

I was dumbfounded. I looked at Esther, who seemed as puzzled as I was, and wondered aloud how he had gotten the number—or even known where I was. And what about the way the waiter said, "Johnny Cash is on the phone for you"—as if the waiter was in the habit of taking my calls? It was the weirdest announcement of a phone call I'd ever had at a restaurant. I couldn't figure it out.

When Esther and I got back to the office, I checked around, and Cash had not called there, and no one seemed to know how his call had found its way to me.

I never figured it out. I am not a supernatural-interventionist of any type, and I assume there was and is some plausible answer to the little mystery, but I have never known what it was.

The paragraph in John's book worked its way around the publishing and press world and into several different accounts of the same conversation. Our short talk seems to have been something of a turning point for John, but the story has mutated a little as it's been reiterated. In one instance, it happened at his lake house instead of on top of my garage. It doesn't surprise me that it has found its way into his legacy, though. It was a moment between us that was genuine on all fronts: two guys facing the Hollywood Mind from the top of my garage, staring straight-on at Beverly Hills.

Standing on the roof of my garage that day, we became a touch philosophical. I said I thought of Hollywood as something of a trap, a gentle trap perhaps, but I still felt as if it would rob one of integrity as easily and in the same way it would confer it. By "Hollywood" I meant celebrity, fame, money, drugs, sex, cars, and all the orbiting weirdness that went with them. John said he knew this too, and the conversation seemed to sink into him. Hollywood, California, was the epicenter of this nonsense, as we both knew, but we were speaking metaphorically.

We were both aware of the importance of sidestepping the dark and disturbing downside of fame, cruel or kind. He said it was important to keep in mind this duplicity of fame. It was to be avoided if possible, but he said that it could be beaten in any case.

By that time, I think, he had become a devout Christian, and I suppose the ideas of basic worth and spiritual causation were active and important in his thinking. He said he hoped to avoid the pitfalls that he saw. I offered that there was no reason I could see that they were unavoidable. All it took, I assumed, was a little self-knowledge, determination, humility, and help from friends. He agreed.

The conversation drifted back to less weighty things, and we came down from the roof. The evening turned out to be a very good time.

At that time, I was facing the slow unraveling of the world I was living in, a process that John had already lived out and apparently moved beyond. My Celebrity Psychosis had taken a grave turn by then and was metastasizing as it morphed into some twisted thought process that served to confuse and cloud every simple issue. Celebrity Psychosis makes it so that being recognized is simultaneously a nuisance and a necessity. It creates a double-bind paradox, becoming an eerie obsession when pursued-avoided. CP's most famous symptoms are observed in celebrities who yell and throw things at paparazzi for interfering in their lives at the same time they pose and smile in hopes of landing a prime position in the popular press.

CP often shows up in the bearer as temper tantrums in public places and, most disturbingly dangerous, as the intensely real-seeming delusions of a narrowed local reality. Under the delusion of CP, celebrities have no qualms about leaving their car parked in a fire lane while they go shopping. They are celebrities, so the rules don't apply.

The first time CP showed up in my life was at the entrance gate to Columbia Studios, where we were filming *The Monkees.* My hair was long, my clothes were shabby, I was in an old car, and the guard would not let me in. I flew into a rage. I started screaming at him—I might have even said, "Don't you know who I am!?!" or some other such foolishness—and no doubt there was a personal insult mixed in as an affront to the poor guard. Of course, he had no idea I was supposed to be there, nor should he have recognized me. It was my second day on the job.

I found out the next day that Davy had been stopped at the same gate but drove through the barrier. The producers gave Davy the broken gate as a souvenir and posted our pictures all over the inside of the guard gate.

That's how it starts—and it just gets worse from those simple seeds. The terrible fact is that those seeds take root and grow, hidden and unseen, tuber-like, underground, until at last they push their hideous bloom to the surface.

This highest and most aggressive form of CP was active in my life right after *The Monkees* went off the air. It had grown to outrageous size and shape and was bigger than my house in the hills. CP was no longer resident in my consciousness; I became a resident in Celebrity Psychosis. I felt the weird, ever-present insistence of some imaginary divine right to be recognized wherever I was—and the entitlement to be there. As one might suspect, it was not a useful approach in any but a society of sycophants who traded on it, and I parked in a lot of fire lanes, mentally daring the parking authorities to tow *my* car—which they usually did. Like many afflictions, CP slows the learning process.

My early experience in music production was with *The Monkees* and all the ancillaries: the records, concerts, huge distribution systems, and Celebrity Psychosis that went with it. Even though that conglomeration of forces was unrealistic as a paradigm for building a new musical group, it was all I had when I started the First National Band. So along with learning songs and rehearsing, I began to unconsciously gather about me the smoke and sparks of the Screen Gems fireworks factory. I had no experience in actually building a successful band, even though there had been some early fits and starts and over time I had met many of the best players in town. Meeting a great player is, to the Celebrity Psychotic, the same as knowing them well and being intimately familiar with their skill and talent; it involves the perception of being an actual part of a productive unit because you happen to have met a key player at a party, gotten drunk with them, and gone out to a club, where you got a good table.

My first tries at a band had been when John Kuehne first arrived in LA. I thought we could use a drummer among us, so I called my high school friend Bill Sleeper and asked if he had any interest in coming out west and joining up. I had no clear idea of Bill's general situation there in Dallas, but I knew he was a decent drummer and had a shared taste with me in music, so that was enough for me to ask him. He said he would give it a try, made the trip to LA, and got an apartment in the same complex that Phyllis, John, and I lived in.

We rehearsed some, and after a short while I met some characters who pushed us along a path of recording and doing some live performances in clubs. The only real job we got was in an outlying casino near Las Vegas, in the tiny town of Searchlight, Nevada.

I was writing songs regularly, but they weren't much more than wild grabs for the brass ring of popularity, attempts to make a living playing and singing the songs of my life—wherever that might lead. However, the problem remained that I couldn't really play well, nor did I know the theory of music, how to read it or write it, or how to lead and inspire other players I might be with. When the casino owner insisted we do covers of pop hits, I was stumped.

He also insisted we have go-go dancers, as they were called, so we brought two dancers with us, one for each side of the stage. One of them had a good voice and knew some popular hit songs, so she ended up singing a lot more than I did. In this way, the Mike, John, and Bill Band, as we named ourselves, ended up actually being the backup group for the dancers we had hired to provide interpretive movement to music we couldn't play. Other than that, we were in great shape.

The band came apart pretty quickly and easily when Bill's mother, who seemed to be well motivated and a good person, came out to LA and took our drummer back home with her. I think she may have saved him from an awful fate, but as I say, I had no real understanding of his circumstances, so who knows?

The band of Mike, John, and Bill had made one record—two songs, one front and one back side—played a few dates, and that was it. The fragile soul of that band never developed enough to be detectable, and that fragility made me wonder if I was missing something, if there was more to a band than just getting together and playing songs.

I was learning, by experience, a little bit of "bandology"—that having songs and players and uniforms and a bit of skill does not by itself create great music, or a great product, or even a good time. There is something more in the glue that creates and holds a great band together than just playing and making a little money. Besides loving the music, it takes inspiration, a point of view, and a workable sense of artistry—and after all that, very hard work and perseverance.

I had only this slight experience in band building, combined with the Monkees and its dreadful CP, as I sought out an agent and a manager and road crew for the First National Band. With my new RCA contract in hand, John Kuehne, John Ware, Red, and I went into the RCA studios in LA and recorded *Magnetic South*, our first record.

The idea of *inclusion* weighs strongly in the formation of a band: what to include and not include is an essential and defining question. It would seem that broad inclusion is a good idea, that the edges of a band might be extended so that many different ideas are working at once. And it is to some extent, but it does not always work harmoniously. Selecting the elements one includes in a band, or any artistic endeavor, becomes an important matter of defining which ones will resonate harmoniously.

With a band, the search starts with songs and then expands to the sounds and instruments and design key that make up the style. A design key is the design element to which all the other elements of the art at hand refer. Often, this design key is thought of as a genre, but *genre* is too loose and imprecise a word for describing the styles of certain music. One gets lost near the edges of genre distinctions. One person's blues is another's jazz.

Nonetheless, there is a widely accepted sense of what defines country music. In the 1950s, country had a style that was different from what it would become later, but the historical and general idea of country music persists. A country-music fan of today has an unequivocal sense of what makes country music country music: it's the background music, or score, if you will, to the life of the working class.

By the time the First National Band was coming together, I had been thinking for years about how the country music that surrounded me in my youth included oddball elements, like "Tico Tico" and "Beyond the Blue Horizon," as well as elements of early rock and roll, which in my case meant Chuck Berry and Bo Diddley.

John Ware seemed to get the idea of this amalgamation right away, and Red Rhodes was happy to contribute to it. Red was in his forties and a punctuation-laugher, placing at least a chuckle after every three or four sentences, like steam-valve relief. When I talked with him about playing "Beyond the Blue Horizon" in a country style, he laughed more than usual and said he had no idea what to play. What he did play turned out to be inspired.

John Kuehne, who adopted the stage name of John London, was along for the ride as well, especially because he had a good foundation in playing standards from the big-band era of the 1940s recreationally with his dad. We all could play twang, but just as important, we all had hours of jukebox-lounge-time coupled with a deep love of rock and roll.

I had a sound in my head that I had first heard in those Nashville sessions I did under the Monkees banner, but until we all played as the First National Band and started learning and rehearsing the songs, I had no idea whether this ensemble could happily or even comfortably play it.

The four of us did as good a job as we could recording. John Ware was generally a strong force in the artistry and direction the band was taking, and he was able to bring Glen D. Hardin, a great pianist who had already backed up musicians like Ray Charles and Sam Cooke, into the studio to play with us for a song or two.

The finished album, which included some of the songs I had recorded in Nashville during the Monkees period, was satisfying. We all were proud of it and felt as if we had found something new and interesting in the musical direction we were taking. But though we were all proud of the album, I was also confused by it. I couldn't tell whether it was good or not. My usual metrics were not revealing much.

The business side of things was also confusing, driven as it was by my CP-certainty that the Monkees model would suffice, which of course it wouldn't, because *The Monkees* was a television show. As an operating enterprise, it was frustrating; it didn't appear to work for starting a band. I discovered that a band's musical system would not govern the outriggers I had lashed to the side of our friable craft—the finance, management, and career captains of the operation. I had thought that the Monkees structure would function well, but it didn't.

I had been greatly affected by the organizational systems of the arts in LA but was more and more confused by them. I could not fathom where the foundations of the music, movie, and television industries were—whether they were "First good business, then find the art" or "First good art, then find the business." I was impressed by businesspeople with artistic flair, like Bert Schneider and Bob Rafelson, but it always seemed as if the bottom line was money. There was a certain limited logic to this, no doubt; bill paying was bill paying.

I tried to learn from the successes I noticed, but they were all clouded in a fog of sorts. In the ambiguities of the Hollywood Mind, art and commerce each occlude the other, making their relationship unclear. More than once, I tried to reverse-engineer the processes of show business only to find myself perverse-engineering them: inverting not the *sequence* of processes but the *nature* of their original intent. There may have been a *Principia* for the Hollywood Mind, but I had no idea what it might contain. The Hollywood Mind was pretzel logic at its saltiest.

In the record business of the 1970s, the road to a hit record was pretty well traveled. Its steps were clear thanks to the control of corporate enterprise. Or maybe not.

It went something like this:

The record was made, and the artist was told to "stand over there for now," meaning, "Don't get too involved in the business; we'll take care of everything." The record would then be manufactured by large East Coast factories and shipped out to stores that took the goods on consignment. The record was identified numerically, something like "RCA Victor 22719," in order for everyone to understand it just enough to get it into the system. 22719 was, more or less, blindly ordered by record stores, which ordered however many copies they were told to order since the goods were free to the store until they were sold.

At the record company's command and expense, the artist waiting in the corner would now visit the record stores and perform the song to a playback of the recording, or maybe with a couple of instruments. Radio stations would play records according to the pressures and inducements of the record-company promotion men, who would tailor these free offerings to the music programmer. The radio station would know whether the public responded to the airplay because the Arbitron rating service monitored the number of listeners at any given time and would tell them how many were tuning in to either 22719 or 14298. The radio station would play more or less of one or the other, depending on what the rating service said the public said in response to what the sales and promotion people from the record company said the record stores were selling from their consignment.

When *Magnetic South* was released, it was the first time I stared into this abyss. It was much deeper and darker than I thought. In the same way that some of the best people might make bad records, and some of the worst people might make good ones, so it was with bad and good business. It was a dense, confusing business on all fronts.

The promotion person from Screen Gems came in excited one day soon after the release to tell me that WFIL, a radio station in Philadelphia, was playing the song "Joanne" from the album. He was thrilled at the break we got. WFIL normally played only pop records, but nevertheless, one disc jockey there had gone against the tide and started playing "Joanne," a nearly acoustic countryish ballad-with-a-yodel-in-it, which to everyone's surprise at the record company had gotten good response from the public. This put "Joanne" solidly in the system and on its way to becoming a mild hit all across the United States.

In a train of thought whose tracks I have never pieced together, my manager—our manager, of the First National Band—thought this would be a good time to leave the US and go over to England and play obscure clubs across the English countryside.

So we made the obviously intelligent move that one makes when he or she stands at the threshold of success: we left town. In the English countryside we played the faraway clubs, to crowds who had never heard the record and whose only familiarity with me was as a television personality. We did the press conference, well attended only because of Hendrix's and Ringo's gracious generosity, and wandered around English society until the specter of success had passed in the US and "Joanne" had drifted into the margins.

It is hard to know, even with *amarcord*, whether it is better in such times to be bitter, crazy, heartbroken, mad, sad, or loony. Not that there is much of a choice. Like trees, artists grow where they are planted, grow the way the wind blows, and grow toward the sun. In the end that is nature's way.

In retrospect, none of this seems as weird as it was or as confusing as it became. The 1970s record business was obviously not natural. It was almost entirely corrupt, and the artists were relegated to pawns, curious and disoriented pawns, not in a game of chess but in a game of checkers.

Each new First National Band record that came out—there were two that followed the first—was issued into the same miasma as *Magnetic South*. Red, John, John, and I played well as a band—we were good as a band of musicians—but the business and the times and the circumstances were working their excoriations deep. The FNB was not sustainable, as promising as it was.

There was another important factor in this picture: my personal life was in shambles. My moral compass looked like a spinning top.

I had three children with Phyllis, my wife, and another child with Nurit, who was not my wife. Both of these women in their own way salvaged what little they could from my misbehavior. Phyllis was resolute and kept trying to make our marriage cohere. Nurit was resolute in making me take responsibility for my child. In both cases, these women were on higher moral ground than I, and I am grateful to them for expecting me to join them—and in some ways forcing me to.

Nurit was more successful than Phyllis in getting me to face my responsibilities. Nurit only wanted me to take responsibility for our child and to support him, whereas Phyllis wanted our whole marriage to become a bastion of mutual affection and trust, and a safe haven for our children. This was not to be, because in addition to all the other lapses of ethics, I fell into yet another sordid and awful affair with a friend's wife, and that affair made me unfit for any relationship on any terms, and I knew it. I cared for Phyllis and our children as best I could with money. It wasn't enough, and I knew that too.

When I saw that the first three FNB albums were not going to be successful, instead of changing the environment or the management or the administrative overhead, which were where the problems lay, I changed the band. The Second National Band came and went in a flash, with only one album. At this point the powers at RCA gave me notice that if I were to continue there, I needed to concentrate on making hit records.

I was back in the same waters I assumed I had just swum out of. I made a record with only Red and me playing that I titled *And the Hits Just Keep on Comin'*. Contrary to the title's promise, the record went nowhere, traded only among friends and hardcore fans. Then I made one final try, with an album titled *Pretty Much Your Standard Ranch Stash*, using the band I had formed for my new record label, Countryside.

Countryside came about when Jac Holzman, who was then president of Elektra Records, and I put together a deal where I would start a label that would in essence be Elektra's country division. Elektra had enjoyed great folk and pop successes, and Jac said he "followed the music," so an LA-based country label seemed like a good idea to him. It did to me too. I proposed that we build a studio in the San Fernando Valley, home of the Palomino Club, and for that studio I would put together a house band around Red Rhodes. Jac seemed to think it was a good plan.

Building a studio band around Red was easy. He knew all the country players in town, the best and the worst, and the idea of joining a house band—kind of like the ones at Stax/Volt in Memphis and at Motown/Hitsville USA in Detroit—had players lining up for auditions. The band that came together around Red was first rate, and the sound was pure Southern California.

Garland Frady was our first artist, and we made an album called *Pure Country* with him. Garland spent a lot of his time during the day selling stuff at a flea market in the valley, and then at night he would record. On weekends he would try to find bookings around town so he could perform. It was a hard life, and he sang like it. He was the real deal.

As Countryside was starting up I still had one more record to make for RCA, and I set about juggling the calendars so I could fully attend to the Countryside start-up and the new album for RCA, and found that I faced solving the unusual problem of which band to use for the RCA album.

The Countryside band was new, and while staffed with very good players, they were not used to the studio work the way the first-call session players around town were. I puzzled over which way to go, whether to go off for a few weeks on my own and use a band of session players, leaving the Countryside band alone to rehearse and make demos, or whether to take the new band into the studio with me. It was my call and I wanted to make the right one.

David Barry was something of a standout in the Countryside band. He was a good piano player and a real spark plug for the rest of the band as a team leader. Country music was not exactly native to him, however. He was a Harvard graduate who was working as a journalist and wanted to be a country music piano player when we hired him to join the band. Red liked him a lot as a person and a player, and David gave the whole endeavor a decidedly classy feel, which as near as I could tell was not his original intent. He seemed to love the country-piano-player culture on its own and for a good while left his background and pedigree untold.

I asked David whether he thought it would be OK with

the other players if I used LA studio musicians for my RCA record. He said he thought it would be devastating for the band at Countryside and advised very strongly against it. I took his advice and brought the Countryside band into the RCA studios in LA for *Ranch Stash*. David had been right. The record and the playing were excellent, but there was more there than just playing. *Ranch Stash* had a cinematic and poetic mission that required some subtlety and some nontraditional thinking by the players. It was clear from the downbeat that an LA session ensemble, however technically superior, would not have had the patience, or the *bandistry*, for this kind of trek.

It was because the Countryside band was a real band coming together around an announced aesthetic that the effort we made paid off. *Ranch Stash* came out exactly as I had directed. The band played the songs exactly as I had hoped, and each member provided real inspiration individually.

The Countryside band had a cohesion and focus that a selected or curated group would not have. This even though the Countryside band *had been* selected and curated for work at the Countryside studios and with Countryside artists. This common ground provided a kind of shelter for the assembled muses.

A band needs at least three players, and thrives with four, because of the nature of harmony. It also needs a place to be and try things out. This place can be a garage or a skunk works or a kitchen or a crucible. Countryside was all of the above—and even more. There is a certain pride of membership that develops and a care for the quality of the work that gets passed around among three or four people.

In the early going I needed to buy a good piano for the studio, an important piece of equipment, and looked around for just the right one. David went shopping for it and finally found a Yamaha C7, a seven-foot-three-inch grand piano that had a crisp, clean sound. He made a great deal for it, and when it was delivered he was thrilled and played it for hours. He pasted a note on it just above the keyboard that said "Please refrain from placing cigarettes, cigars, or other carbonaceous materials on or near this piano. If at all possible, use the piano in the Palomino!"

Ranch Stash closed my RCA career in fine style, and again, poor sales. Sadly, by then the world had turned a little and the songs were no longer as fetching as youngsters, and they were lost into the vaults of RCA until RCA itself was finally lost.

I turned my full efforts to making Countryside work, and although I did not know it, I also started turning my life into a country song.

8

I would like to die on Mars, just not on impact.

—Elon Musk, CEO of SpaceX

The Hollywood Mind is seasoned with certain residents who I came to know as Hamburger Movie Tycoons, people who have made personal fortunes in other businesses besides Hollywood. They come from fast food, land development, construction, or computers—any number of entrepreneurial endeavors that have made them extremely wealthy in their field.

Typically, at least in my direct knowledge, they are good men and women who are more or less beneficent and think they can help make a difference in the arts, can help make better records or movies, and, most important to them, help save Hollywood from itself. Some are proud, with the arrogance of wealth and associations. Some are genteel, with a good heart and purpose. All are lured to Hollywood like a thing drawn to the heat of a flame it cannot see, with no notion of what or where this Hollywood is.

The Hamburger Movie Tycoons cannot be deterred. I think it's safe to say that before they come to Hollywood, they have never experienced the phenomenon of the terrible Friday Night

Flight—watching tens or hundreds of millions of dollars disappear in one hour, starting at 5:00 p.m. on a Friday, on the opening night of a movie that has taken years to make and is 250 percent over budget. It had all the right qualities for guaranteed success, but no one showed up. Nothing ever quite recovers from a bad opening. It is one of the more astounding capital occurrences, a nuclear-bomb-like devastation of wealth and value in the blink of an eye.

I came upon the scene of a minor Hamburger Music Tycoon crash shortly after Jac Holzman and I made the deal to start Countryside Records. This tycoon—I'll call him Ralph—was building a studio in a California ranch house on a few acres in the San Fernando Valley, and compared with motion-picture-making crashes, this music foray was just a parking-lot fender bender. But it was upsetting to him.

I became friendly with Ralph and commiserated as he regaled me with stories of his entry into the Los Angeles music scene and record-business world. I made him for a good guy, with a decent goal, but he was utterly naïve as to the workings of hardball Hollywood production in any form: music, movies, or TV. I was embarrassed that I knew so much about that awful side of the business. He did not understand what he had gotten himself into. I resisted all his offers to hire me as a consultant, or any attempts to get me to take his money. I never used the phrase "Hamburger Tycoon" in his presence, although I invented it there.

This tycoon was morose, saddened at his failure to create a studio hub for the record business he wanted to start. So after my offer to rent the house for the Countryside studio on a long-term lease, take over the half-finished, nonworking, poorly designed and poorly built studio, and build it out to a state-of-the-art facility, Ralph reacted as if he were witnessing the arrival of an angel.

Once the studio was finished in the little ranch house, Countryside Records had come together. It also came apart very quickly.

After Garland Frady, we signed several other acts and started making demos and rehearsing, but just then Jac called to tell me he was leaving Elektra and the deal for Countryside was being handed off to David Geffen, who was coming in to take over. Geffen, an ex-agent and manager, was an executive star of the moment and had no use for me or Countryside. He gave me the masters we were working on and offered to sell me the studio if I could raise the money; otherwise, Elektra would take over the studio it had built and paid for and leave me with the masters. It was a nice gesture, fair enough.

Under the new deal, I could stay in the studio and use it for a while, but I needed to find funding quickly and set up a new distribution system. I started looking around among the few people I knew in the show-business world, but they were not interested; then I wandered into depths I did not know existed, full of people I did not understand or recognize, a world made of shadows on the wall. I discovered places where music-business people administered the arts like cruel slum lords, stealing copyrights and intellectual property and insinuating themselves into the process without adding any value. They did not know what the process was. They only saw the money.

Ralph, the Hamburger Music Tycoon, saw opportunity and again offered me money and all sorts of perks to keep Countryside going as a business, with him as a funder and partner. He was perhaps not motivated purely by the money, but still I knew better than to accept his offer. He called me up late one night to tell me he had figured out how to solve all the problems of the music business and how he would help me run a new Countryside Records. He said that we should adopt a strict policy that we would "only record hits."

In this way, he reasoned, all the time and money wasted on recording records that weren't hits would be saved, and we would quickly get into profits. Artists and distributors alike would line up to be a part of Countryside. I said I would think about it, but I didn't, and instead courteously closed discussions with him. I knew that to persist would lead to an ultimate sorrow for him and that he would end up in worse shape than when he found me.

Shortly after the collapse of the Countryside deal at Elektra, a whole sequence of unexpected events started, and I found myself in free fall. Every seam in the sack of my life started to split, and all its contents started leaking out. My affair with my friend's wife became even more horrible to me, but I didn't know how to retreat. Let's call her Kathryn, because that was her name. We were thrown together by circumstance, and maybe it was because I was getting desperate that I fell in love with her, or maybe it was really true love. I didn't know how to tell. I only knew the attraction was impossible to resist.

I wasn't sure how Kathryn felt, though I suspected we each were a life raft for the other, and in some uncertain way had become each other's next steps along parallel paths. Even so, I could not shake the terrible feelings I had at betraying my wife and my children and my friend, all of whom had trusted me. It was certainly a nadir for me, a point as far as possible from where I wanted to be.

I had no opportunities as an actor, a player, a singer, a songwriter, or a producer, given my sales history with RCA and my recent crisis of confidence in any ability I might have to pursue goals along those lines. Even those I thought of as friends received me warily.

I had naturally reached out to my mother, whose fortunes were waxing and whose company, the Liquid Paper Corporation, was expanding in leaps and bounds, causing a stir in the office-supply business. Maybe, I reasoned, she would like to go into the record business with me. She was surrounded by traditional businesspeople and sent her top execs out to the San Fernando Valley to meet with me at the Countryside studio, examine the opportunity, and look at a possible fit. I can only imagine how thrilled they were to be sent to meet with the loony son of their chief executive.

It didn't take long for Mom's business team to figure out how underpowered my enterprise was, how incompetent I was as a businessman, and how much they wanted to get out of there. Their advice to my mother was something like "Run away!" It was not the thing a mother wants to hear, but the message picked up a little extra volume and urgency when she discovered that leaving my wife and children to flee with a friend's wife was a real option for me.

David Barry, the Countryside piano player, was the voice of some hope. He told me that he met someone who had just bought him a car and he thought maybe she could help me. She was part of a traveling commune that was coming through town, living in a school bus. He assured me these were not the kind of hippies the conservative press was bashing at the time. These were clean, well-heeled, gentle, and peaceful people who smelled of incense. He thought that the woman who bought him the car might be happy to lend me some money to keep Countryside rolling while I got on my feet. I didn't have the heart to tell him I had no feet, so I agreed to meet her and see what was up.

As David had said, the hippies were really more a commune

of yogis. They were a beautiful bunch, with long flowing hair and fit and trim bodies dressed in colorful tie-dyed clothes or white yoga pants and shirts. The women were pretty, the men were handsome, and they were all healthy and very, very high. They were following a form of Hinduism and trying to live an ascetic life. Their trip looked Keseyian, and even if the bus they were in wasn't actually named Furthur, they were immersed in the developing counterculture of communes and shared lives. They were educated, calm, and radically left of center, and Countryside must have seemed to them like a good alternative-music enclave—except for the politics of country music, a not insignificant problem. Bringing them into my world, or me into theirs, would create a weird conundrum in my ever-growing sample box of conundrums, but I had little choice, and I privately thought of their presence as a blessing, the slight touch of the spirit of the Merry Pranksters' stopping by the ranch and nodding their approval.

Part of the school-bus entourage was a fellow who was introduced to me as Ajatan. Jots, as he was more often called, was a big smiler and happy yogi who was fascinated by Countryside, the Countryside studio, and all that surrounded it. He was not a fan of country music, but he and I still got on well. He and his brother, who was a greengrocer in Topanga Canyon, served as a local contact for the traveling band, and the grocery store as a rest stop on the emerging counterculture highway that headed north out of Los Angeles. This group was the first look I had up that road, into what was to become the Northwest Corridor, the new world of settled American Hippiedom—new technology, new religion, and new enterprise, and the first glint of the horizon of the rising Whole Earth.

The lovely lady who bought David the car lent me a little money to keep the lights on, and the merry band started gathering at the ranch and having meals there, which they supplied and cooked and were delicious, as long as you didn't want meat. While I'm not a vegetarian, I was happy and easy with their presence and their approach to society, to things like cooking and chores and finances and definitions of acceptable behavior. I liked the simple joys, and I was starting to look closely at their alternative lifestyle, one that didn't require hit records or television shows. After a few weeks, as the yogis left for their Shangri-la of Northern California, I watched them go with some sadness and a nascent desire to follow them.

Kathryn and I had made a mess of our spouses' lives as well as our own, and between us we decided that the best thing to do was to make a quick exit—maybe even follow the trail of the hippie-yogis. Through all this breakdown, though, Celebrity Psychosis still dominated me, and I entertained the thought that I could make a record in the Countryside studios as a parting gesture; then Kathryn and I would move north just behind the hippie bus and set up a new record company in Carmel, where we would live in my mother's vacation home. I was sure my mother wouldn't mind.

Of course she did, but she didn't say so. My request had gone from needing lots of dollars to save a failing business enterprise to needing simple shelter for me and my girlfriend. This she could provide, and she did.

I asked Phyllis to divorce me, gave her my portion of everything I shared with her, and promised to send money regularly for the kids. She was devastated. I was clueless.

This tragedy faded into the distance as my great nonsense train pulled into another station, and I was sure I would soon be joining hippies who smelled of rosewood, setting up a record company in a resort community, making a record that was sure to lift the general level of consciousness simply by its presence on the planet. What did it matter that none of this was coming together in any justifiable, or reasonable, or even understandable way?

Of course, it mattered a great deal.

What was really happening was I was running off with my friend's wife, leaving two sad, angry mothers and four innocent kids behind, along with a failed marriage and a pile of unwanted recordings. What was really happening was I was at the bottom of the darkest box canyon I could have been in, without a shred of sunlight.

It is truly said that, only by the blessings of universal order, from such a point there is no way to go but up.

Deep in the bowels of sorrow, in the songs of the hard-laboring, slow-growing, painful life that is mortality, there is embedded a concept shared among country and blues writers and musicians, called High Lonesome. Those two words describe the deepest pain experienced in this life—a pain so intense that to merely describe it is to experience it in some degree.

This High Lonesome is beyond the reach of anything the human senses know. It cannot be seen, heard, or felt physically. It's accessed only through the heart and soul. It is the essence of loss—lost love, lost chances, lost life—and nothing is ever sadder or more difficult to bear. It is wanting to love—feeling the need to love, deep and real—and having no place for it. It is affection, pure and sweet, with no one to receive it, no one to know it, no one to give it to or share it with, so this feeling sits and wails like a lost child in a desert, nothing for miles in any direction but its own sorrowful sound—a cry not for food, or shelter, or power, or money. This sadness cannot be assuaged by any finite element.

High Lonesome had been the unknown and unintended theme of my life, even when my life looked to an outsider like an example of great success. Buried within the life of all mortals is one resounding and echoing heartbreak after another—one despairing moment repeating and repeating—even if it is unrecognized. High Lonesome is the feeling that accompanies it and is the purest blue the mind can paint.

I always knew I would live full time in Northern California one day, if for no other reason than the weather. But the quality of life and its pacific and beautiful nature entirely suited me as well, and my flight there with Kathryn seemed like as good a time as any to try to bring this nature into my life.

I had been surrounded with the aesthetics of the hippies for a while—pleasant enough—but the yogi life seemed more interesting to me. Among this new group, I could study the yogi writings. I could read and ponder the Upanishads and the Bhagavad Gita and even *Be Here Now.* I might follow their yogi trail. I might even live in a school bus with them and do asana in rest areas.

But the music was another thing. I needed my own, such as it was, and such as it had become.

Importantly, I was getting the ever-clarifying notion that I was actually writing my life with every song I wrote. It was too dim to see clearly at the time, but in *amarcord* it is plain, that with every word I wrote, with every note I sang, my life was fashioned, a life that I would conform to as it appeared.

The prose of the Indian ancients I started reading was familiar and resonated with what little I remembered of Christian Science. Mary Baker Eddy wrote, "Truth is real, and error is unreal. This last statement contains the point you will most reluctantly admit, although first and last it is the most important to understand." This theodicy seemed settled but still contained many questions whose answers were higher than I could reach. The yogis seemed to have opened another door into the same place. "Maya"—the perceived reality of life, an illusion—"is the Soul erroneously imagined," so it is written in the Upanishads. Perhaps there was a doorway to new paths here that would lead me out of the awful wilderness I felt trapped in.

I wrote myself through this door of escape. It was the only one I could see and understand. I wrote and recorded *The Prison*.

In *The Prison*, the songs and the story that accompanies them are about the gap left between the seeming reality of a finite prison and the metaphor of infinite freedom. Here prison walls nearly—but never finally—close inside the metaphor of finitude-within-Infinity, and so there is a gap, an opening, a way up and out, practically unseen by me until I wrote it down. It was truly the song of my life as it was unfolding verse by verse.

In *The Prison*, the protagonist, Jason, discovers this gap in the prison. It is a space where two exterior walls do not meet but leave a clear escape, symbolizing the ever-present spiritual sense of eternal and infinite Truth, even as that sense seems surrounded and incarcerated by finitude. Jason walks through the gap and out of the prison but soon thereafter falls into a night so dark and cold that he is sure he has made the final mistake. Crumpled by fear and fatigue, he falls into sleep and into a lonely, tragic place where all he can do is be still and wait.

From this fearful sleep he awakes to the dawn of a new day, a shining sun, and by its light discovers that the prison is of his own making, that the prison is not a fact of life but a dark and temporal belief of corporeal sense. With this new discovery he forges forward into another, higher life—not the life of an escapee or an ascetic but a life of infinite renewal, with a certain promise: despair may not disappear immediately, but it will lessen until it ceases, leaving only the living facts of Infinite existence.

I wrote down the story in prose and married it with music and lyrics, so *The Prison* would become a "book with a soundtrack." I wrote and recorded it in just over a week, with me and Red Rhodes in the Countryside studio before I left for Northern California. We put several musicians on it: I played guitar and drum machine, Dasher Kempton played synth and piano, Chura played congas, and David Tate and a yogi choir sang along with me and Donald Whaley. It was an unlikely band made of casual observers, each of whom had something to offer.

When it was finally complete, it was a ragtag recording technically, with some indistinct problems and some glaring ones, but it captured the spirit of the work. The book and record were a package to be read and listened to at the same time. It was a good idea, but in practice it was not widely accessible.

Even so, it was an angel of catharsis for me. It disconnected all the injured, angry, disappointed, disabled ideas and actions, and cut them loose from the pain of one another, and then embraced them in my admission, remorse, contrition, and commitment to reform, my genuine effort to make right in my community what I had made so wrong. It reduced the lattice of pain and fear to rubble, then swept the rubble away with a clean broom, into a dustbin of illusions.

Kathryn and I packed our things and moved out along the trail of the hippie-yogis and landed in the Carmel Highlands. She had been in commercial production for television before we moved, and I was happy and not a little surprised to learn that she was a good and willing partner with a skill for handling a cold sales call. She tackled the job of setting up distribution for our new one-record company by calling out to independent record distributors to find out if they were interested in handling our product, meaning *The Prison.* Most said no. That did not stop us from trying, and we ordered a stack of records and strove ahead in earnest to make the record company work.

The yogis had moved north to Sebastopol and stayed in touch. So did the IRS, which transferred my delinquent account to a local office, and as pleasant as the IRS officer was—and he was civil indeed—he kept me essentially penniless. I was cut off from any of the assets I had created, such as songs and records and all my other work that had produced or might produce royalty streams. In the mind of the IRS, that was all their money until they were paid.

On a few occasions, the yogis paid a visit to the house Kathryn and I rented in the Carmel Highlands. We had moved there after a few weeks at my mother's house, once the IRS decided on a living allowance for me. The yogis encouraged me to read the book *Be Here Now*, the autobiographical story of how Richard Alpert, a Harvard professor of psychology and a close friend of Timothy Leary's, became—after intense self-experimentation with LSD, a journey to India, and the discovery of his guru—Baba Ram Dass.

I found the book interesting; it fascinated me how close some ideas about the illusions of materiality were to Christian Science teachings. When Jots—the smiling yogi who had been so fascinated by Countryside—called one day and asked if I wanted to go with him to visit Baba Hari Das, who had given instruction to Ram Dass and was living in Northern California at a development called Sea Ranch, it sounded like a fine idea.

Baba Hari Das—or Babaji, as he was called—was voluntarily silent and communicated by writing. Jots told me he would be sitting on the floor or on his bed, so I should be prepared for that. When we met he was sitting on his bed, a slight man wearing a dhoti and a white shirt. He had dark brown skin, flashing deep-brown eyes, a beard, and long dreadlocks piled together atop his head, and he was gracious and very hospitable. I sat across from him on the same bed, and he asked what I did. I told him I was a musician and songwriter.

"What kind of music?" he wrote speedily, with a piece of chalk on a small chalkboard, almost as quickly as one would normally speak, in a clear, nicely rounded cursive script.

"Mostly rock and roll," I answered.

"What is rock and roll?" he wrote.

I said I would play some. I went to the car, got my guitar, came back, crawled on the bed, sat cross-legged, and played Chuck Berry's "Johnny B. Goode."

He burst into the widest grin and bounced along with the rhythm. He may have been silent, but of course he could hear perfectly. When I was finished, he asked me to play more, so I played a few more Chuck Berry songs that I knew. In each case, Babaji's smile grew wider; he seemed enraptured by the music. The more enraptured he was, the more delighted I was to see the music connect like that.

After about an hour of me playing, and Babaji listening and bouncing along, I put down the guitar and we started a conversation—mostly mundane—about his trip to the United States and my shows and music, about yoga and Ram Dass and *Be Here Now* and what Babaji's plans were. He said he was thinking of moving to Santa Cruz, but that would depend on whether his visa could be sorted out and whether his sponsor would be able to find a place for them to settle. I told him I lived a little south of Santa Cruz and to please stop in and visit, that he was welcome to stay the night, or even a few days if he needed to.

A short while later he called—an operation that consisted of someone else on the phone talking while Babaji wrote his questions and responses. He said he was coming to Santa Cruz and wanted to visit for a day or two. I said of course, come ahead.

I didn't exactly know what I was getting into, because Babaji's arrival brought with it his traveling entourage and a whole outside community of people wanting to meet and talk to him. My little house sat on the side of a hill with terraced gardens and overlooked a great expanse of the Pacific Ocean. The house was older, built entirely of redwood, with small rooms and one kitchen and bath but a very large main room with a huge stone fireplace. The room was big enough for Babaji's entourage, all of whom sat on the wood floor until it was completely taken over by a school-bus load of hippie-yogis a few orders of magnitude larger than the original I'd met in LA. It was a swarm of people in and out, cooking and cleaning and caring for the children, remarkably well ordered and serene, and Kathryn and I were very happy to have them all. Kathryn had read *Be Here Now* by then and quickly got on the same page as everyone else. It was thoroughly delightful—peaceful, conscious, and calm.

After a few of these visits Babaji moved to Santa Cruz and set up his yoga center in the hills there. He and I spent many hours alone in conversation during that period. We had time enough alone to talk deeply about yoga, world religions, philosophy, the science and order of being, and soccer. Because he had to write, the conversations about spiritual things were necessarily slow and sometimes slowed to a crawl, but they were always highly charged with meaning.

I started going regularly to visit Babaji at his ashram, but as his followers increased, it became less and less intimate, and the close times on the bed at Sea Ranch and on my living-room floor in the Highlands were fading.

Babaji has written and published an entire body of work,

so his teachings are best left to his own words. However, there was one incident I will mention that had a deep effect on me. I was at his ashram one morning as he was starting *satsang*—a kind of sacred gathering among yogis, usually in the presence of a teacher or guru. It is like a church gathering, but in Babaji's case it was fairly informal. Often at these gatherings, I would sit by his side at his invitation. From there I could see his chalkboard and would read what he wrote to the crowd. In the early days the crowd was small, somewhere around fifteen or twenty people, and they would ask him questions on theology and scriptural interpretations and so forth.

On this particular morning I sat beside him as usual and was happy to see him as usual. A young couple made their way forward and sat a few feet from Babaji. I could see them clearly. They had a young boy with them, around seven or eight years old, and he seemed quite disturbed, struggling with what appeared to be a severe chronic illness of long standing. The parents seemed more or less used to it, although they were clearly unhappy. The child writhed and twitched in a kind of internal agony. I felt an instant, almost overwhelming, sense of love for the family, a deep concern and care and compassion for the child.

After a few moments and a few questions from the congregation, during a silent pause, the mother asked Babaji if he could heal her child. I don't remember with much more clarity than *amarcord* affords, but I recall that Babaji took a short moment to think and then wrote on the board, *"No. But he can."* Then he nodded to me to read it to them as he held it up for all to see.

I read the words out loud to the little family, and when I read the words "But he can," Babaji pointed to me and smiled. I was surprised.

I was unsure what to say or do. Babaji continued to point at me and nodded a yes, meaning, "Yes, him."

I sort of wagged my head in a gesture that was a cross between "No I can't" and "I have no idea what he's talking about, or why he said that."

The parents looked at me longingly and, I thought, in confusion. It was a most uncomfortable moment, because in their long looks was the incipient question: "Why not? Since he says you can, why won't you heal our son?"

The truth to my own mind was unequivocal. I hadn't the slightest idea how to heal that child, even with my upbringing in Christian Science.

I'd had many healings through Science, and those healings were verifiable in my own experience and in my own thought. When Phyllis and I had called a Christian Science practitioner to help us with our infant child, who had all the symptoms of jaundice, the practitioner healed him overnight. Our child went to sleep the color of a carrot and woke up looking normal. I didn't know whether this was a common occurrence, one expected by medical doctors, only that it happened. When Phyllis was injured in a car accident, the same CS practitioner came to her side and three days later what had appeared to be life-threatening wounds were healed, and she was up happily cooking a large Thanksgiving dinner with me. Again, I did not understand where this fit in nature, but it happened as I have written here.

I had usually been the one healed and not the one doing the healing; my own verification was from the experience, and the experience was always anecdotal. The healing experience in metaphysics always is, because it happens differently every time it happens. But those present know it has happened, testify to it, write about it, trade stories among themselves, and in this way many come to reasonably depend on metaphysical healing. If anecdotes were data, the Christian Science Publishing Society's library of thousands of sworn accounts and witness-verified testimonies of healing would be overwhelming proof of the effectiveness of spiritual healing.

Sitting next to Babaji at that moment and looking into the eyes of those parents filled me with compassion and an understanding that of all the arts, the healing art was the most demanding, the most important, and the most loving.

I stayed for the rest of the *satsang* but left immediately afterward, saying nothing to anyone. The moment with Babaji and the sick child and his parents had shaken me. I realized that I had looked to Babaji and to the practice of yoga as a healing practice, among other things; as a relief from the burdens of illness and incapacity, as a cure for ailment. In this moment I was unsure what the yogic practice was and felt as if I had somehow missed the point.

Back in the Highlands, Kathryn and I talked in depth about what Babaji could have meant, and I finally resolved that I did not know and might never, and the best way I had to think of it was to let it stay in my thought as a moment and leave it as it was, etched in *amarcord*.

Kathryn and I concentrated on setting up a record-distribution company and getting *The Prison* out as our first release. Because it was a curious piece, to say the least, the going was slow and arduous. The pushback from the press had been devastating; the reviews were aggressively disdainful or cruelly dismissive. But the hippie community I had been orbiting was enthusiastic and embraced the work. Those who enjoyed it needed no rationale, and they were encouraging in their enjoyment. Hope sprang.

We had not managed to sell any records to speak of, only a few hundred, and it looked as if a concert presentation might help open the work to wider appreciation. I decided that I should figure out a way to perform the piece live. This would be difficult, since the work required careful listening and reading at the same time to get the full intended effect. I tried to solve the problem with a presentation where I would read the story and then sing the songs in the interstices of the storytelling. It was a clumsy fix, but it connected with the hippie-yogi culture. I tried it out at a small college north of San Francisco in a presentation that Jots set up. The reaction was very positive, and this gave me more hope.

I decided to try using a dance troupe that would perform to the music, and maybe there would be some way to make that work with the prose as well. I would read the book, the dancers would dance, the songs would inspire, and perhaps all would be fine.

I found the choreographer Carlos Carvajal and his dance troupe in San Francisco, set up a concert performance of *The Prison* at the Palace of Fine Arts, and began regular rehearsals with them. Even though it felt natural to me, the rehearsals revealed something amiss, ungrounded. I started to feel there was something missing that I could not provide.

I was in my late twenties, and on top of my flagging confidence in *The Prison* as a play, my mother was beside herself with worry about me and my future, especially now that the counterculture bus had made a stop at my studio. Had it not been for the fact that she liked *The Prison*, she might have tried to persuade me to leave the arts and show business behind and join her in the office-supply business, but she didn't. Her marriage was coming apart as well by then and she said she had found some comfort in listening to and reading *The Prison*.

However, her enjoyment of it did not lessen her reluctance to accept into her life the yogis who had wound their way into mine. Her Carmel visits did become more regular, and our discussions more pointed. She was certain that the hippie element was not spiritual or even cultural but political at its root, and that it was bad for America—and she began to aggressively push this idea. She rejected their spiritual teachings out of hand and encouraged me to stay with her religion and politics.

But my mother was inarticulate to a fault, and even her very good intentions were thwarted again and again by this failing. Her capacity for feeling strong allegiance to her politics and religious doctrine was mixed with an even stronger incapacity for explaining that allegiance. In our conversations, however deep the goodwill between us, this confusion—between explaining a feeling and merely having a feeling—ran time and again, and again ran us aground. She became yet another siren on yet another shore, and it was disturbing. My confidence in the play flagged.

I didn't realize it at the time, but my notions of a band as a system—like the internal combustion engine as Chick had explained it—were far from accurate. My conception of art-as-applied-science set me at odds with many doctrinal practices, religious as well as political, and with cultural pursuits and capital industry. But I was not alone in this. Indeed, the whole nation was struggling with a new imperative for society, business, politics, and religion. What had started as a dance with LSD and Merry Pranksters, with rock and roll and alternative lifestyles, was taking deep root in the cities and suburbs and forests of Northern California and driving cultural, political, and economic change. Everything was changing. New systems were emerging, systems of thoughts and ideas, systems of living and systems of tools, and I was watching from the epicenter.

A band by its nature brings together its members' diverse and contrasting ideas and harmonizes them. This shared viewpoint first unifies everyone, then creates an ensemble that strengthens the voices into a choir, and finally raises its message from the mundane to the inspired. Seen in this light, the demands of being part of a band are very different from the demands of being part of the usual industrial hierarchies.

What developed most prominently for me during this time was a question about how to determine whether a system was natural, or more to the point, whether my instincts were to be trusted. So far the answer was a clear no. I was happy to set aside my instincts and my shallow ideas of evolution, since both had regularly betrayed me. But without gentle nature pushing me along, identifying the systems it supports and causes to prosper, I was lost for motivation. The fringe mantra of the seventies, "If it feels good, do it," would not serve. I could not shake the idea that a higher principle than that must be at work.

I was now in a different kind of mess, but it was the same dilemma I had faced for years. I loved my mother and knew her intentions were good, but her politics and practice of metaphysical doctrine were not helping me any more than Babaji's good friendship and curious words had.

Trusting my instincts was no longer an option for me. I felt what I needed was a dependable, understandable, and intelligent sense of an actual governing principle, a gravity of mind, an organizing, governing Nature with a capital *N*. This did not separate me from science or God, but it did set my thinking against the prevailing winds, popular opinion, blind faith, religion in general, and politics in particular.

Christian Science considered scientifically was still vague to me, but I saw truth buried within it that set aside my shallow sense of order and replaced it with a willingness to accept a higher natural order—the real laws of nature, even if I didn't fully understand them.

The overarching metaphor for *The Prison* was the understanding that a puzzle stops being a puzzle to anyone who solves it; the solution appears at first to lie through a doorway, but it is a doorway from one side only. Once one is through that apparent doorway, it is easy to look back and see through the illusion of the door. This simple metaphysical fact, while comforting, was not enough, because it was far from complete as a moral basis for living well and right.

My mother understood this dilemma because she shared it to a degree, and she gently and positively encouraged me to at least listen to a leading Christian Science teacher, a man named Paul Seeley. She had recently been to see him and was impressed with his understanding of the teaching. I agreed to give him a listen. It was the least I could do to show my gratitude for all my mother had done for me. As it happened, he was giving a talk in San Francisco when I was going to be in that area giving a performance of *The Prison* to a group of college students.

I attended the Seeley talk dutifully, and when I arrived, I was surprised at how large the crowd was. Christian Science churches, like all the other churches, were struggling along after the culture shock of the 1960s, and the services were usually held for smaller and smaller congregations. But on this afternoon, at this church, it felt like a rock concert, and the buzz was palpable. The church looked as if it seated close to a thousand people, and the hall was full, as was the balcony. I could not get in to find a seat, so I stood on a landing outside the balcony, where I had a partial view of the side of the stage.

I knew little about Seeley or his reputation in the church. He was a Princeton philosopher and a Harvard lawyer who had begun his work in Portland, Oregon, in 1910 and still lived there. He had lectured and taught for years in the Christian Science church, and reportedly once saw Mary Baker Eddy as she passed in her carriage. He was something of a legend. I could not see him well since I was looking down at him from the balcony, but I could see that he was dressed immaculately in a dark suit, had snow-white hair, and appeared to be somewhere between the ages of sixty and ninety.

I was more curious than interested. I had heard all the stories of healing over the years and had lived among those who practiced, but I had never been able to grasp the fundamentals of Science, or whether it even was a science at all. I knew even less about Christianity and had only a shadow of an idea about what people meant when they talked of God or Spirit. The yogis had a beguiling culture of spiritual worship and practice, in that it was serene and peaceful. The other religions I knew of appeared to be stacked against me and seemed arbitrary and wrong since they were full of scolding and reprimand, which were toxic to the artistic nature and pursuit. It would take something of real substance to overcome these feelings, but I was content to be at this lecture because my attendance discharged my promise to my mother to keep an open mind.

From the moment Seeley started to speak, I knew I was in the presence of something special and unique in my life. The first impression came from how he spoke: eloquently, like an old-time lecturer. He used no microphone, but his voice had no trouble filling the entire hall. He had a commanding presence and spoke loud and clear, with no placeholders like *um*, *and*, *uh*, or *anyway*. Second, his words were authentic, like a great lyric well sung. He had hold of the basic idea of Science in a way that I had never heard expressed. He carefully unfolded and unpacked the ideas of Spirit and God so they registered as natural and normal. There was no mysticism or supernatural sense; rather, these were facts of existence to be reckoned with and used as part of intelligence. His individual intelligence was as clear as any I had encountered. There was a depth to his inspiration and a clarity to his explanations that put his message a great distance from the jumbled preaching of the rehashers who thumped a Bible and warned of disasters. Seeley spoke about things he knew of. He spoke of Spirit, of our everyday use of it, of our place in it, of our relation to it, all in the same way Uncle Chick spoke of an internal combustion engine. Chick knew what he was talking about, and by listening I knew he knew.

Both men exemplified what they were talking about, exemplified what they knew, but in Seeley's case these were questions about Life and Being and the foundations of Existence. The talk was over in about ten minutes, but in that ten minutes I knew I had been in the presence of the highest mind I had ever encountered, speaking truth as I had never heard it, establishing in my understanding what was in his understanding. These were ideas I could examine, ponder, and accept or reject according to my own internal compass.

It was Nature at its highest, most beautiful, and—most important to me—at its most artistic and useful, and it was completely and clearly normal. I figured if anybody could teach me Science it was Paul Seeley, and now that I was excited to learn it, I would have to search him out and see if he would.

My mother was happy I had gone to see Seeley, but I didn't tell her about my reaction to his talk in any detail. There would be time enough for that. For now, I was up to my armpits in rehearsals for *The Prison.* A lot of people were working on spec with the idea that after our first boffo opening, the seats would be full, the ticket sales would keep us rolling in money, and everyone would get paid.

On opening night it didn't take long into the performance for me to have the feeling I was a sitting duck. The critics were out in force, and it was a massacre. The lead newspaper critic wrote a one-paragraph review with the headline "I Was Imprisoned by a Monkee," and it got worse from there. Fortunately, such critical reception did not hurt the record sales, since there were no record sales. I felt especially bad for Carlos, since he and his troupe had done an excellent job, and his choreography had seemed just right and very expressive of the underlying ideas. Sadly, the whole ship sank. *The Prison* opened and closed in one night. I was down to my last dime and a couple of slim options.

There were other recordings left I had pulled from the ruins of Countryside, but they were all in a state of disarray in the trunk of my car, so to speak. Only two pieces of music had been finished before the Countryside collapse. One was a soundtrack I wrote for a biker movie called *The Northville Cemetery Massacre*, a low-budget, Roger Corman–esque exploitation feature made by Tom Dyke and Bill Dear, a cameraman/director from Detroit I met in my last days at Countryside. Bill had wondered if I would write the soundtrack. I asked how much the budget for the music was, and he said zero. He wanted me to do it for free, and I said OK, on the condition that he couldn't ask me for anything specific and had to take what I gave him. He agreed, and we had our deal, so I had that album such as it was.

The other was an album by Swami Nadabrahmananda, whom the school-bus yogis had wanted me to record. He sat cross-legged on the floor of the studio and played the harmonium as he sang raga time counts in a kind of mantra holy-music exercise. I liked the music he made. It had a cadence I later recognized in hip-hop, of all things. I recorded about two hours of music, with him accompanied by tabla and sitar. I had no idea if it was good or not, but I was pretty sure I couldn't sell it.

For the other Countryside artists, whose projects were at various stages of development, I thought the best thing to do was to return the masters to them and let them have all the rights. I didn't feel as if I had held up my end of the bargain, and in some ways I just didn't want them to get hurt or ensnared in the inevitable Countryside crash.

Those three pieces of music were all that really existed, and of those three, only *The Prison* was mine and complete, and *The Prison* was now earning the same revulsion from the press and public that I had lived with for a long time. I desperately wished that *The Prison* might be my *Vase with Fifteen Sunflowers*, but it clearly wasn't.

The night of the closing and opening of *The Prison*, I got drunk on scotch at a small bar next to the Palace of Fine Arts, where we had performed the concert/play. Kathryn and I had not seen the reviews, but we both knew that the show was a disaster. After the performance, the attendees had silently shuffled out like prisoners. As we sat there neither Kathryn nor I said much. The hippie-yogi dance had turned into a grave disappointment and neither of us knew what to do next. The only plan I had was to drive to Portland the next morning to see Paul Seeley. I didn't want that connection to slip away and had made an appointment to meet him. As I sat there, I drunkenly prayed to the God of all drunks to lead me to the Truth and that Seeley would be the real deal.

9

It's time to move on to the next step in the psychedelic revolution. I don't know what this is going to be in any way I could just spell out, but I know we've reached a certain point but we're not moving any more, we're not creating any more, and that's why we've got to move on to the next step—

—Tom Wolfe, quoting Ken Kesey in *The Electric Kool-Aid Acid Test*

On the day of my appointment in Portland with Paul Seeley, I arrived a few minutes early. I stood at the entrance of the building where his office was and looked up, squinting my eyes and steadying myself from the lousy hangover that followed me from the night before. The building was thirteen stories, built in 1913, and though it was small by Portland standards, it loomed over me in my debilitated condition. I hurried in before I fell down from dizziness.

Seeley's fairly small two-room office was about halfway up the building and modestly furnished with some regular office furniture and a few bookshelves full of books. When I came in he was seated, dressed in a suit and tie, and he stood up to greet me and offered me the seat across the desk from him.

I could see that he was quite mature but very alert and focused. I told him I had seen him speak for a few moments in San Francisco and was impressed with what I heard, that I had been raised in the Christian Science church and was familiar with the teachings, but that he seemed to have an insight he could offer. I told him that I hoped I might learn more from him.

He was cordial, somewhat casual, very soft-spoken, unlike the powerful speaker I'd heard in San Francisco. As he sat in his chair and pressed his fingertips together, he asked me, please, to tell him something about myself.

I can't remember exactly what I said, but he listened to me in a way that showed me he heard me clearly and understood precisely the meaning of every word I said. I gave him a little of my history, and told him that I had just come from what seemed to be the failure of a recent project. I also told him I was depressed and lost for direction, and keenly interested in gaining a larger understanding of Science.

He thought for a moment, leaned back in his chair, and began to talk to me in extremely slow sentences about Christian Science, now with the same clarity and understanding I had seen from the balcony in the church in San Francisco. He spoke so slowly that I had to change my way of listening, from anticipation and expectation to patiently absorbing the thought value of the words he was choosing. He unfolded for me some of the simple and useful ideas of the teachings, ideas I had heard while growing up and had encountered recently in my life and in the arts, but each word came forth as if I were reading a beautifully written text.

Sentences, long and complex, fit together in paragraphs in a way I had never encountered in conversation. The sense of what he was saying was deep, but what really grabbed me and held me was the way the words formed great paragraphs of meaning that completely revealed aspects of Science. It was as if I were hearing the ideas for the first time in a perfect and lucid presentation of a discovery. This was very far from party chatter, or a usual conversation between businesspeople, or even between a student and a teacher. These were arrays of ideas that formed images of a world that came into thought clearly as he pointed them out. He was almost like a tour guide who was showing me things in a previously unseen and startlingly beautiful place, objects as ideas, ideas that I had not seen.

He pointed them all out to me just as I needed, or wanted, to see them. If a question popped into my mind, he answered it in the next sentence he spoke without my saying a word. If I wondered silently at an idea, he unfolded its origins, simplicity, usefulness, and practicality, again without my asking a question. He spoke of a spiritual Science, a Science of Spirit, that was a body of knowledge and infinite wisdom ordinary and normal but glorious as a sunrise, and told me everything I had come to hear as if he were pouring water into a cup.

After he had spoken for several minutes he looked at me and said, "How does that sound?" I exploded in laughter. It was the laughter of gratitude—the laughter of Hallelujah.

At first I was embarrassed because I was afraid he might think I was laughing at him, but instead he laughed with me, in a kind of "Isn't it wonderful?" moment that happens sometimes between friends attending a delightful event.

Seeley knew of what he spoke and shared it completely and fully with me, and at that moment the only thing I could think was *I should never take another drink of alcohol again.* All I wanted to do was to learn what he knew and how to think as he thought, and I knew that I would not get that from any other place but my own clearheaded thinking under the tutelage and guidance of a higher mind. Drugs would not get me into this state, nor would anything other than my own spiritual sense and willingness to learn. I knew that I had to approach this revealed state with absolute humility and patience, with receptivity and gratitude, and I knew that Seeley was to be my teacher and guide into this ever-present unseen world.

When I returned home I sent Seeley a letter asking him for class instruction—the formalized method of instruction in Christian Science provided by the bylaws of the church—and he sent me an application. I dutifully filled it out and returned it, and heard back from him fairly quickly. He said he could not accept me, that I was not yet ready to hear what I needed to hear to benefit from instruction.

I was devastated. I think my mother may have ruined my chances for being accepted on that first application for class with Seeley, because I used her as a reference and she did not approve of the fact that Kathryn and I had betrayed our respective spouses, run off together, and even worse, were not legally married. This would have been a lot for her to forgive. The application I filled out and sent to Seeley included a request for references who had information about the applicant's work and family status. I suspected that my mother had been candid and forthcoming about this, and had included her opinion of it in her responses to the questionnaire. The weight of the opinion of one's mother is like no other. The effect of this weight varies depending on the individual and the circumstance, but I think, in general, the effect is greater in the single mother–single child relationship than any other possible family configuration. In this relationship, the mother's opinion is extraordinarily intense and influential, and while the influences are greater, the relief valves are fewer.

I answered the question about marriage on my own application candidly. Kathryn and I were cohabiting at a time when such arrangements were not acceptable to the church, or even legal in many states. But the question of cohabitation was not specifically asked on my application, so I put *divorced* as my status, since that was true.

Discussing the question with Kathryn raised an issue between us that had gone untended. I was still reeling from the betrayal of our spouses, a betrayal that had become part of our relationship. Kathryn and I had fallen into each other's arms in a passionate embrace, and I had used that passion to justify all that came afterward, including the betrayal of my friend, her husband. It was a flimsy foundation to build on, but I thought it was all I had.

My mother had flown out to try to talk me off this ledge, and pointed out that passion and lust were governing me, but I took all of it as rebuke and scolding. The alternative—ending the affair—did not have any purchase in my thinking and I dismissed it out of hand. This dismissal was validated in my own mind by the intensity of the affair and the physical satisfaction it offered. However well intentioned my mother was, however right she was, to my benighted mind her trip out seemed meddlesome.

I did not discuss the issue of infidelity in our two marriages in the early going with Kathryn. However, the application to Seeley had moved the ethical and moral questions involved to the top of my mind, and I finally wondered aloud to Kathryn if we should make an effort to find some steady ground to build on, some kind of moral rectitude that would redeem the infidelity. It was one infidelity out of many in my life, but I had always thought of them as justifiable. Now that had changed.

The social mores of the time were negative pressures against infidelity, as were opinions of a certain type of thinker, but these were nothing compared to my own internal agonies. Compared to Seeley's, my mind seemed like a dumpster of dishonesty and despair, and for this pain there was no sign of relief, no forgiveness.

I said to Kathryn that I thought we should get married. I did not get the sense it was important to her, but she agreed.

We were married in a civil ceremony, just the two of us across the street from the courthouse in the home of a qualified official and two witnesses, but as I feared, there was no magical feeling of relief for the misconduct, no comfort or inkling that I had corrected a wrong. I still had the overwhelming sense of having gotten out of balance with universal order.

Kathryn and I kept trying to build a home. We started acquiring more records to distribute in the business, and we tried to settle into a routine that included my children, to create a family for them as their individual mothers had, but all of it had an empty, unstable feeling. I missed my kids, and this added to the weight I was carrying. The marriage felt like an attempt to put a damper on the societal pressures and stop the spinning of my moral compass. Without this compass functioning, I had "no direction home."

I knew that Seeley held class once a year, with thirty slots for students. After waiting what I thought was a proper amount of time, I applied to him again for next year's class. In this application I made two changes. The first was to change my marital status to married; the second was to *not* use my mother as a reference. For whatever reason, Seeley accepted my second application and gave me a place in his 1976 class.

I was happy to have access to an instructor and practitioner of Seeley's caliber, and Kathryn said she was happy for me, but I think she may have wondered if I married her only in order to get accepted, which wasn't the case.

I left for Portland, Oregon, in August of that year and, like many others before me, came home a changed man.

Class instruction in Science requires hours of guided reading and study, but most of the focus is on the Bible and the writings of Mary Baker Eddy, so I took all those with me and set up a small library on the little desk in my plain but comfortable room at the Mallory Hotel. The class lasts twelve days, six days a week, with Sunday set aside for church services. Classes are limited to thirty students and may happen only once in each student's lifetime, although continuing study and learning is provided through annual meetings of each class with all other classes a teacher has taught. Seeley was ninety when I attended and had been teaching for decades, so the alumni numbered over a thousand.

The class itself was held in a Christian Science church in Portland in a pleasant room in the Sunday School. Windows across the back of the room filled the space with light from outside. We were each given an assigned seat and a small notebook. When Seeley appeared that first day, he was immaculately dressed in a suit and tie, exactly on time, and took his place without ceremony at a desk at the head of the class.

He welcomed us and then began his opening lecture, speaking at a pace as slow as when I had first met with him. It was a pace slow enough to allow me to copy down his lectures word for word, so I did that every day. When he read he did so without glasses; he heard perfectly any questions that were asked, and only occasionally consulted notes as he elucidated various points. The lectures took place over four hours, from 9:00 a.m. to 1:00 p.m. each day; then we were dismissed and handed copious reading assignments that took the rest of the day. After the lectures I would walk back to the hotel, settle into my room, and do nothing but read, study, pray, and meditate, then sleep until the next morning.

I cannot describe here all I learned in that class; I believe that everyone who is instructed in these classes has a different individual response. What I learned and took with me related directly to my life as an artist and my desire to set down carefully an aesthetic foundation I could trust.

There is no hierarchy to these ideas as I present them. Each idea opened its own door for me, and I can trace each of those ideas back to the thoughts I was having as I wrote and recorded *The Prison*. In class instruction, the central idea of an infinite existence that is immediately at hand and available was demonstrated and explained in a way I had never thought of, and it revealed to me my own infinite mind, a reflection of this great and infinite being. It set me free from my confused sense of finitude.

The grand entrance to the teaching was through the door of spiritual sense, through science and art, the beauty of holiness, and an awakening of the active ideas of immortality, the definition of God as infinite Mind, Life, and Truth with which we could become intelligently acquainted, and by which we could enter the realm of the real, where we could find the God-provided ideas that we could use to build, heal, and love our fellow man and ourselves.

The first stone in the foundation came to me in the discovery of a new approach to science and ethics, an awareness of the many facets of these disciplines. Ethical navigation points were revealed to include the *finite* and *infinite*, *complete* and *incomplete*, as well as *right* and *wrong*. From this new standpoint there was the promise of an ever-unfolding understanding of even higher concepts of science, ethics, and morality.

Another stone was the idea of speed and process. I was taught to understand the importance of the natural pace of the artistic processes, the speed of the emergence and unfolding of ideas that was aligned with nature, neither too slow nor too fast. I began to sense these changes in process and learned to identify them for what they were. A high-speed manic sequence would indicate a push away from the natural order, while too slow a speed was an indication of drag or laziness. It was a simple metric I could use to focus my aesthetic pursuit and refine and clarify the ideas I was using in developing projects. Patience must have her perfect work. I remembered well the "easy speed" of the London art scene with the Beatles and other artists of the time, and how I was first made aware of this natural pace.

I was introduced to the important distinction between the *real* and the *unreal*, between *belief* and *fact*. Imagination was held distinct from belief, and belief distinct from fact. Truth was real and eternal. Error was unreal and temporal.

Finally, the assembled foundation stones unfolded the *sustaining* Infinite. The Infinite was revealed to me as continuous unified existence. The word *all* became inclusive of everything that existed, and *all* was *infinite*. Every moment was pregnant with infinite possibilities.

As an artist, the usefulness of the infinite idea could not be overstated. It allowed me to access spirit and spiritual ideas. *Infinite* and *Spirit* were identical and destroyed barriers and eliminated gaps. The continuity of numbers, notes, and colors established plurality in infinity. I could see that infinity was as near as my own thinking, extending far beyond dreams and imagination, into the metaphysical realities governed absolutely and entirely by harmony. I was included in this, not merely observing it, and I understood this inclusion in infinity as complete.

This clear teaching brought me to a threshold that allowed me to see the limitations of all I had done up to that point, and revealed a wondrous new landscape of being I had never seen. While I was expected to walk over this threshold, I saw, for the first time, that I was continuously provided with everything I needed to do this. I was shown the key and lock, and lovingly, patiently, gently shown how to use them both by depending on infinite mind. Surrounded by these magnificent ideas, finitude became a precisely limited tool.

⁂

Back at home, with these ideas in heart and mind, I awoke to a new dawn and a new view of my whole life. I wrote the songs for a new album, which I called *From a Radio Engine to the Photon Wing*, and started looking around for the funds to record it. I had gotten a call from an acquaintance at Island Records who was interested in perhaps setting up a distribution deal for Pacific Arts, especially if it included any new works. I established Pacific Arts in 1974 and it was my production company. There was no interest in *The Prison* as it was, but I could include it in a deal for overall distribution, and with a small advance I would be able to record *Photon Wing*.

The songs for *Photon Wing* were unlike any I had written, both lyrically and musically. I wanted to capture some of these new teachings in song. One song I particularly liked that bloomed from all this was "Rio," and I wanted to find a good band to play and record it. Perhaps it would be the anchor of a new album of songs.

I thought about the Nashville cats and called David Briggs, the piano player who had been on those original Monkees sessions when we had cut "Listen to the Band." I asked if he could get that same band together for me. He said he would try, but that it would probably have to change a little.

The more I played "Rio," the more I liked it and the more it developed an off-kilter lilt that a reggae bass part would enhance. In San Francisco I ran into a bass player named David MacKay, who was in a reggae band that impressed me. I asked if he would like to go to Nashville with me to record, and he seemed happy to accept.

Briggs had assembled a first-rate band for me by the time I got to his Nashville studio, Quadrafonic. It was not the same as the Muscle Shoals team, but what a great ensemble it was. Briggs played piano, Jerry Carrigan and Larrie Londin played drums, Weldon Myrick was on steel, and David MacKay was on bass. I played guitar on all but one tune, when Lonnie Mack came in to join us. MacKay, being something of an outsider, was accepted into the Nashville sessions professionally, as was proper, but I could see that he was not allowed much more than that, even though the bass part he played on "Rio" was a signature for the song and set the tone and pace that contributed greatly to the popularity the song attained.

I started teaching the band my new material. The vibe was different from what it had been in the Monkees sessions. The musicians were the same first-rate players, the sessions were exciting and satisfying to me, and I was overjoyed to be playing again and playing at this level, but the material was not as easily accepted as it had been in the Monkees sessions. These were clearly songs with little possibility for airplay, and I was obviously unconcerned with chasing hits.

The sessions were far outside the musicians' usual calls for high-speed arranging and performing in service of potential hit country singles. At one point, when I brought up the song "Navajo Trail," everyone essentially walked out on me. The song had a feeling and mood that, to me, evoked a high Southwestern romanticism, a poetry of skies, mesas, and vast stretches of wilderness that combined to make it a touch surreal. But when I announced it, they all took an unscheduled break. They were worried, because, as one of them later told me, they did not do "that kind of music" and thought I might be making fun of them, treating them like a cowboy band instead of the world-class musicians they were. In bandology, a cowboy band was a strange critter that played western music, and these musicians were not used to playing country music that did not have a pop hit as an ultimate target.

My reason for including "Navajo Trail" in the sessions had nothing to do with old-time western campfire music, of course. I wasn't asking them to play a clichéd and long-gone style. I thought of them as consummate musicians, and I was glad and relieved when they all returned from the break. I played "Navajo Trail" for them the way I had arranged it and led them through a performance that, in the end, they all agreed was exquisite. I was thrilled with it, too.

But the star of the session was "Rio." It was the first part of a diptych that included "Casablanca Moonlight," and since the combined length was over thirteen minutes, everyone rightly figured it had no chance for airplay. Nonetheless, they all took another step up the ladder of music for music's sake. It was their playing on this piece that made it my favorite of the session.

After the Nashville sessions for *Photon Wing*, I came home and delivered the record to Island Records, which would handle sales and promotion, and there was further agreement that "Rio" was the standout. If I could edit "Rio" out of the diptych and cut it down to around four minutes for airplay, then they thought it might even make a single. I sensed an unspoken opinion that the rest of the songs on the album were too unusual and not very likely to get played on the radio at any length. I was used to this perception by now, but since "Rio" was my favorite song, I was happy to get a commitment from Island to promote it.

Island Records was owned by Chris Blackwell. He usually lived in Jamaica and ran his enterprise from there, but on one of his rare visits to Hollywood I was asked to come meet him. Chris was reportedly from a large, wealthy family, but that was more rumor than fact. In fact, Chris was one of the few authentic people I met on the business side of the music industry—without question the best record exec and music curator I ever knew. He did have a distant connection to fortune, but he was very far from a Hamburger Tycoon and had been raised, as far as I knew, within the bounds of Jamaican music. His list of accomplishments in the music industry is long, unequaled, and very impressive. One of his more notable accomplishments was introducing Bob Marley and the Wailers as a mainstream rock-and-roll presence, lifting Marley from the wings to the center stage of global music.

Chris was the genuine article as a music man, and there were probably none better. By the time I met him, Island was one of the great prestige labels, and he was revered. I felt privileged just to be a part of it. At the time he was light-haired, well tanned, with a big smile, and always dressed in light short-sleeved shirts, pants with rolled cuffs, and either no shoes or flip-flop sandals. He was a striking and welcome figure in the sea of Hollywood Minds and Celebrity Psychotics, and I instantly liked him.

I was drawn to Chris immediately and could see that I was in the presence of someone who was grounded in his music the same way I was in mine, but who had deeper roots, who was immersed in it spiritually and physically. It was serendipitous and poetic that I had chosen a reggae bass player to underpin *Photon Wing* in general and "Rio" in particular.

Chris said he liked "Rio," thought it was a good record, and that it might actually sell some copies. Then he asked a question that set me and the entire record industry in a new direction that would forever change the way music was received and embraced. He wondered if I would make a promotional clip for "Rio" that he could use to promote it in London and Europe.

I hadn't any idea what a promotional clip was, but I sensed an artisanal approach at work in Chris's request that made me agree to produce one without hesitation. I would do the research to get some understanding of what a promotional clip was when I went back home to Monterey.

Unlike in the US, all television in Europe was state-owned at the time, so only a few government-controlled stations provided all the television programming in each country. As a result, anyone in those countries who watched television watched these one or two channels, and typically the programming contained an hour or so a day of music. This music usually consisted of the pop tunes of the time and territory, and the visual component was a short film of the band or performer singing the song as they looked directly into a television camera. This short film was called a promotional clip, a promo clip, or just a clip.

It was an odd way to deliver pop music. When Italian television was playing a clip of a British act, it would be disconnected from the rest of Italian television's regular programming day, offering only a blurry look at an international landscape. But it worked, probably since it was the only television program anyone could watch, and the promo clips sold lots of records.

I didn't find all this out at once. Various execs at Island told me that all I needed to make was a film of me performing "Rio."

In their mind, that meant me standing in front of a camera and singing along with the record. However, in my mind, the assignment triggered a remembrance of scenes of every Hollywood musical I had ever seen, from Fred Astaire and Ginger Rogers dance numbers to Disney musicals and *Fantasia* explorations, all the way up to and including *A Hard Day's Night* and *The Monkees* TV shows.

I wrote out a kind of shooting script for "Rio" and "Navajo Trail" that consisted of a sequence of scenes I thought would be good visual components for both songs. They were the text equivalents of what I wanted to see: women in fruit hats dance by, Nez suns himself on the beach, Nez flies through space, Nez sings into old-timey mic, Nez dances by with woman in red dress, Nez rides up on white horse. The aesthetic came together around little more than dreaming up what I wanted to see as the song played, the same way I'd thought about what I wanted to read while *The Prison* played.

Then I called Bill Dear, with whom I had remained in friendly contact, and asked if he would be able to come help me film this. I told him I could pay him a little something. He said yes.

With her background in TV commercials, Kathryn instinctively knew what would need to be done to bring together a crew for a production, although she had no direct experience in doing it. She agreed to explore how we might pull this off and started working with Bill to produce a budget.

Island Records had no allowances for this. The clips were expected to be produced by the artist or their management and were usually done so quickly and cheaply that cost was no factor. No one seemed to care much whether they contained any content other than the visual of someone singing the song. I had a very different idea, and as Kathryn, Bill, and I began to sweep things together into a pile to see and understand that idea and how we might execute it, we each found a place to apply our particular skills.

A new band came to life in my life. Like everyone, we didn't know we were a band until we started playing together. At this stage, it was just Bill, with camera equipment he was willing to contribute to the mix, and who could shoot, direct, and edit; Kathryn, who had production skills she could lend; and me. I would write and perform. It was a good, balanced fit for all of us. The band would emerge.

Bill wondered at first how the scenes would fit together, and it took some effort for us to understand each other. Bill was concerned about *continuity*, and I didn't know what continuity was. Continuity has to do with the way independent shots, filmed at different times, are made to fit together to create a whole, so that a door opens the correct way in both shots to make it appear as if they are contiguous and part of the same scene. As you can imagine, continuity is a big deal to a filmmaker.

As Bill tried to explain to me what this was and I tried to explain to him what I saw in my head, we pretty much talked past each other for a while. We never argued, but it was hard for us to get on the same page, as it were.

Nevertheless, we had many happy dinners and conversations because we laughed a lot. Bill was a hardcore Monkees fan and had a good sense of humor himself, and together the three of us threw ourselves into the production with at least goodwill and high hopes. It didn't make much difference to me, or perhaps to any of us, that while we were all good at what we did, none of us knew what we were doing collectively. A lot of this would have to be improvised.

BMI, a performing rights organization, had been collecting money for songs I had written whenever they were played on the radio. After Kathryn did the budget, I was able to get enough of an advance from BMI to pay for the production of the "Rio" clip, as well as a clip for "Navajo Trail"—or so I thought. The budget was $25,000. This was considered astronomical at the time. The stand-and-sing promo clips were usually a few hundred dollars to produce—if they were made at all.

On the first day of shooting it became pretty clear that we were not going to hit what we were swinging at. We had way overestimated how much we could shoot in a day, and also underestimated how much it would cost. The images Bill was shooting were superb, and his crew was hanging together under Kathryn's management, but we weren't getting as much footage as we thought we would, and we finally ran out of time with only about half of what I had written making it to film. Some of it was footage for "Rio," some of it was for "Navajo Trail."

We were using the standard technique of shooting to "playback," which meant the record was played while we shot film and I would lip-sync along to the recording, so all the footage was more or less locked to the portions of each song in which I was on camera singing. Where lip sync was unimportant, the footage was shot without me on camera, with the idea that we would put the sound on picture in the edit.

As the edit days came up, all three of us approached them

with some confusion and concern that we had driven into a quagmire and really had nothing that would cut together—certainly nothing that would look continuous as a whole. But we were stuck and had to move forward with what we had and see how far it got us. At least we were having fun.

In the edit bay, we were assigned a switcher named Danny White, and to our good fortune it turned out that he enjoyed doing special tricks with the video switcher and could produce all sorts of electronically generated visuals, colors, feedback, and such with just the switcher and nothing else. It was unusual to discover this talent in Danny, because it was unrecognized as a skill in the business at the time. He said he had taught himself to do it by sitting at the video switcher and playing around with it during his off-time.

Bill was a good cameraman, a competent director, and an even better editor. I had a lot to learn. I sat up in the back of the edit bay and watched as Bill and Danny struggled with the footage we brought in, trying to make some sense of it and get something out of it. From time to time I would make a comment about what footage might be inserted into the clip, but for the most part I was quiet and listening. We quickly ran out of the footage we had shot for "Rio," so we started dipping into the silent footage from "Navajo Trail." It was our only option.

The important thing to me was that the whole video flow with the music and be musical itself, with visual edits made on the beat of the music so the music drove the images. I would sound off every so often, saying to move that picture here or there to match the musical beats and nuances. I was highly sensitive to the song and music; Bill was highly sensitive to the image and editing. As we worked together, something extraordinary began to unfold.

As each new piece of footage—whether a short interlude or a distant shot, whether from "Rio" or "Navajo Trail"—was laid against the soundtrack, continuity began to emerge. As the clip grew in length and different footage was added, the continuity became stronger. Danny would season some of the edits with wild transitions, tame by later standards but novel for us, and a smoothness and point of view became clearer and clearer as a music video came to life.

At a certain point about halfway through—I can't spot it now or remember exactly where—the song overtook the images and began to provide a narrative structure the images did not have on their own. The whole was more than the sum of its parts. Unknown to me at the time, this shift from pictures driving the narrative to sound driving it was almost unprecedented as a production objective.

When the song came fully forward and became the primary intention, the idea of the song, the spiritual value of the song, took over and was realized by all the images on the screen. The significance and meaning of the words were expressed on another, higher level that had appeared—much as a phantom chord or harmonics become audible on adjacent piano strings. The song gave the images a meaning they didn't otherwise have. It was exciting to me and apparently to the other people in the edit facility, because one by one they all came by, peered in, and stayed, watching this edit process unfold.

Bill and I didn't discuss the process at all, but we were both obviously excited by it and getting more intrigued and satisfied with each new edit. By the time the first complete edit was finished, almost all the other rooms were empty, and everyone was in our edit bay watching "Rio" play over and over.

It was a repetition for me of the "Listen to the Band" session in Nashville, but here the video component had shot the whole project skyward at a tremendous rate and revealed a space that had been only partially visible while we were shooting. Bill and I were ecstatic. The loss of a shooting day's footage, and not having done what we first tried to do, and the puzzle of fitting together images filmed for two different songs—all of it was overtaken by this extraordinary new birth, the music video.

None of us had ever seen anything like it—and yet it contained some of the legacy of every film ever made. We had invented nothing, had created nothing, and yet by the action of an artistic process we knew nothing about, we had been present at the birth of something.

I couldn't wait to show "Rio" to the staff at Island Records. Bill flew home to Michigan and showed "Rio" around to his family and friends. None of us knew what would come next, but we all knew something had started in our presence that was going to propel us for years to come.

The final product of the session was recorded on a video recorder/player made by Sony called a U-Matic, which produced a large, boxy tape cassette that I could carry around with me and play for anyone else who had a U-Matic. It was the industry standard for showing and trading tapes among the small community of television producers and agents, but it was extremely rare among the general public. In fact, the whole notion of video recording was still in its adolescence. When I took the cassette over to the Island Records office in Los Angeles, the staff gathered around and watched, and laughed, and finally applauded when it was over. The head of the US division of Island asked me, "What is this for?" and I responded, "I'm not sure. Chris asked me to do it."

I had indeed made it in response to the request I thought Chris Blackwell had made, but it was hard for a casual observer to imagine what this little film might be for. To American eyes the little film was a white elephant, a trinket, fascinating and entertaining but with no apparent application among current television outlets. In the US, the music video had been born an orphan, without a place to be played.

But this was not the case for the European stations for which Chris had wanted the promotional clip. I made plans to travel to London to meet with Chris again and to personally present the clip to his staff of promotion people who worked in Europe.

When I arrived, there were around thirty or forty promo people in a recording studio listening to the newest releases and watching the clips that had been made for them. As far as I remember, Chris was not at that meeting. I was asked to sit inside a booth where I could watch through a glass partition; this way I would not disrupt the meeting. It was fine with me.

I sat through about six or so film clips and noticed that the crowd was listless and a bit distracted. This seemed like a required meeting, and many in attendance seemed eager to get through it and leave. The promo clips were exactly as they had been described to me: someone standing in front of a microphone, singing into a camera, in what was apparently an amateur video setup.

When "Rio" came on, the room went electric. After just a few seconds, everyone's attention was riveted on the screen, and the talking and whispering stopped. As the film played, the crowd became more and more engaged, laughing at the right places and nodding along. When it was over, they all stood up and cheered. I was glad they did not know I was there. I would have been embarrassed instead of thrilled, like I was.

The audio record of "Rio" was rejected outright by the radio industry. First, at over five minutes, it was too long a song in an age of Top 40 hits, all of which came in at around two and a half to three minutes. Second, it had an odd reggae undertone but wasn't a reggae song or record, so it didn't fit any format the stations were playing. It was understandable to me but very frustrating to once again have a song held back from airplay.

I had hoped they would program "Rio" on *Top of the Pops*, the highest-rated music program on TV in the UK, but *TOTP* said it had a policy that it would not play promo clips and that all artists had to perform live. I was unhappy about this since I had no way to perform "Rio." I didn't have a band that could travel to play it and didn't know anyone who might help me form a band quickly in the UK. As such, "Rio" reached only No. 28 on the charts in the UK and never even charted in America. In other countries it came in at a very high position, well into the top ten in most markets, selling especially well in Australia, where the music video was warmly received and where the music TV shows that played a rotation of promo clips were happy to play it.

Back home, happy at Island's reception of the music video but sad that we hadn't cracked the US or UK record market at all, Bill and Kathryn and I kept sailing on the discovery of this new form. I kept trying to think of a way to expand the reach. I felt certain this format of presenting music had a lot of value and added greatly to the art form.

I was not alone in this, but I was also not unopposed. Many times when I played the clip, people would tell me flatly that they hated the idea of a visual accompanying music. Typically, these were people who closed their eyes when they listened to music. They didn't want any of the other senses to disturb the sound experience. I understood their point, but in my mind, this form was not just an add-on to pure audio. It was a new form altogether, and only certain types of songs and music would fit this merging with video. It seemed natural to me that there would be a division between songs delivered in music-video format and songs delivered in an audio-only format. The two formats might not fit all music but they seemed compatible to me and not mutually exclusive.

Bill and I had become good friends, and after a while he announced that he wanted to move to California and was thinking he might like to settle near Monterey. I welcomed the move and was glad we would be able to work together more and develop the music video.

I was sure I was going to need more music if that was the case. Bill, Kathryn, and I all were wondering whether "Rio" was a fluke or whether it really was an art form, whether it really could be written and produced on purpose, according to a given standard.

I had shown the video to my mother, but she had to buy a U-Matic to see it. This she did willingly, but I don't think she ever used the player beyond the few times she played the video. She didn't understand the purpose of the video much more than any of us did, but her artist's eye could see there was something at work in it that pointed to a high artistic space. She was impressed, and she said so. She wanted to help if she could. It was a welcome and sweet connection between us.

The little record company Kathryn and I had started had begun to put out more and more records, but I could never manage the finances to come around to its full support, and the company was always behind financially. I could see at the time that the main problem was me and my inexperience in finance and business, but I didn't know how to fix it. I was not a very good manager either, so the company struggled along the brink, even while it was picking up larger and larger distribution partners and more and more artists.

I thought it a good idea to write and record another record, perhaps to energize the record company and create music that Bill and Kathryn and I could use for more music videos. I was conveniently and foolishly overlooking the fact that the problem

I'd run into with "Rio" had not been solved: there was still nowhere in the US that played music videos. In fact, no one in the general public had even heard the term *music video.*

I have learned, and had learned by then, that no one really invents anything. When I say I had learned it, I mean it was my own personal dogma about creativity and innovation and I assumed it was true; it seemed to me at the time that most new ideas came from connections between prior ideas. I didn't know then, and don't know now, how true this is, but I clearly and definitely remember where I was and what I was doing when I *invented* MTV.

But as I say, I didn't really invent anything and was only one of the thousand fathers that were part of its birth. Before the idea occurred to me, I had never thought of it or heard of it, and when it did pop into my head, it seemingly came from nowhere.

One afternoon in 1978 or 1979, I was driving east along Carmel Valley Road and into the valley, having just turned off Highway 1. In my mind I was trying to find the analogy or metaphor I needed to understand the music video and where it fit in my life. This was in the context of Bill's arrival in Monterey and our constant conversations about film, television, and so forth, all framed by "Rio," what it was and where it fit.

I thought, *Well, the music video is sort of like a video record. And audio records are played on the radio, so a video record should be played on video—on television. There should be a broadcast component for the music video just like there is for records.*

There was no US broadcast outlet for music videos, as I had just learned with "Rio," but at that moment it was obvious to me that it could be built and should be built. It was an idea whose time had come. Perhaps I could build it or figure out how someone else might. I thought of everyone I knew in the broadcast business and came up with, on the one hand, the people who despised me like Lonesome Rhodes was despised, and on the other hand, the one or two who would still talk to me, even if they didn't like me. One of them was Jerry Perenchio, who had been my agent when I was in *The Monkees.*

Jerry tolerated me as far as I knew. I respected him as an agent and a businessman and knew him to be tough, direct, and highly intelligent. He had gotten into business with Norman Lear and started a company called Embassy that was doing, among other things, original programming for syndication. This seemed like it might be a good place to pitch an idea for a program that would play music videos. Even though music videos didn't really exist yet, I had no doubt they would. If I had stumbled into it, then certainly others would as well.

I called Jerry, and he seemed happy to hear from me and willing to sit with me and talk. I went to LA and showed him "Rio," and to my delight he said he thought it was terrific and wanted to get involved somehow. He thought he might be able to sell it as a movie idea or perhaps the basis of a television show. I told him my idea about it being an art form that could find its way onto television and become part of the TV-programming spectrum the way records were a part of the radio-programming spectrum. He instantly understood and agreed, and he assigned one of his lieutenants—a young, bright, natural salesman named Gary Lieberthal—to develop it with me and try to sell it as a first-run syndicated program. There was a convention coming up for this kind of business model in the spring of 1978 in Anaheim. It would be attended by television-station owners and buyers for these types of shows. Jerry suggested we try to be ready for this.

I thought it was a great opportunity, but first we needed a pilot.

I went home and told my band, Bill and Kathryn, about the meeting and what it looked like our next steps should be. "Rio" had been picking up some speed in Australia, since Australian television was actually playing the video. *Photon Wing* had gone gold there, and while that meant only around twenty thousand units, it meant a lot to me. It was my first hit record. John Ware and I, along with David MacKay, put together a band, and with a good promoter and solid sales headed to Australia to try to stoke the sales of the record and see what the music video was doing there. I wanted to see if I could learn anything about the new form.

I got to Australia in November 1977, just as summer was starting. As I was walking along a street, someone came up to me and, without prompting, said, "Hey, I really liked your popclip," and kept walking. Popclip? The Aussies even had a name for these things. I waved, smiled, said thanks, and made a mental note as I kept walking.

The tour was an overall success, and back home I told the story of how a random stranger on the streets of Melbourne had called the music video a "popclip." I thought this could be the name of the show.

I thought about how a half-hour daily show might work and remembered my first experience with *American Bandstand*, a show that essentially did the same thing in the 1950s that Embassy was trying to do in the 1970s. *Bandstand* came on five days a week—I imagine it was tape-delayed from a studio in Philadelphia—and Dick Clark played a series of songs while kids in the studio danced to them. I thought *Popclips* would make a wonderful daily afternoon show right after school, in smaller markets, so with that in mind I tried to think of the best structure for it.

I started exploring to see what other music videos the big record companies might have. I assumed there would be at least some promo films like the sing-into-the-camera ones Chris had wanted me to make, and these would suffice for a pilot we could play for the small-market television-station owners as a sample of the strip-show they were buying.

I was surprised to find out that nothing like those clips existed in America. There were of course concert-documenting films, but that wasn't the same thing. I reached out to the television stations in Europe, but no one had anything. The promo clips were usually thrown away after a record had its run. Most of them never got on the air, but even the ones that did and were associated with hit records weren't archived or saved. I had dreamed up a show that had almost no content available for it.

I knew that Bill and Kathryn and I could produce more videos if we had the artists, the money, and the time, but we had none of the above, and I had no real idea how to solve the problem. So I focused more with Bill and Kathryn on how to set up the presentation: what the set might look like and who would present and play these music videos. The concept of a VJ—a music-video DJ—was easy enough, but what would be the setting for that person? We had to see them, of course.

Bill thought it might be a good idea to build a futuristic studio set and put the show in outer space, creating the idea that *Popclips* was coming from a space station far away—maybe even from a distant orbit around Earth. The Video Jocks, as we started calling them, would be living and working on the space station and doing this show. Bill had a pretty good sense of the special effects he could do with just a camera.

I thought perhaps the best thing was just to play the music videos back to back, like a Top 40 radio station, and use voice-over and graphics between the videos. This was easy enough to do, provided we could get our hands on anything to play. I dug deeper and deeper into the promotion departments of record companies, and I thought more and more about shooting some on our own.

In the end, I was able to find a few other promo clips I could include in a *Popclips* pilot that we could take to the convention. Jerry and Gary and I were not a band, but we all had high hopes for *Popclips* selling. As it worked out, we ran head-on into deeply entrenched opposition. The convention was attended mostly by station owners—which is to say, rich old white men. They were all looking for cheap programming, going from booth to booth trying to find either reruns of sitcoms or old movies they could buy cheap and use to counterprogram against the networks. *Popclips* was an anomaly. As the head of Chris-Craft Industries—the owner of KCOP in Los Angeles—said to me, "Music will never work on television, and I will tell you why. If you put me against Barbra Streisand's new album and TV special in prime time, I can beat that show with a third-time rerun of a 1940s movie on my little local station that sells used cars."

The awful part was that he was right. The big prime-time specials built around musical stars always had a hard time, even if it was Streisand, a huge star and beloved entertainer. Mr. Chris-Craft-Stations could indeed get better ratings with a cheap old movie, but he did not have the vision to see what *Popclips* was. The amazing part of that conversation was how wrong he would become.

Sadly, though, his was the voice of that whole convention. As Gary would later joke with me after MTV became a billion-dollar property, "You were the guy who invented MTV, and I was the guy who couldn't sell it." It was a good-guy joke, but not really true. Gary was a good salesman, and it wasn't his fault we couldn't get clearance to launch the show. Jerry was the greatest salesman I ever knew, and even Jerry couldn't make the format fly at that time.

Jerry finally said, "You better take this back. I can't sell it. Give me back the money I invested in it, and we will call it quits on this. Good luck."

It was a fair enough walk-away, and I settled up with Embassy and started looking around, once again, for another way to go. Whatever perceptions were driving Mr. Chris-Craft-Stations had no influence on me, and I was convinced the music video was the face of popular music even if we couldn't see it yet.

I decided to call and check in on Jac Holzman, now happily retired in Maui, and ask for his advice about next steps. Knowing Jac to be a no-nonsense and insightful guy, I felt I would get a good honest look at *Popclips* from him. He was intrigued when I described it to him, and said, "Let me see it," so I sent him a copy of "Rio" and the pilot I'd done with Embassy. He called right back and said, "You should call John Lack at Warner Bros. and show him this. Something is going on there that this might fit."

I immediately contacted Lack and sent him the package. Lack got very excited, and with good reason. As I was later to find out, John was a real music lover and had been brought into a peculiar transitional moment in a partnership between Warner and American Express. The companies had gotten into business on a project called QUBE that makes sense now but was then before its time. It was an interactive television hookup they were testing in Columbus, Ohio, that allowed people to shop from a black box on top of their TV—essentially online sales but before there was such a thing as "online." The QUBE project had been shut down, and all that was left of it was a transponder on a satellite, the basic pathway of cable delivery. Warner and American Express owned this very expensive bit of gear together and didn't have much of an idea what to do with it. It was useless without programming, and it had a cost of millions of dollars monthly. John told me that the general idea was to set up another channel to program additional movies alongside TMC, which was Warner's movie channel.

They had just hired a fellow named Robert Pittman to program TMC2, as they were calling it, but no one was all that happy with the idea of launching another movie channel, or so I was told. So *Popclips* and the music-video idea came in the door like a fresh and beautiful breeze.

"What are these music video things?" John Lack wondered, asking me the same question I had now heard over and over. I explained as best I could that I didn't exactly know, that I had more or less fallen into it, but if one thought about it for a while, there was an analogy between records and radio and music videos and TV—not, as I had just learned, traditional or syndicated TV, but a new kind of TV that played videos twenty-four hours a day, like a radio station, and would be the point of connection between this new form and whatever potential audience it might have.

John got it almost instantly and, like the Embassy guys, got excited. Unlike them, he was not pushed into an existing business, but had an existing technology. I agreed to come to New York and meet with his boss and whoever else, do some strategic planning, and see if we could figure out what we had on our hands.

I told my lawyers what I was up to and they agreed to help, but they saw lots of problems getting from the idea to the product—legal and rights problems mostly. Still, there was something embedded in the idea of the music video that gave me confidence that all those problems were easily solved. The music video had the ability to deliver content in a way that was powerful and compelling and that rolled through all resistance in its path. I had learned by now to leave it alone and follow it, rather than try to jump on its back and steer it. All I could do was get it set up and see where it led.

In New York a few decisions were made to see if there was a way to quantify this new programming form: how to buy more music videos, what to pay for them, what to charge sponsors. By now everyone knew there were not a lot of these music videos lying around, and that free programming was not dependable. But everyone also strongly suspected from looking at "Rio" that the music video had arrived, and that "Rio" was a harbinger of more to come. The task quickly became figuring out how to program the new form and to whom. Someone, not me, suggested that they run the concept on Nickelodeon, a channel Warner owned that was running programming for kids. I agreed to create a series of *Popclips* episodes and see how they tested.

I kept hunting around the record companies, and slowly music videos started popping up buried in the vaults. The Buggles' "Video Killed the Radio Star" was to become famous. Split Enz, out of New Zealand. The Mighty Towers of Babylon. Paul McCartney. Debby Boone. It was an odd bunch to be sure, but the videos I was discovering were getting more complex and interesting—turning into real music videos. I was finally able to get about fifteen of these together. This would be enough to put together a few episodes for testing. "Rio" remained the standout and was the reference standard for all the rest, but the "rest" filled out the episodes and proved the concept.

Bill, Kathryn, and I, along with lots of help from the crews we were training around Monterey, put together approximately eight *Popclips* episodes. I say *approximately* because the conceit of the show was to use the same clips across several of the episodes. These short episodes would be the model for twenty-four-hour programming. For the purposes of Nickelodeon, there were eight different episodes delivered, but they ran them over and over and over. I don't know for sure, but I would not be surprised to learn that they swapped the music videos among the episodes and reedited them so they had some semblance of variety.

Whatever they did, the ratings went sky-high, or in the analogy I like to use, buried the needle. Everyone was ecstatic, and Warner and Amex convened and wondered how to go forward now that they had a clear signal the idea would be well received.

As for me, I was happy the shows had tested well, and the conversation I now had with John Lack was about developing a production structure that would start the new cable channel rolling. They had named it MTV. Good name.

My option was to continue with Warner-Amex and operate the production side of the channel, but it took me only a few seconds to realize it was not for me. I had only wanted an outlet for the music video and the ideas I had for filmmaking—short-form films that would stitch together to create an overall feeling and have an artistic presence. Producing for a cable channel seemed like a dead-end road—in the sense of the cul-de-sac of a luxury housing project. Life might be good, but I would be stuck in that small circle, so I politely declined and went back to my little studio and house in Monterey. I had been paid well for *Popclips*, and my little band had all made a few bucks from that production, so I was happy to settle deeper into the life of an artist and produce programming for the new outlets that would develop.

By this time, perhaps partially because of my legitimate marriage or the success of "Rio," but very definitely because of my Christian Science class instruction, my mother had opened up to me and begun offering more and more support for me, the record company, and productions I wanted to do. I happily accepted her encouragement and generosity, and her gifts provided me with the capital resources to record another album and start doing more music videos.

Going forward, I wanted to do more than music videos; I also wanted to do short pieces of film that revolved around a point of view, a kind of pictorial and filmic representation of life as we live it. But I knew not to discuss that with Bill or Kathryn. They were both happy I had the funds to make the films I wanted to make, but they did not seem interested at all in the philosophies or any of the aesthetic principles that were driving me. I wanted to explore matters of the heart, to use the arts to give a voice to the cries of sorrow, to open the compassionate soul. They did not confront me or ridicule me to my face, but I would catch the occasional eye roll.

The only plain indication of the disdain with which Bill was beginning to look upon my writings and film ambitions came at the beginning of work on a series of short films I was pulling together. I wanted it to be funny and comedic, but I was also writing some rants and some rages into the mix of absurdities and pratfalls and goofiness. As the director, Bill suggested that he come on camera and shut me up in the middle of a rant about gasoline prices. "Michael. Michael! Nobody wants to know from social. Comedy. Music and comedy!" he shouts as he waves the camera off and sends everyone to the next set.

He was right. His way was simpler and funnier, even though it was at odds with my intent. Artistically I felt that something was missing and that there were much deeper and richer topics to be played with in doing these short pieces, but Bill was quite right to keep the "social" out of it. In this fashion the short film came together in a much better way than I could have imagined, since it gave everyone a chance to contribute and a kind of creative license. It was frustrating to me to leave out the "social," but I could see that the piece was going to have, like *Rashomon*, many perspectives around the same point, none of which quite describes the whole. The little piece Bill did for the camera was used to start the whole film, and was very likely its saving grace. In the end it was better because it was funny.

I called Bill Martin, an old friend I knew from my Monkees days, to see if he wanted to contribute and write and perhaps even perform with me. He was happy for the work. Bill had a special dust of mirthful madness he sprinkled around him and utterly cosmic riffs about nearly anything. Bill was what I called a "walking writer," just what I thought we needed. Now the band had a fourth member, and the four-piece band distinguishes itself from the others because of the extended harmonies it enables.

The title for the project that popped into my mind was *Elephant Parts*. Like the music video for "Rio," when I showed the now hour-long film around, no one knew what it was—or what it was for—or how it would be programmed. When I announced that *Elephant Parts* would be the name of the film, people thought it sounded funny, but no one seemed to know what I meant by it. I nevertheless enforced its use by executive fiat, without discussion or collaboration, just because I was paying the bills. As it came together, it was very different from what I anticipated, with much more in substance and laughter than I had imagined. I was proud of it and grateful to everyone who had helped.

I hired someone to try to sell it into syndication, but the form was still too outré, still off the radar of conventional television, even as MTV was insinuating itself into the lives of millions of adolescents. I couldn't sell it to a broadcaster or on home video. The money I poured into it lay there and stayed there.

Other than that, things seemed to be going well. I was happy living the life of an artist, gaining a little each day in that direction, and I felt as if I was starting to get my moral and ethical feet under me. I felt sure the business side would come around.

Then, in May of 1980, my mother died. She was fifty-six.

CHRISTIAN SCIENCE READING

10

The void awaits surely all them that weave the wind.

—James Joyce, *Ulysses*

While in California I received a call from a close friend of my mother's asking me to come to Dallas at once, and I did. My mother had apparently been felled by a stroke and was taken into a care facility. When I got there, she was in bed and appeared unwell. I tried to comfort her and cheer her up, but we could not communicate too well verbally. I hung one of her favorite pictures on the wall of her room, the small oil painting by Georgia O'Keeffe titled *Taos, New Mexico* that she had purchased not long before. She smiled when she saw it, and there was a familiar contact between us through the art. There was an appreciation we shared, of the painting and each other.

She died peacefully in her sleep two days later. While I was at dinner that night I got the call that she had stopped breathing, and by the time I returned to the facility, she was gone.

I was sad to lose her. I was stoic to a degree, through the funeral and the good wishes and kind concerns of her friends and mine, the gifts of food and the gatherings, but there was a time after all of it when I was standing alone in her house and began to cry uncontrollably for a time longer than I could count or can remember. It was High Lonesome in its most acute, severe form. Every pore wept, every beat of my heart hurt, every breath I took was cold. I missed her presence, naturally, but more than anything I felt left behind, left out, and lost. It was selfish of me but I felt I was friendless at that moment, that she and I had encountered a barrier on our journey that I could not see past as she ran through. I did not despair for her well-being; I held a certainty of her individual continuity and life. I had the unshakable sense that she was fine where she was. The feeling of loss went deeper than all of that. For a time I was inconsolable, but I did not let it show. I missed her.

Mother and I had talked daily, almost never about anything other than things spiritual. This was a pattern from since I was as young as I can remember. Bette was not glib or particularly quick or funny, but she was a deep thinker and could be very loving. So the conversations concerned how we each were dealing with what mortal life was dealing us.

Some years earlier my mother had said to me that she wanted to give all her money away, to get down to owning essentially nothing and live an ascetic life. I admired her for this and told her so, but the goal seemed an impossibility to me. Too much water had passed under the material bridge. Nevertheless, I understood her desire and her motivation. The money was a mark of success, but it had become a burden to her, and not all that easy to give away. She felt it slow her and divert her from the spiritual sense of life, the truth she had practiced and loved.

She was also depressed, as she had become estranged from the board of the Liquid Paper Corporation. The men she hired to run the company had joined with her ex-husband to push her out. There was much acrimony and many harsh words. It was devastating to her. She had settled into an awful, destructive kind of warfare over property and control. The board devised a solution: the company should accept an offer and be sold to Gillette before the rancor among the management destroyed the business. She reluctantly agreed to this, but only under the condition that after the sale, all the executives she had hired would quit. I never understood her logic in this, if there was any, but I had a suspicion that revenge or some kind of punishment may have been active in her mind, as well as a great sorrow. Whatever it was, I have no doubt that it killed her.

Even though I didn't know exactly why my mother had wanted to give her money away, I suspected the reasons. Hers was not sudden wealth, but it was great enough to get her name in the papers and to put her life under scrutiny. As I saw it, wealth and success were not married in her mind the way they are married in the mind of a lottery winner or someone who strikes oil. For her it was a gate slowly opening on materialism, letting it loose on her lawn. It had even taken some shallow root.

She bought ermines and jewels. She built a large and in my opinion beautiful home, and she lived with servants and cooks and the attendants of her business. She bought a Rolls-Royce. Actually, I bought the Rolls-Royce on her behalf, at her direction. I think it may have created one of the unhappiest episodes in her life.

She had trouble buying cars because she had no tolerance for car salesmen, an obvious generalization she refused to correct, and wanted nothing to do with them. So the few cars she bought got older and broke down. When I returned from London the first time, I told my mother about John Lennon's huge Rolls Phantom V that had picked Phyllis and me up, and suggested that she buy a Rolls; then she would never have to buy another car. It would last forever, or so I foolishly thought.

She combed through magazines and finally picked out one Rolls-Royce whose shape she liked. It was a 1963. This was in the early 1970s. When I pointed out that it was a used car she responded that I had said it would last forever, so what difference did it make? She didn't like the way the new ones looked, thought they were overpriced, and she very much liked the way this model looked. She had a point. I offered to shop for one for her.

After a little searching I found a prime example in LA that was white and recently restored. She thought it was beautiful, bought it, and brought it back to Texas.

She had flaming red hair that she began to dye redder and redder as she matured and her hair turned grayer. At one point I asked if she knew the natural color of her hair and she said no, she thought it was all gray, but if she could have her hair any color she decided she liked orange. In her white Rolls and orange hair, she and her second husband made the society rounds of Dallas.

One late evening after the symphony, she and her husband and another couple were driving home along the empty Dallas tollway when the car died and rolled to a stop on the side of the road. It was late and they were a perfect mark for the car full of thieves that rolled up behind them and, with drawn guns, approached the four in the car and demanded money. My mother was draped in hundreds of thousands of dollars' worth of jewels, and they took all of them except her bracelet. As she told the story, when one of the men demanded the bracelet, she had been unable to open the latch and could not get it off her wrist. She told the robber she couldn't get it off and he said, "I guess I'll just have to shoot it off there, then," to which, she said, she calmly replied, "Oh, please don't do that." The robber thought better of it and left.

I can only understate the trauma the incident caused her and the deep soul-searching that ensued. The great display of wealth attenuated quickly after that. She sold the old giant white Rolls and bought a new small one in a subdued metallic beige. She stopped wearing the furs. In her mind, both were big steps out of the trappings of wealth, as they are so properly called.

We discussed on many occasions the slow degradation of the quality of her life as the wealth increased; we talked of the shadows that lay long across the pool in her backyard and obscured the spiritual values she cherished, and of her real reasons for living, which were unconditionally directed toward finding God. To her, wealth was not evil per se, nor was money undesirable, but she struggled intensely within the constraints of financial freedom and the weight of expensive material objects. She may have fallen into a tub of butter, but she never lost sight of her unending search for truth. Truth with a capital *T*.

Her efforts to assimilate the wealth made me recall the second time I went to see and stay with John Lennon. While we were sitting at his piano, he asked if I wanted to see his car. It was an odd question, I thought, but I said, "Of course." I remembered the long liquid-shiny solid-black Phantom V that had picked Phyllis and me up at the Grosvenor House that day, and how there was a moment when the enormous car's errand—picking up the somewhat scraggly only-two-of-us—seemed incongruous and strangely out of place. The car was nearly new and almost twenty feet long, a symbol of status, state, power, and money. In the context of the rock and roll counterculture it seemed an anomaly.

We walked out to his garage on that particular evening, and when he opened the door and I saw it, it made a kind of perfect sense. He had painted the big black car bright clown-yellow and covered it with hand-painted multicolored psychedelic images in panels and scrolls that made it look like a huge circus wagon. Years later it sold for millions as an objet d'art. The way it was painted became more valuable than the car itself. As far as I knew, he did not drive around in that car to any great extent, and finally parked it in his garage, where it sat for private display as sculpture.

My mother had a similar problem of assimilating her wealth, but without the attendant celebrity. While she was alive, in what looked to me like a sincere first effort to disperse the money she had made from the sale, to in fact "give all her money away," she started a couple of foundations—the Bette Clair McMurray Foundation and the Gihon Foundation—and began transferring her estate a little at a time into them. But by the time she died, she still had a sizable personal fortune. The foundations did not have the same joie de vivre that Lennon's circus car did, but they were on the same train of thought. Great wealth from a sincere effort, arts, humanity, or good business creates a conundrum. The wealth is not the object of the success at hand, but such wealth is perceived by many as an end in itself, as a reason for living. This did not seem to be so for Lennon, and I knew for a fact it was not for my mother. The two, however, solved the problems in their own way, and the foundations were a good fit for my mother's individual goal, as turning the Rolls into a circus wagon was for Lennon.

The sale of the Liquid Paper Corporation had been consummated only about a year before my mother's passing, so the corpus of her estate was quite large. After the IRS settled up with her estate, there was enough to be a generous inheritance for me, but very much smaller than the press—and everyone I knew—imagined. Still, an inheritance of this size for someone like me, raised as I'd been raised, and living as I had been, was like a cross between a tsunami and a Category 5 hurricane but with winds over two hundred miles per hour. It was the most curious mixture of total destruction and a new expensive broom that swept clean the mess and replaced things as it went along.

Money cannot really be controlled, because in essence it is

ephemeral, spiritual, and constantly in motion, moving back and forth between perceived states of frozen and liquid. In one time frame it is stagnant and in another it is like a typhoon. It can be ridden for a moment but it will run where it will, almost as if it has a mind of its own, which it clearly does not. Its actions are more of a mystery than a science, as most economists will testify. The only thing that is made with money is more money. The idea that one can somehow set up a wind farm in a windstorm is an ignorant one, revealing a lack of awareness of the forces at work.

After my mother passed, it was a bad time in general for me. I didn't have much of an idea what I was going to do with my life, much less with the foundations she had started or the remainder of her estate. It felt disrespectful to think of money at this time, but it was an enormous and increasing presence and it seeped in, like wind through a cracked window. I began receiving calls from people who offered congratulations as well as condolences. I didn't know what to say, so I said thank you to both.

Weirdly, amid the deep sorrow, I was also confusingly comforted. Now that I had the money to do some things I was truly yearning to do, I began to think of what else I *might* do. I began to think of money as causal—I felt that whatever I could think up, the money would facilitate and even create. I made no effort to argue against this notion, since I didn't know any better at the time. I was happy to have a new art form, embodied in "Rio," to introduce to the public and was motivated to pursue the culture that I was sure would follow it. I knew that Bill Dear wanted to direct a movie, and now I had enough that I could also unilaterally produce a movie that he could direct. All of these things had been possibilities before, but now they were becoming realities. Now that I had the money.

This time, I thought, Bill and I could write together and produce a real movie, with a director of photography and a line producer and real movie actors. I could see to it that Bill had whatever he needed, and we could make a movie that was designed to simply and directly sell popcorn—a fun movie, a comedy of sorts, at least a few jokes, with a tad of action and a simple narrative.

We could do it cheap, as features go. "Rio" notwithstanding, we had pulled together *Elephant Parts* for a low price and made it look expensive. We used low-cost camera tricks and got help from our friends. Now that I had the money, I could produce a real Hollywood movie and send it around the world.

Bill would have his chance to direct a feature and move into the society of other filmmakers, to meet heroes of his like Steven Spielberg and Sam Raimi, possibly even work with them. I thought it was a way to offer my gratitude for the help he had been with "Rio" and *Elephant Parts.* And while I knew nothing of the movie business as such, I could learn it quickly. I had been successful, in a way, with these other efforts, and now I had the good fortune of an inheritance to make a low-budget movie feasible, and keep it completely under my control. I could let Bill do what he wanted, pretty much.

And so it happened that—within weeks of my mother's passing, as the tears stopped, leaving me silent in my contemplations of the next steps in my life—without even the slightest indication of a costume change, money began a masquerade and donned the appearance of being able to make things happen, to stop sorrow, to create worlds of imagination, to create friends. Money was an ever-present, unending wind in the sails of my little boat, and it would create, build, and establish wonders. In those few seconds, filled with thoughts of the good work I could do, I became a Hamburger Movie Tycoon.

The wind that brought my main thought—*I can make this happen*—through the door also closed the door behind it and locked it. Whatever lessons my mother had learned from her wealth she carried with her to her grave as I fell into the same tub of butter.

Days after my mother died, I met with the board of the foundations she had set up, which consisted of the two women who had helped her organize them, Patricia Hill and Maryanne Henneberger, and me. Each foundation was focused in a different area, with the McMurray Foundation making grants to assist women generally and women in business specifically, and the Gihon Foundation focused on operating a program supporting the arts. I asked Patricia and Maryanne if they wanted to continue the foundations or just close them and disperse the funds. They both said they would be happy to continue if I wanted to, so we came to the decision to keep them going as long as we could, given that the funding given by my mother would now slowly decrease over time.

With that decided, we kept making grants along the lines my mother had started. I thought for a brief while about continuing to fund the foundations from the inheritance that came to me, but since they had already been funded, I thought I would stay the course with building my production company, Pacific Arts, with the idea that at some point I could possibly fund the foundations as she had: with profits from a successful enterprise.

Fortunately for me, my mother had left the estate in good shape and under the wise executorship of competent men. The beneficiaries were clearly identified and there were no conflicts or contests. She was very generous to all her family and loved ones. Unfortunately, my business was held together with tape, and it would take more than a windfall of money to make it stable and secure.

It didn't seem to make any difference how hard I worked at it. I couldn't get the business to grow any legs to support itself or nourish a band of execs and administrators. So far nothing I was doing was making money. I had put the money my mother had given me before her death into Pacific Arts, and it had scrimped along. Then, when the inheritance landed, I was able to consider doing more projects, expanding its expenses without any real idea of how to expand its income.

The distressing part is that I had no clue what was wrong or how to fix it, and this ignorance was now being sustained. I had money to throw blindly at a problem that was not only hidden but systemic.

The problem was, of course, that I had started to depend on the causality of money and had stopped trying to form a band. Had I stayed with the band dynamic, I might have seen that it made no difference how much I could pay a musician; if there wasn't a band sensibility, the player would only do the job and move on to the next gig. No creative return would develop, and certainly no loyalty. The key element of a band is the sense of family created when it plays together, so that when the music is made, everyone rides the joy. It is not called "playing" for no reason.

At the time, music videos, the main output of my current band, had very few places to play, but we were only a few years away from the migration of the Internet from its military roots into the general culture; Vint Cerf and Robert Kahn were writing the protocols—TCP/IP—that would make the distributed network available to everyone. All that would be needed was a personal computer, like the one Woz and Jobs put together in their garage in Los Altos in 1976.

And while the band that *had* recently formed in my life had produced another artifact, *Elephant Parts*, that was starting to gather a little steam, the idea of home video was just starting up, and there was no real distribution system in place. The studios were eyeing video as an ancillary source of income for their movies, but *Elephant Parts* wasn't a movie. Videotape was virtually unknown, and the presence of video players in homes had only started to build.

The best idea I could fashion for developing a market and selling *Elephant Parts* was to move Pacific Arts to LA, where perhaps I could attract some executives to help me, and could try to expand my distribution business by buying or licensing other products and producing more of my own. I could do that because I had the money and could support the move. But it was a move in the wrong direction.

I had the money to move anywhere, yes, but the self-importance that came with the money hid from me the real parties and fun the cyberculture was having, the technology bands that were playing and the garages they were playing in. All around me, literally down every block in every garage, Silicon Valley was coming alive with band after band after band, starting companies that would eventually become the large-scale leaders of the world. The new cyberculture, the new creative centers, the new garage gardens and indoor plants—the seeds of all these had been sowed in the seventies, and they were now sending up shoots and young blossoms to the north, up the Northwest Corridor, toward Seattle. The cyberculture was following the counterculture up the coast, led by Stewart Brand, the Grateful Dead, Ken Kesey, LSD, and a whole new young world of Merry Pranksters.

I took LSD a few times in the 1970s, enough to get a pretty good feel for the drug and to open myself up to it enough to enjoy it. I got my first hit from Owsley, the famous acid maker from LA, since he was the main distributor for a while, and then I got a few doses from a friend who always had it lab-tested for purity since he was afraid of getting a bad dose. I never had a bad trip; there were ups and downs, but for me the ups far outweighed the downs. There was very little known about the drug at the time, but once I took it I could see how different life looked. This view was very far from alcohol-, tobacco-, and cocaine-induced perspectives, those produced by the big-money drugs. My trips with LSD were as pleasant as the lore around them promised, with doors opening as expected. Then I took it a few times more, as a sacrament to see if there was higher light than dancing in only one corner of the universe. The last couple of trips carried a message that was part of the trip itself—the message was "*You don't need drugs to reach this space, and you will come to a point where you will not take them anymore but still reach the same state of mind.*"

Once, several years before I took class instruction with Paul Seeley, while *very* high on acid, I opened the Christian Science textbook *Science and Health* and started reading it just to see how it fit in this mental landscape. I was astounded to see how the same frame of mind I was in at the time was present in the writings. I read *Science and Health* for hours straight, continuously amazed to be reading something that conveyed the same clarity and powerful insight I was experiencing. I finally stopped all drugs once I met Seeley, but I was fascinated by the way the ideas and reality I was taught in class were as familiar, as high, and at least as profound as any of the ideas and the reality that acid had showed me.

Through the 1960s and '70s there developed a certain class of thinker, made up of those who looked closely at all aspects of culture and society from the very different viewpoints that acid and cannabis brought in. I was good friends with these people, and won't put their names here, but they were close enough to talk to and insightful enough to discuss the drugs. I was essentially on the sidelines of these new thoughts and ideas, but close enough to witness them and understand where they were coming from. Even then, I had only a slight idea of the effect the whole counterculture was having on the developing cyberculture.

Wozniak and Jobs had created the first Apple computer in 1976, the same year I went through class instruction. I have no way of knowing whether they were high or not, but I was not surprised when Kary Mullis said he had been high on LSD when he had the inspiration for inventing the polymerase chain reaction method. He was awarded the Nobel Prize for this outstanding, beneficial work in 1993. Since then I have learned from research that Francis Crick said he was high on psychedelics when he thought of the double helix, and there were other examples like this. I assume that some of this information is suspect, especially given the way rumors float around and among bands, but I also assume that some of it is true.

From my personal experience I can understand how the psychedelics—or entheogens, as they are now called—could have stimulated some very powerful new ways of looking at things and bringing hidden analogies to light. The more I looked into the new high-tech world, the more surprised I was at the similarities between that world and the counterculture of the times. The fragrant gardens and groves to the north seemed indistinct, almost like Elysian playgrounds, removed from business. The idea that this would become the financial and intellectual capital of the world was only a faint gleam of sunlight on fresh-growing fields. Unfortunately, it was too faint for me to see at the time.

The shiny object that drew me in was Southern California and Los Angeles, the center of media distribution. I thought this distribution center might work for new media as well. As the base of installed video players in homes grew, I assumed that home viewing would be a good business to develop, as well as a good sales base for original productions. So I decided to set up a distribution company in Los Angeles and produce movies and videos that I could sell through it. My first full-length movie would be *The Adventure of Lyle Swann*, the movie Bill Dear and I were writing.

I also started buying and licensing documentaries—or "nontheatrical titles," as they were known—for the catalog. I licensed the entire series of Jacques Cousteau documentaries on the ocean and sea life. I licensed an Agatha Christie series. I licensed foreign films like *The Official Story*. I was surprised they were available to license, but I shouldn't have been, since the thinking at the time, aside from general ignorance of the burgeoning home-video business, was that once a show had been on television and played a few times, its value had depreciated to nothing. All the producers of these documentaries were delighted that I was interested in licensing these "leftover" rights and that there was yet another market developing for them.

I licensed or bought everything I could, and as it turned out, I acquired them a few years before I could sell them as videotapes. I was still years ahead of the market, and for some inexplicable reason I had no sense that I wouldn't be able to sell them immediately after getting the rights. I was certain that people would want to program their own television sets to suit their own schedules, choosing what to watch and when. The bottom line was that in just a few years I had purchased the rights to what was now the largest nontheatrical video catalog in the world, but sales were slow, to put it mildly. I was finally able to recover some of the cost—but in a way I never imagined.

⁂

Though they stem from the same root, Celebrity Psychosis and the Hollywood Mind are quite different. CP is fully delusional. The bearers justify their actions through the *perceived amount* of their fame. The recognition and the fame validate and confer power and authority, specifically the authority to give opinions on subjects about which the Celebrity Psychotic knows basically nothing.

The Hollywood Mind, on the other hand, is not delusional but is instead based on the *actual value* of public acceptance, specifically in the form of retail sales. In the Hollywood Mind, little thought is given to aesthetic principle or how spiritual and artistic value is created and measured; it curates art based strictly on the broadness of its appeal and its commercial value. Income in the form of *money* is the metric of the Hollywood Mind, whereas *power* is the metric of Celebrity Psychosis.

The Hollywood Mind, despite the name, does not exist only in Hollywood, although Hollywood is the largest collection of Hollywood Minds in the world and, as such, is the Galápagos Islands for studying the evolution of the phenotype. But the Hollywood Mind can be found in many places and many industries. That the business of Hollywood is underpinned by the arts makes the HM thrive there, since the arts are considered only a matter of opinion until they make money.

By the time my mother's estate was settled, I began—for what reason I can't say—to recognize Celebrity Psychosis when it would appear, and it began to fray and fall away in bits and pieces, disassembling like a vampire in sunlight. Recognition became meaningless and obscurity appealing, but the crumbling, corroded infrastructure of CP remained intact just enough to cause confusion. The inheritance had replaced the window dressing of CP with the mentality of a Hamburger Movie Tycoon, and the logic of the Hollywood Mind lingered as well, having crept in and set up a rationale for the new Pacific Arts offices in LA.

Bill and I hammered out a script for *The Adventure of Lyle Swann* in my and Kathryn's home in Carmel, and once we had something shootable, I thought it would be a good idea to leave Bill to his own devices, directing as he wished, free from any influence by me. We hired Harry Gittes as the producer for the film, and Kathryn and I took off for a vacation in Greece.

It wasn't as class-A crazy as leaving the country in which I had a hit record starting up, as I did with "Joanne" in 1970, but it was close. If anything requires hands-on management and care of cash flow, it is shooting a movie. The motive to let Bill and Harry have their way was a good one as far as the humanity of it, but the result was not as good as the motive. Bill deserved a chance. I could provide that, and I didn't want to muck with this project as much as I had with *Elephant Parts*. Leaving the project in the hands of Bill and Harry was not a bad idea, but it wasn't as good an idea as staying.

By then, *Elephant Parts* had won a Grammy. I had been delighted with the critical reception it received and was just as happy to learn it had been nominated for Video of the Year in 1981. The National Academy of Recording Arts and Sciences had never bestowed such an award before, and they only awarded one more, the next year, to Olivia Newton-John, so my Grammy turned out to be a rare Grammy. It may have been that after the award, NARAS officials thought the music video was a passing fad. The video was so far outside their usual channels of production and distribution that no one knew what to do with it, only that it had shown up on the scene and gained all sorts of attention from and influence within a large group of viewers, most of whom were kids. As it worked out, shortly after the Grammy for Video of the Year was discontinued, the MTV Awards took it up, leaving NARAS behind.

Orphan though it may be, I now treasure the award, even though I didn't know how to take it at the time. The mixed feelings may have come from the incipient notion that such awards are the spoils of hard-fought competitions. I did not like the idea of artists pitted against each other, since the essence of artistry includes diversity, individuality, family and friends, all the direct opposites of competitive efforts for the same ultimate position.

When *Elephant Parts* won, I was wildly excited in spite of myself. I accepted the award without a word of thanks to Kathryn or Bill from the podium. In fact, I left off all mention of the production team and made a joke instead. The joke was this: after I walked to the podium and accepted the award, I said, "Thanks very much, and now that I have this national exposure, I'd like to take the opportunity to let everyone know I have one chrome wheel for a 1963 Camaro that I would like to sell." I meant it to be a Tuesday absurdity—something one lonely hippo might say to the other. Instead it came off as insensitive, weird, and eccentric, and was met with soundless stares. I was embarrassed.

Additionally, the acceptance speech received no actual "national exposure," since it was *not* televised. The award was given during the preshow ceremonies, where they honor arcane technologies and practices, like the award for the best instrument created with yarn strung across an old fence.

While I was in Greece, Harry and Bill shot *The Adventure of Lyle Swann*. I returned eager to help, if I could, in getting *Lyle Swann* ready for distribution in theaters and *Elephant Parts* distributed on home video. With almost amazing precision and perfect aim, I once more started shooting off my own feet, one toe at a time.

I had bought a billboard on Sunset for *Elephant Parts* and

put on two large-scale publicity events, one each in New York and LA. The expenses piled up as fast as any public interest did, and at what I assumed was the height of public awareness, the pinnacle of the marketing effort, I said to my tiny staff, "Now! Now, is the time to really push and sell *Elephant Parts*! Now that we have their attention!" In a live twist of an old joke, they all asked, "Whose attention do we have?" For all the accolades *Elephant Parts* received, there were still no buyers in the still very niche home-video nonmarket. Other than its funny name, no one had any idea what it actually was.

The band of Bill Dear, Bill Martin, Kathryn, and me finally came apart, and although we were all more or less civil to each other, a great silence had come over me and Bill Dear, and things were particularly troubling at home between Kathryn and me. Kathryn refused to join me in LA and insisted on staying in Carmel. She said Los Angeles gave her a headache. I couldn't blame her for this, but I was lonely in LA and things were getting more and more difficult and distorted there all the time.

Without each other to console and counsel, Kathryn and I both began to sink under the weight of the distance and, to a great degree, the new money. It is very hard to describe just how this happens, especially since many people seem to carry around an idea that money confers a kind of social and financial security. Thanks to my mother, I started to learn something different, but she was gone too soon to advise me, leaving no further instructions.

I have talked to friends who have become Masters of the Universe and made billions of dollars, and they all have the same two concerns in common. The first is that they feel as if, in some unexplainable way, their wealth and success is a fluke, like hitting the lottery. Second, they fear it will all suddenly vanish and leave them wretched and homeless, living under a freeway overpass.

Add to this general malady of supermoney the specific quirk of windfall wealth and you get some idea of the pressures that build. Just at the time one thinks they have solved all of life's problems, life delivers a package of new ones, bigger than the last and with more intricate lacings. One of the lessons I was learning, and that I have tried to explain, is this: "Never complain about the air-conditioning in a private jet."

This nugget came from riding in a Learjet in the 1960s on a Monkees tour. The model was new—more or less a converted fighter plane with plush seats where there used to be fuel and ammo. Five people were snug, and four comfortable, so it was pretty nifty for a band. The big problem was the huge air-conditioner vent that sat right behind the rear seat and blew out and over the back of it to cool the entire cabin. It had a gale-force fan, so if one sat in the rear seat, it howled like an arctic blizzard and blew like a Florida hurricane. It was a miserable seat, and it made for a miserable ride.

Hopping out of the Learjet at a destination, I complained about this to someone waiting for me and got a look I will never forget. It was a mixture of *You dreadful spoiled rich bastard* and *What a no-talent jerk you are.* Hence the admonishment to my loved ones: don't complain about the air-conditioning on a private jet, and I don't mean to do it here.

I have regularly looked to the skies since my mother's passing and thanked her for her generosity and love. The money may have made me crazier than I was, but the money was providential and I will be forever grateful to her for it and for all the other good and selfless things she did for me. May we all be so fortunate.

But in the moment, Kathryn and I did not discuss this looming weight of the money, first because we were hardly aware of it, and second because we were caught up once again in our own infidelities—the residual of the beginning infidelities that had started our relationship, and thus provided no foundation for us, and the latest infidelity I had fallen into with another on my own in LA. Had there been greater intelligence at work and greater understanding, as well as a little self-discipline, then the money as madness might have surfaced as an issue to be analyzed. But there wasn't, and it didn't.

With the new money, the new business, my personal artistic career, and the philanthropic foundations all converging, I was in the confusing center of conflicting purposes, and something had to give way or grow together. I wanted to grow into an ability to manage all these things and not get run over by them.

With *Elephant Parts* now sitting on the shelf, waiting for a seismic shift in the media market, I hit another rough patch in finalizing *The Adventure of Lyle Swann*. Bill was called away to do a commercial, and I had to hire a new editor. There was no music, so I pulled something together for that. And I was running very far over budget. But we stayed afloat and steady through these little rapids, and at last *The Adventure of Lyle Swann* was ready for distribution.

Thankfully, Bill came up with the title *Timerider*, which took the place of my bookish Lyle Swann meta-reference title, and I set about getting distribution. I got nowhere with any studio or even old friends. I showed the movie to Jerry Perenchio, who told me it was the worst film he'd ever seen. *Timerider* wasn't that bad; it was only that Jerry was that good. He had his share of dropped balls, but he knew a good thing when he saw it, so when he told me that *Timerider* was not that *good thing*, it was a real blow, even though I didn't agree with him.

In the backwaters of the movie-distribution business I found a little company in Utah that agreed to distribute *Timerider.* It went out of business on the day the film opened. In a fit of despair and anxiety, I bought the distribution rights back from them, against the counsel of everyone in the Western Hemisphere, and set about trying to sell it to television and, through Pacific Arts, to the home-video market, which had finally peeked out from behind a lettuce leaf growing in the tangled agriculture of Hollywood movie studios.

However, Pacific Arts was too young and ill-equipped to handle these kinds of sales at that time, and *Timerider* languished on the shelf right next to *Elephant Parts*. Like a real Hollywood Movie Tycoon, I got my first taste of a Friday Night Flight, when the money flies away upon an opening of no sales, and now I had to learn how to manage the aftermath. I was learning quickly that money would not solve many of my problems; in fact, I was starting to understand how it would actually not solve any.

I had been more careful and thoughtful with the foundations than with Pacific Arts. The foundations' wealth wasn't my money, and my approach to that money was different from my approach to my own. I was in charge only of preserving and increasing as much as possible of the corpus and seeing that the foundations' finances were used to the benefit of society and community.

The McMurray Foundation's mandate was simple and straightforward: its grants simply needed to benefit women, and especially women in business. This was a joyful and most fulfilling exercise, and I started to love it more after each quarterly meeting.

The Gihon Foundation was a little more difficult, since it was generally focused on supporting the arts. While there was not too much in the foundation's bylaws about how to do this, I'd had enough talks with my mother while she set up the foundation to have a good sense of the overarching spirit in which it was created. *Gihon* was the name of one of the rivers reputed to have flowed from the Garden of Eden and was a word my mother pulled from Mary Baker Eddy's *Science and Health*, where it is defined as "the rights of woman acknowledged morally, civilly, and socially."

I understood the intent of the Gihon Foundation, but not so much how to find a program for it. My mother had collected artworks for a while after she had the money and was in the process of building a museum for the foundation to hang them in. I didn't know much more about what she intended, but I knew we did not have the money in the Gihon Foundation to continue to buy paintings. In any case, I could not fulfill her vision for the museum. I was sure it would have been beautiful had she built it, but I was also sure I couldn't build it with her unique vision.

Understandably, many of the paintings she had collected were by men, but it occurred to me that it would be a good idea if they were all by women. This would serve two purposes. First, it would benefit women, which seemed right to me and in accord with the definition of *Gihon* my mother had used, and second, it would give me a point of departure for curating the collection. I had developed an artistic sense I depended on, but it was more focused on music, recording, design, writing, and performing and producing live events—not on paintings, about which I knew almost nothing. I couldn't tell much of a difference between a good and a poor painting, but I could tell the difference between men and women. After some study and much conversation with art conservators and auctioneers, I sold the men's paintings, and with the receipts from that, bought art by women, mostly on the basis of gender but also on the basis of aesthetics. To my relief and delight, the collection turned out to be impressive and high-quality.

My mother's time raising me as a single mother was difficult, to say the least, and one of the elements that made these times so hard was the simple fact of the anxiety she suffered as a woman in a society and a culture that was controlled by men. She was pushed aside again and again for being a single mom—not an unmarried mother, mind you, just simply single—and from my vantage point as a ten-year-old boy and onward, I watched in despair and sorrow the way she was treated in certain situations by men who were not one percent her equal. To say the Gihon collection resonated with me as an adjustment for those times is a colossal understatement.

We created a program to send the collection to smaller towns, most of them without a museum nearby, and set the artwork up in high-traffic public areas like shopping malls and parkways and such. This way the people in a little city that might never see these paintings would get to enjoy them, and there would be the potential to inspire.

Foundations measure success with unusual metrics, and I found it hard to know whether we were actually doing any good. I discovered among other foundations a general tendency to count things up and bundle them together in a way so that the counting and bundling matters more than the things themselves. Many foundations count the number of vaccinations given and the number of meals served, and that becomes their measure of success. I was not moved by this tendency, however. To me a foundation's metric needed to provide some idea of the importance—the spiritual and emotional value—of the foundation's work and freely convey that to the public. The metric needed to take into account how *good* the meals were, not just how many were served, and to pass that value on as part of the nourishment. For Gihon, this was hard to do. Art traffics in good and bad, in aesthetics that call forward the spiritual senses and either satisfy them or not. As far as I know, there is no quantitative metric for that satisfaction. For me *Guernica* is one of the great antiwar statements, but I don't imagine fifteen *Guernicas* would be any more impressive or make me any more antiwar.

Running the foundations might be enough to completely satisfy me as a life's work, but without a dependable sense of the level of good they did, I would remain unrequited.

I had been brought into the foundations when I was dead broke, when my utilities were being shut off and food and gasoline were scarce in my household. It was hard for me to accept my mother's invitation to become a member of the board and help her give her money away when what I wanted, and what I felt I needed, was for someone to give me a check. It was hard, but not impossible: after the first meeting I attended, where we made grants to struggling mothers, I was hooked. The emotional and spiritual return in this activity was overwhelming and much more significant and satisfying to me than sales numbers. The emotional high was satisfying in a way that making money was not, but I thought there must be a place where these two objectives could meet and where the emotional return meets the satisfaction of a profitable enterprise.

I was proving to have a lot to learn as a businessman, including how to exercise good business sense while keeping true to what motivated me and made me happy—to find among all this some sense of well-doing as well as well-being. I felt certain they were not mutually exclusive. I supposed they were likely mutually supportive, perhaps even symbiotic. I didn't know if it was true, but it seemed worthwhile to try to find out.

11

It's all part of a cosmic unconsciousness.

—*Repo Man*

After *Elephant Parts* and *Timerider* had come to rest in my archives, awaiting further developments in the home-video business, other events started pushing me down intertwining paths in a way I did not and could not have planned. I believe this preceding phrase might be written by any human at any time. These intertwining, unplanned paths are something we all share, and I am not sure why their appearance in our lives should be such a surprise, but it always is, at least to me. It's easy to think of these confluences of events as random, but this does not seem natural. Douglas Adams taught me that calling a colligation *random* was a lazy way to say "I don't know, it just happened." I was growing into an understanding of systems, and a principled system comforted me in a way that a supposedly random system could not. This did not mean I let go of the spontaneous or serendipitous nature of living. I was happy to trust the pilot when I got on a plane, but I simply wanted confidence that the engineer who built the plane had not been playing dice during his task.

Around this time, Bill Dear went his own way, as I had suspected he might. He was able to set up a movie at Universal called *Harry and the Hendersons*, a movie that I thought suited him. Meanwhile, Harry Gittes, who had produced *Timerider*, brought me a script he thought I might want to produce, written by a young UCLA film school grad student named Alex Cox. It was called *Repo Man*. I was smitten.

Repo Man was a hard-edged script that came from a punk sensibility. The script was a bit of a mess narratively. It didn't have an ending—or rather it had three endings, and like a person with three watches who can't tell what the time is exactly, the ending was vague. The opening, however, was nearly enough on its own: On a lonely road in the desert a single 1964 Chevelle Malibu weaves, crossing back and forth across the center line. A motorcycle cop spies the car and quickly pulls the driver over. The driver is obviously under high stress, on drugs, or drunk, and barely conscious. The cop demands to see in the trunk. The driver, soft-spoken and very far out of his normal state, gently pleads, "Oh, you don't want to look in there." The cop demands the keys, walks to the rear of the car, and slowly opens the trunk. As he does, a light appears in the crack and gets brighter and brighter as the trunk opens until the light is brilliant high-intensity cosmic laser-greenish-white, as bright as the sun—and the cop vanishes.

That was on the first page, and I asked myself, *Do I want to see the rest of this movie?* The answer was a resounding yes! Clearly, one way for that to happen was to produce it myself. I also found something of my own sense of humor in it. My humor had ranged free in *Elephant Parts* and I'd been in absurdist's heaven while making it, but *Repo Man* took a step I didn't know how to take artistically. It was unrestrained and had an angry, dangerously hilarious undertone that expressed a sincere yearning for understanding in the same breath as a punitive impatience for politics or malfeasance.

It would be an easy film for me to back artistically, but I also decided I wouldn't throw money at it, as I had with *Timerider*, and expect the Throw-Money-At-It god to make it all come out right—which is to say, to make it make money. This time I would consciously construct a deal that lined all the elements up in the most productive way. I wasn't sure exactly how that would work, but I was certain that it was possible. I finished reading the script and asked Alex and his producer friends if I could have a meeting with them and explore possibilities.

I liked Alex quite a bit as a person. He was imperiously tall, rail thin, with an orange mohawk and a face that was jolly and cartoonish in spite of the threat of his intellect, which I thought was formidable. His two producer friends, a movie-star handsome Peter McCarthy and a Lennonesque Jonathan Wacks, were much more mainstream arts-crowd casual, with a certain confidence that signaled to me they could be trusted to get the picture shot and edited. I was relieved to find them nowhere near the usual Hollywood producer/agent style—no suits and loafers or attitude. All three seemed much more a product of the new wave of the counterculture that was emerging in the Venice environs of Los Angeles. Alex wanted to direct the movie and I thought he might go far as a director. This looked like a great band forming, and I was happy with the thought that I might be included. These three were living a hard life in LA as young filmmakers, a life that I would have liked to share in somehow, although by now I was starting to understand that in most of my contemporaries' eyes I was Daddy Warbucks.

As bands go, the *Repo Man* team was nearly perfect as just the three of them. Three-man *bands* are usually power bands—distinct from, say, cocktail-lounge trios, which are event bands. And the *Repo Man* band was nothing if not raw power. The way they careened through filmmaking was a joy to watch and a terrifying ride. It was as if they wanted to leave a scar on the world as their artistic legacy.

I was sure this would be a fun punk band to watch play in gritty downtown LA, a forgotten city melting in the heat during the summer of 1983. Its infrastructure was crumbling and its citizens had fled to the beach and the suburbs, leaving it a distressed hull, listing badly, pierced and tattooed. I longed to actually play with them, but it was yet another band I wanted to be in but couldn't. I would stick to business. *Elephant Parts* and *Timerider* had been hard and expensive lessons in management, and I did not want to repeat them.

I consulted with some of my advisers about how to set up a deal for *Repo Man*, and the structure that seemed best was called a "negative pickup" with a large studio. *Negative* in this context referred to the film negative. The basics were that I would finance the film, and the studio would agree before we started filming to buy it from me on completion, assuming it was true to the script they read. This way the *Repo Man* band could have complete freedom from the studio overlords, and I would get all my money out when I delivered the picture, in addition to keeping a healthy percentage of the gross income from first dollar going forward, which I would share with the filmmakers. I set that deal up with an executive team at Universal Pictures that really seemed to understand the script and its potential. Only a few months later I delivered the film, but to a completely different executive team, this one from the Golden Age of Hollywood, where movie stars made musicals and vivid Technicolor war movies.

When I delivered the movie to the new Universal team, the Hollywood Mind immediately deemed it unreleasable. In the screening where the Universal staff gathered to first watch the film, there was an implacable silence at the end as everyone shuffled out uncomfortably, except for one woman—I never knew who she was—who turned to the sullen crowd and yelled at the top of her lungs, "What is the matter with all of you? Don't you know what you just saw? This film is a miracle! You should be cheering!" I knew she was right—she was the voice of the film, of course—but she got no response, and the crowd avoided her.

Fortunately, one small theater in Cambridge, Massachusetts, got a print and started playing it. It ran in that one theater for a year, and it wasn't until some young staffer at Universal listened to the soundtrack and pushed for the soundtrack's release that the movie began to surface. The deal I made with the studio turned out to be wonderful and nearly prescient about its future success. I got all the production money back when I delivered it, and as the picture and the ancillary rights started performing, the residual and royalty checks got bigger and bigger. The picture finally went into net profit and still makes money for all of us as I write this, meaning the *Repo Man* band gets a regular check, along with me and others.

A project like *Repo Man* carries a lot of gravitas with it, and the creative return is immense, even if the monetary returns are not immediate. The script was innovative in the way it drew in the culture of its time, and the filmmaking looked very different from other contemporary films. The actual ending did not pop into view until well into the production. Alex said he thought the character Miller had been overlooked and lost, and that the craziness of his ramble at the burning trash barrel had been forgotten in the twists and turns of the rest of the film. He wanted Miller to have a real connection to another place and to have access to that place through the powers that lived in the trunk of the Malibu as he rescued Otto in the levitating car. They would rise together in the glowing vehicle as it swept through the skies of muddled downtown LA and disappeared. I thought of it as a rich moment and good ending but told him he should decide. It was his film, and I would deliver it as he made it, as long as it was close enough to the script to comply with our commitments.

Over time the film set deep roots in its base of fans and appreciators. I was proud of it, and of Alex and Peter and Jonathan and the cast and crew—all of them who put it together. I was also afraid the Hollywood Mind could not grasp the film or where it fit in moviedom. *Repo Man* taught me how to make a decent deal with the studios, and it also taught me patience.

It took several years, but the cachet and respect I gained from its borrowed light were nourishing to me. I had not experienced it since the First National Band, another slow starter that now lives in its own pantheon, to my great satisfaction. Simple though it is, when people come to me for an autograph on a piece of *Repo Man* memorabilia or say a kind word about the FNB albums and their place in music history, there is a connection that feels especially good.

The Hollywood Mind's focus on the money metric is not a flaw so much as a commitment to an arbitrary standard that limits the opportunity to create something of lasting and life-changing value. Making money is fine, as far as it goes, but the more I looked away from the HM, the more I saw different intersections where great things gathered, and where good ideas flourished in unexpected ways. Hollywood Mind movies are part of the popcorn and sugar water business in the end, and as such there is no gain stage for a film but time and acceptance. I think a good film lives in the heart of its filmmaker as always good, regardless of the money it makes. Moneymaking doesn't satisfy the artistic yearning, doesn't satisfy the search for meaning, doesn't equal the personal reward of discovering tiny gems among stones.

Over at the foundations, fresh rains and new growth were stimulating me, too. We received a request for a grant from the Sundance Institute, which needed money for a writers' workshop and for the launch of the Sundance Film Festival. It was an easy yes for me because of Robert Redford's involvement and also because writing was an area I understood.

A bit later, I became aware of a program at the American Film Institute called the Directing Workshop for Women that needed funding, and Gihon was able to provide those funds within the foundation's program guidelines. I was drawn to it because there were no women directors making films for the major studios at the time. The few in history had come and gone, and women in film were an oppressed class among an oppressed class. This rankled me, and it felt not only morally right to help remedy the problem, but it was the kind of problem that government policy was not likely to address. A secure, high-powered, enfranchised woman did not present herself immediately as someone in need. But the field was as clearly skewed against the high-powered working woman as labor-intensive work was against the low-powered disenfranchised one. At Gihon we resolved to fund the Directing Workshop for Women, and did so for several years.

Through this funding, I met the director of AFI, Jean Firstenberg. She invited me to join the board, at first because of Gihon's funding of the DWW. Later, as we became colleagues, it became clear that we shared a mutual goal of opening the industry to women in a way that it hadn't been. I was happy to have a board seat and help carry this idea forward.

One of the more pleasant days for me at that time would

involve having lunch with Jean Firstenberg, Jamie Hindman, and Bob Gazzale (who would later become president and CEO of AFI) and discussing philanthropy and how to measure its effect. AFI had been started by a presidential order from LBJ, as part of a government effort to stimulate and build the industry, but as government funding waned, it fell to Jean and her cohorts to figure out how to raise money from the film community and how to justify the existence of AFI. I was having the same problem of validation and justification for my mother's foundations, although they were tiny by comparison, so it was helpful to me to compare notes with an essentially philanthropic organization that had to continually update and validate its existence. Such is the work of many foundations and charitable organizations.

One day I was having lunch with Brandon Tartikoff, head of the entertainment division of NBC and at the time the youngest executive to run a network programming arm. He had given me a cold call after attending the Sundance Film Festival, where he saw *Elephant Parts*. I didn't even know that *Elephant Parts* was at Sundance. He had suggested we get together and explore some ideas about doing a television show.

At this lunch he told me a story about a very senior television executive who had been at NBC some years earlier. The exec was driving home after celebrating having won a season in the ratings, and he was a bit tipsy. It was late at night, and he ran through a stoplight at the Beverly Hills Hotel, where a cop was waiting in the parking lot. The cop pulled him over, and the exec, in a lapse of judgment, handed him his driver's license with a hundred-dollar bill behind it. The exec explained who he was and what he did and that he was coming from a big one-time celebration, how sorry he was, and how much he would appreciate it if the cop would just let this go since it was a very unusual circumstance.

The cop said, "Not only did you run a red light, but you're intoxicated—and you also attempted to bribe an officer. I'm taking you in to the station."

The cop packed him up in the police car and drove him to the Beverly Hills police station, where the cop started writing him up. The exec said he would like to make his phone call, and he made his one call to the actor Jack Webb, who was famous for playing Detective Sergeant Joe Friday of the LAPD in a television show called *Dragnet.* It was the dominant crime show on television at the time, and Webb's Friday was the most famous cop in the US. The exec asked Webb if he could help him out. Webb came to the police station, and the exec was released in twenty minutes.

Brandon told me this story in the context of how television created its own reality, and at that moment I knew I had met a soul mate. Years later a relative of Webb's told me that this same story was told many times but with various movie stars and studio heads at its center, and was probably apocryphal. All that mattered to me was that Brandon understood it for what it was. Piercing the media veil and using its fictions to solve problems was a reality if I ever saw one.

Brandon seemed to me like the perfect executive. He was affable, with an easy, quick smile and a classy self-deprecation that lifted those around him, and he looked preppy, like the Yale graduate he was. Conversation flowed seamlessly and easily between us. We didn't discuss the philosophy or deeper meaning behind television, but we didn't need to because we shared an unspoken fascination with everything that was going on in that world, and we could both tell we were looking at the world of media from the same perspective.

Brandon had a well-known reputation for nurturing shows

he liked. He seemed to enjoy the creative process, and I thought that deep down he might like to be a producer. The seat of the entertainment director at a network was one of the hottest—in both the best and worst senses—of all the positions in show business. Brandon handled it well.

He seemed to have an intuitive understanding that a television program could create something other than what was in the programming, and then program whatever that was, like actually playing the phantom chords on a piano as the primary chords. This multilayered approach would have a far-reaching effect on television, and especially NBC under his stewardship. His idea to incorporate aspects of a music video into something like a comedy video was born of this understanding.

He had first contacted me because, the way he tells it, he was standing in the lobby of one of the festival theaters at Sundance having a conversation when raucous laughter started getting so loud he couldn't hear the person he was talking to. He went to see what all the fuss was about and saw that the crowd was watching *Elephant Parts.*

Brandon wanted to talk about doing a series like *Elephant Parts* for NBC. I said sure, but that I had no idea how to get *Elephant Parts* on television and asked him to share any ideas he might have about how he saw it working. He said he thought it would be interesting to do what I had done with *Elephant Parts*, musicians and music and bits of lunacy, but with comedians—to make comedy videos much like music videos.

I understood immediately what he wanted, but not immediately how I would be able to do it. He was suggesting that the new music-video form might work for a stand-up comedy routine the way it worked for a song, and in pursuing this new form, he could avoid the dreaded comedy sketch. Sketch humor was the fallback for many network comedy shows, and it had taken on a slow-moving, predictable plod, with lots of the same crossed eyes and funny costumes that defined vaudeville. Stand-up was *not* sketch comedy or situation comedy. A stand-up routine could be as vital as a song well sung, could have all the same openings for sudden uproarious riffs, and in the right hands could even be performative.

It should be easy, he said. Call up Steve Martin and Robin Williams and a few of the other big comedy stars, and they will come and make these comedy videos with you for your new network-television show. He actually made it sound easy, and I accepted.

Of course, I could not just "call up" Steve Martin and Robin Williams, except to hear them say no. They were big, expensive stars and had no intention of wasting their hard-earned fame on my little TV show. I would have to search the comedy clubs, find the talent, and then write up the routines they were doing as some kind of counterpart to the music video I had done. I had to assemble a writing team and a film-production team. Bill Dear's other projects were by now well under way. He agreed to help out on a few of the comedy videos, but I could see that, especially if the show got picked up, I would have to set up a much larger production team.

I started crawling the clubs of LA and New York, looking for stand-up comedians who might resonate with the idea of a comedy video. I hired Ward Sylvester, one of the Monkees producers, to help find talent with me. The work was great fun, night after night—almost nonstop laughter with some dreadful silences.

One comic who immediately understood the dual reality of television was Garry Shandling. I saw Garry on a talent-scouting evening in LA; he did a routine about dating Miss Maryland and I thought his material would work perfectly for the show, which we were now calling *Television Parts*. I asked if he would stop by and try to hammer something out. Garry was like Douglas

Adams, very funny just hanging out and having fun. He was a comedy writer first and a performer second, and his writer's eye gave him an ability to detect the comedic undertow of an otherwise normal situation that unintentionally reveals itself as bizarre, like a pet parrot that says something embarrassing and outrageous when company comes. His delivery was self-aware and he would laugh as he told these stories. His laughter was infectious and a great pointer for those who were slow to come to the joke. A script came together for the Miss Maryland routine pretty easily between us.

The first video we shot was built around going on a date with the beauty queen whose life had essentially stopped when she won her crown. Everything since for her had been post-awards-show goofiness, including her insistence on sitting on top of the backseat of Garry's open convertible as they drove to the restaurant so she could wave to the nonexistent crowd, the obsequious way she thanked the waiter and other patrons, and the outfit she wore—a ball gown, scepter, Miss Maryland banner, and tiara.

It was very Garry, and made a super comedy video. The Miss Maryland bit made me think the show might even be a hit. Everyone I showed it to broke into peals of laughter, including Brandon. I started inviting almost every working comic I knew, or saw working, to come by and try to put together one of these new comedy videos. Often as not, I used Miss Maryland as the touchstone for describing the concept.

I hired four writers to help the comedians wrangle their stage material into comedy videos. Michael Kaplan and John Levenstein were young Yale graduates who had seen *Elephant Parts* and contacted me—easy enough since Kaplan's father was my attorney at the time. They were both quick and super funny and worked well with the comedians. The other two writers were Jack Handey and Bill Martin. Bill, of course, had worked on *Elephant Parts* and he had also made another long-form video with me called *An Evening with Sir William*, about an absurdist eccentric billionaire living in a castle and doing old-time drug riffs to himself, to the camera, and to Rogar, a pet sea monster that lived with him. It was Handey's first television job, although he had worked some with Steve Martin. Jack showed up one day with "Deep Thoughts," funny bits he had written but wasn't sure what to do with. I started laughing at the first one I read and couldn't stop. I could see them as little snippet films done in a satirical-somber "messages of high inspiration" voice-over style. I sent a second unit crew out to a beach to get the background visual, a romantic sunset shot of a lavish picnic being swamped by a wave.

The writers and I all bounced ideas off each other and the comedians who came to audition, and it was a constant whirl of riff after funny riff manifesting as little comedy moments. What happily did *not* manifest in the writers' room was what one of the *Television Parts* comedians called "a pathological need to make other people laugh." The comedy was natural—stand-up comedians sharing their own funny way of looking at things with other professionals.

We tried writing routines that we could shoot as comedy videos, but they usually weren't funny. We were trying to cast one of these soft and desperate skits, and Lois Bromfield came in to read for a part. She was bright, attractive, blonde, and would have been good if the material had been better, but it wasn't and she wasn't. Those of us sitting on the audition panel said thanks, but I stopped her before she got out the door and asked her about her career as an actor: How was it going? What was she hoping for? She said that she wasn't an actor but a comedy writer and stand-up comedian. I asked if she could do some of her stand-up for us. There were only three of us in the room, and we got nervous because we knew the request was potentially embarrassing for all of us if the routine went wrong. But without missing a step, Lois started on a routine and all of us nearly fell off our chairs laughing from the first sentence. By the end of her stand-up-without-an-audience I had given her a segment of the show. We titled it "Sorority Girls from Hell."

From that we had confirmed for us the difference between a comedy sketch and a stand-up routine. Stand-up was a performance—much like a musical act—with all the power and presence of that event. It had to be delivered like a song.

The completed pilot was funny—Martin Mull made a video about home safety; the Funny Boys did one set in an "Irish Language Lab"; and there were others, all featuring the same incessant absurdity. Editing brought the first hint of the only trouble I would have with the network. The executive in charge of the show was a highly competent and dedicated television guy who believed almost religiously in the power of the laugh track. I tried but could not get *Television Parts* past him without a fake audience laugh—as when a humorless person pushes a button on a machine. I was sure the laugh track was a mistake, but I agreed to throw a huge party and screen the pilot while recording the laughter of the watching crowd. I argued that laugh tracks annoyed me and broke the comedy spell, but maybe it would work if they were real laughs. The TV guy agreed to the laugh track party, as long as I paid for it. As it finally worked out, the laughter from the real audience was so loud and long that it sounded fake and was unusable, but the pilot sold and Brandon ordered eight more.

The eight episodes of *Television Parts*, each one with a fake laugh track, came and went in the summer of 1985. It was the lowest-rated show on television for every episode, except one time when it was next to lowest. I'm not sure it was the laugh track that torpedoed the good work of the comics, but I'm not sure it wasn't.

There would be no more orders for *Television Parts* episodes from NBC, but I was gratified to see Garry take off into his own orbit with *The Larry Sanders Show.* He used the concept of talking through the fourth wall that he had learned in *Television Parts*, and he graciously gave me and the show great credit for that, saying it was the foundation of *The Larry Sanders Show.* Other comics, like Jay Leno and Jerry Seinfeld, landed on their feet as well, having passed through the *Television Parts* doors. The show took its place in all our lives as part of a seminal past.

During this time, Brandon and I started talking casually about setting up a movie partnership between Pacific Arts and NBC. He wanted to make movies like *Repo Man*, but his television sensibility made him nervous about such movies for the same reasons the Universal execs had been nervous.

During one spitballing creative session with him, he told me he had just gone to visit the old black-and-white printing presses in Florida that had been used for the *National Enquirer.* They had been repurposed by a band of ex–Harvard journalism students to put out the *Weekly World News*, a never-let-on ironic newspaper full of outrageous made-up tabloid stories. This paper was distributed through the same grocery store system that had distributed the *National Enquirer*, so it showed up at most of the checkout stands in the US. Brandon had become fascinated with it after he learned that the issue that had sold the most copies—in the millions—was the one with Bat Boy on the cover. Bat Boy was just what the name implied—a half bat, half boy. He was supposedly a feral child, raised in a cave of bats, by bats. Brandon thought Bat Boy might make a good movie. The notion of it made me laugh out loud.

Brandon also wondered if the Monkees could figure into this show somehow. His idea was to set the film up by calling it the *Weekly World News* and have the main conceit be that it was the local newspaper of the town of Weekly, Mississippi. I added that maybe Weekly was the town where mythical pop characters retire, since they can never die, and the central character would be Elvis. This made him laugh.

We decided that the movie should be about the Monkees, now plenty long of tooth, who have been invited to Weekly, which is to say forcibly retired. They would be given the job of community relations, taking care of Bat Boy and Elvis and others. I told him I happened to know personally that Dwight Yoakam did a really funny Elvis impersonation, and at this we both laughed as hard as we could. At least we had our Elvis. He would have been great.

NBC Films and I made two movies together, *Square Dance* and *Tapeheads. Tapeheads* was my favorite of the two because it was silly and adolescent fun, the kind of kid-anxiety comedy that was perfect for its time. The music was top-drawer R&B-meets-wacko-Mark-Mothersbaugh genius. When I showed it to an audience of their peers, the two stars, John Cusack and Tim Robbins, tested very well, and the reactions made me, NBC, and our theatrical distributor wild with excitement. The Hollywood Minds were all atwitter, and I was sure that at last I had gotten one over the fence. This would move me from simple Hamburger Movie Tycoon to Official Hamburger Movie Tycoon with a Hollywood Mind.

Unfortunately, our distributor was the De Laurentiis Company, and it went bankrupt only a few seconds after buying the film from me and NBC Productions. I held on to the video rights, and I still have them and take them out from time to time and look at them.

Unknown to me, Brandon was in the target window of the headhunters for Paramount Pictures and would not be at NBC much longer, but even had I known that, I was sure by then that I had to get farther away from the Hollywood Mind. I had no dependable process for spotting projects that would make money and then putting together a system to make that happen. The theatrical movie business, both in production and distribution, was wearing me down in a way I did not think I could be worn down, and I wasn't happy about it. It seemed like a good time to focus a little more on a business I understood. The *Tapeheads* heartbreak was the finale of my movie-producer career.

The distant thunder was coming from home video, and by this time I had the largest catalog of documentaries and non-theatrical titles in the world. I thought I should buy some business suits, settle down in LA—even if I didn't move there full time—and concentrate on building the new home-video business.

At the time, two other events had occurred that would shape my life in ways I could not have imagined.

First, Vint Cerf and Robert Kahn had just completed writing and establishing TCP/IP, the new Internet protocols. The migration of the ARPANET to TCP/IP had been officially completed in January 1983, when the new protocols were permanently activated over a new networking system called the Internet, and by the late eighties there was smoke from a distant but very great fire.

Second, a young woman named Victoria Kennedy had seen the *Television Parts* episode that included the hilarious Lois Bromfield "Sorority Girls from Hell" bit.

I had no idea at the time who these potential band members were, or that the instruments they played even existed. I could not have imagined the kind of music they would bring into my life.

12

I was walking through an empty hangar at the Santa Monica Airport. I had learned to fly years earlier and decided to use that airport as something of a travel depot. I was living in Santa Fe at the time, and the process of commuting back and forth to LAX on commercial airlines was full of problems. I bought a small plane I could use for a commute, settled on Santa Monica as my LA-area destination airport, and was now looking for a hangar—along with a little office—in the airport.

I found one that was small, with just enough room for my little single-engine plane. It had a kitchen and a bathroom with a shower off to one side, and a mezzanine for a workstation. It even had an expansive ocean view when the wall-size hangar door was open.

I hung large artworks, many of which had been in my mother's home, on the walls, and placed comfortable, contemporary, high-tech furniture here and there. It became a fine place with a cool design, much more than just a huge garage. When GM built the EV1, an electric car, I got one of the first available and set up a charging station in the hangar, and that became my LA car. As LA digs go, the hangar was ideal, and very modern: a little plane and an electric car and my office all in the same space, surrounded by art. On a clear day, with the door opened to the ocean view, the space represented a departure point for all possibilities. I loved it.

I told the architect Frank Gehry about this at dinner once, and he was keen on seeing my setup, since he was thinking of getting more space for his Santa Monica offices. We had met during one of the Gihon Foundation's programs and struck up a friendship that followed on after the council's work was done. I thought of him as an exceptional architect, a truly artistic thinker and an all-around lovely guy. His work had been through some harrowing trials but was finally proving itself to be some of the greatest architecture of all time, and his business was starting to flourish. When he mentioned seeing the hangar, I said, "Sure, come by anytime and I'll show you around." It was a privilege.

Frank was looking for a much bigger space than mine, so we walked around some of the larger empty hangars. We were joined by four or five of his minions and fellow architects. One hangar we looked at was extraordinarily impressive, over fifty thousand square feet of clear span that created a spectacular open space with ceilings almost three stories high. Our little band was dwarfed by it as we walked along.

I said to Frank that I had always wanted to get a huge space like this—plain, big and open, safe and contained—and then set up a system of open areas like an island within it, basically just floors at different levels that would combine to occupy one large area in the center of the hangar. Then, with careful lighting and sound control, I could make the living spaces mostly separate but still conjoined, flowing into each other by stairs and ramps, a wall here and there, with the purpose of each room determining the flow to the higher and lower spaces.

The big open space would control the overall temperature, but the smaller areas might have their own climate zones, like sleeping areas, bathrooms, and kitchens, all protected by an overarching space. "I would love living in something like that," I said.

Frank responded, "That's what everyone wants."

I laughed, as his remark let me see momentarily through his artist's and architect's eye. The idea of a huge open space with living areas and work areas established here and there, flowing into each other as needed, was nothing less than the planet Earth. Not only was it "what everyone wants"; it was what everyone had. Recognizing this in Frank's remark opened a new window for me. From it I could see just how vast possibilities were, and importantly, how they were all right at hand. That moment with him was an important step for me in understanding how the local, practical applications of big ideas came into being from resources as near as thought.

It had started becoming obvious to me in the early 1980s that I was not cut out to be a Hamburger Movie Tycoon, or any kind of tycoon for that matter. The Hollywood Mind was unnatural to me, and it was folly to get into a business where I would have to compete against others for whom it was natural. After *Television Parts* and the various movies were completed, I focused more and more on building Pacific Arts' home-video business, putting my individual artistic efforts aside to see if I could make the little company start and run.

It was doing a pretty brisk sales business but was not making a profit, and I had no idea how to turn that around. I kept hoping I was only a little ahead of the times, so I kept putting money in the company to cover the shortfall while I waited. I thought the answer was more and more sales and better and better ideas, rather than better operations, which at that time were a complete mystery to me. The operation of a business on a profit-and-loss basis is very far from the operation of a band on a good-and-bad-performance basis, and I was lost. VHS rentals were growing, so there was reason for hope, but an idling business still burns fuel.

In the cooldown from my time as a Hamburger Movie Tycoon, I tried a few novel ideas with the Pacific Arts distribution system. We potentially could sell videotapes to many video stores nationwide, and the Pacific Arts system was good at that delivery even though it was small.

Video rental stores had sprung up in the early eighties, and in just a few years customers were coming into stores, usually once a day, renting a video for the evening, then returning it the next day, so the stores had an ever-expanding need for product. Looking around the stores, I saw that customers didn't have a good way to see what was available, nor did they have a way to preview home-video product.

I thought it might be a good idea to release a weekly videotape containing previews of coming attractions and reviews of current releases. Customers could pick up the tapes at checkout stands for free; they would be supported by advertising the way magazines were. I went so far as to Hamburger-Movie-Tycoon a prototype program and put together a band to create and produce it. I named the program *Overview* and produced the first issue, but the idea faltered. The market closed behind it like water in the wake of a passing boat. It was a good idea, and a band of very good players came together around it, but as it turned out, the band was playing the wrong song, in a weird key, with a bad arrangement. From corporate sponsors to video store owners to the retail customer, nobody understood it. The band had no audience.

⁂

Bands are natural, and they come together more or less spontaneously, but they also tend to come together around a strong point of view. Band members coalesce because of the implicit understanding that they will be part of a larger whole, but a band can only become so big. Three- and four-piece bands can manage within their own structure to keep a balance among the members, but any more than five or six and the band starts to morph into an orchestra, and an orchestra is distinct from a band.

In the end, performance is everything a band is about, the only thing it is about. It is the final measure of a band. Hundreds of millions of people will listen to a good band perform. In the right skillful hands, these performances can become *performative*, can create something that is accessible no other way—hence the phrase "You had to be there." These performances inform the consensus about a great band.

There is a moment when a band comes offstage after what everyone agrees was a particularly good performance. It is not a moment that can be faked or created like a party laugh. It is true, a real moment of appreciation, each for the other. The camaraderie is real, and in that moment there is a special creative return, a kind of fulfillment that comes with a successful effort, not only for the art of the performance but the science of it, the appreciation of how difficult it is to play well. It is a shared space that can only be honestly shared.

Music that is crucially important to only a few people is as valid as music loved by millions. This is an aspect of the arts that the Hollywood Mind doesn't understand but tries to exploit by trying to make a performance seem true when it isn't, or to seem more valid than it is. In the arts this is called "hype"—the falsifying of a moment. In the industry it is called, more formally, "marketing and advertising"—even though it is still hype. In the arts, hype is toxic and gives off a warning rattle and foul odor. This kind of hype is easy to spot.

In business and law there are certain boilerplate concepts. Most people know and understand them even if they are not businesspeople or lawyers. They are simple ideas that form part of the fabric of society and civilization. One of these simple ideas is the "covenant of good faith and fair dealing." It means that if you agree to something, then all parties must be honest with each other; they are bound by the agreement they made in "good faith." If one crosses this line, it is known as a "breach of the covenant of good faith and fair dealing."

This covenant is present in nearly every written contract as a statement of general principle and exists in some form in all cultures all over the world. It looks fragile because it seems so easy to break without getting caught. There are classes of thinkers who routinely ignore this basic civil covenant or who see it but do not heed it. And yet it reaches deep into our lives.

When "Rio" became a hit in Australia, I got offers to come and play there, so I put together a band with John Ware, David MacKay, and Al Perkins and went down for a series of shows. While there, I started to get the usual interview questions about the Monkees, and I wondered at the press and the general consciousness that developed according to what a person might read in a newspaper and gather from news media in general.

My own early experience involved a willingness to believe most everything I read, trusting the journalistic ethic to see to it that if I needed hard truth, I could depend on the media. There had to be a good reason, or so I thought, that Walter Cronkite was the most trusted man in America while serving as the news anchor for CBS in the 1960s and '70s. I assumed it was integrity. Now I was starting to suspect it might just be television.

My time with higher thinkers like Seeley had given me pause; I had taken time to think through and thoroughly examine processes, systems, and ideas. In Australia I decided to try an experiment. It was nonscientific by any measure, but I had in mind that it might teach me something about veracity and the origins of trust among mortals. If only a crumb, it would be interesting.

I had an interview scheduled with a reviewer from a prestigious and well-known Australian newspaper, and he arrived a hail-fellow-well-met. He had read my press release, he said, and had only a few follow-up questions.

As we sat down for the interview, before he asked the first question, I told him that I was going to lie to him. He was taken aback, then seemed a little nonplussed and asked why. I said it was because I didn't trust the press, that I didn't expect him to tell the truth, so neither would I.

It was confrontational in the extreme, but I was careful not to insult him personally. I said that I expected him to lie, but I supported the remark by the outrageous claim that this was what I assumed the press did in the ordinary course of business, just like politicians, because they had to—that mendacity was endemic to their agenda, which was to attract readers in order to sell advertising. I conceded that there was probably a certain amount of information that was corrupt before it got to them. So, I told him, I had decided to work the same angle from my side.

I said that some of the things I would say would be true and some false, and it would be up to him to figure out which was which, according to the normal standards of journalistic responsibility. He asked how he would tell the difference between when I was lying and when I was telling the truth, and I said, "You won't. That is the point of a lie."

No doubt he thought I was a jerk, and the space between us cooled by degrees. The interview started cautiously and I put on my best behavior, sincerely assuring him that I felt no personal animosity toward him and that we were both just part of a curious cycle, with no one to blame for the outcome. As he relaxed, so did I, and for a bit there were no lies I could tell, nothing false I could say that would seem credible. I didn't know whether he was playing the same game or not, but he, like me, seemed sincere and interested in the subject of the interview, which was the Monkees.

Then came a point where he asked me about the sales of the Monkees records, and I saw the chance. It isn't too well known, I said flatly, that we sold over thirty-five million records in 1967. More than the Beatles and the Rolling Stones combined. The numbers were so big it was hard to count, I continued, but on a worldwide basis, as the numbers came in, it was finally resolved that we had outsold both bands. I left it there—any more and he would become suspicious, if he wasn't already.

He diligently wrote all this down, and I wondered for a moment if I had chosen *too* outrageous a lie to tell, but it turned out it had been just right. The next day in the paper, there it was, printed as fact.

Over the years I saw that fabrication pop up time and again in publications, more and more respected, and I became amazed at how a lie perpetuates itself. This conversation happened in November 1977, while I was still in the arms of the new phenomenon of the music video. I have never said a word to correct this misinformation until this writing. I just kept nodding my head in agreement when people would bring up the "fact."

I bring it forward here because, by the mid-1980s, this notion of hype and creating something from nothing had started to infect my business in a way I could not see and could not stop. In my personal life, away from the market, even as I had fallen into an affair, I had started to understand the fundamental importance of trust, and becoming trustworthy had moved to the top of my active endeavors. But there was a kind of hucksterism in corners of the business world that I found myself constantly tripping over. Such was not the case in the arts or in philanthropy, or even among the majority of businesspeople I knew and did business with, because they were usually honest and forthright and I could usually see the traps and falls. But I could not see it when ordinary people broke trust or purposefully and maliciously lied in a business deal. I simply couldn't imagine people being that evil.

Pacific Arts' home-video business kept growing, but as the gross sales got bigger and bigger, the losses grew right alongside them. The more money the company made, the more money the company lost. I studied the balance sheets, learned debt-to-equity ratios, ROI calculations, P&Ls, and other metrics used in running a business. It all made sense to me, but there was a screw loose somewhere, and I started to realize it was me.

In a last-ditch effort to steady the business, I looked around in the catalog I had amassed to see how I might improve things and was struck again by the fact that it was the largest catalog of its type and, I thought, of the highest quality. Maybe I needed to find a good brand to market it under. The most recognized and beloved brand at the time for this type of programming was PBS, and many of the titles I owned the video rights for played regularly on PBS. I thought perhaps I could license the PBS brand, use it to sell these titles on home video, and pay PBS a royalty. It would be found money for them, since I would handle all the sales and distribution and even add some titles to the line that they had never played to increase the royalty flow.

I also had it in the back of my mind that after the business righted itself, I could give it all to PBS at no cost—just donate it to them as a profit center they could use to finance more high-value product. It seemed like a good plan.

PBS was intrigued, but was also concerned that Pacific Arts

was operating at a loss. In a kind of final move in my Hamburger Movie Tycoonism, I offered to personally guarantee the deal and see to it that royalties due to them would be paid. That seemed to cinch things up, and we launched the PBS Home Video label in 1990.

What I did not know at the time was that some of the staffers and management at PBS had begun acting in bad faith, reacting to pressure from the highest levels of the organization. The main question being wagged around the boardroom was "How did Nesmith end up with the video rights to all these titles?" The answer was straightforward. I had bought them over the years. At the time I bought them, conventional wisdom held that once a show had aired on television, its value was used up. The home-video rights were a mystery to this side of the Hollywood Mind, and the result was that home-video rights were cheap. I bought all I could find while the HMers shook their heads in disbelief.

I was not deeply affected by their ridicule. I learned early on as a performer that ridicule is standard-issue. One gets very thick-skinned and persistent. I kept buying rights. I also knew that even as it struggled for acceptance as a viable channel, at some point MTV would be worth a billion dollars, and as I watched the Internet come to life, it slowly dawned on me that one can never pay too much for software. Programming for television was software in the home-video business, and that was starting to dawn on everyone, including the powers that governed PBS. Maybe it's not quite Moore's law, or even an axiom, but this guideline gave me enough light to see by.

That's why they started to lay a plan to snare my rights and take them from me.

The contracts between us were such that PBS could terminate unilaterally at a certain time, and they knew that doing so would send Pacific Arts into bankruptcy, since it was already running at a loss. If they could get the licensors of the titles I had licensed to go along with them, once they were free of Pacific Arts, PBS would then have the titles to use as they wished and could set up their own distribution system, or make a more favorable deal with another distributor.

The main problem for them in all this was that if Pacific Arts filed for bankruptcy protection as it failed, that would keep the titles from being available to PBS. PBS had to make it so that Pacific Arts either could *not* file for bankruptcy or could be tricked into *failing* to file for it. I know this only because these PBS meetings, where the Pacific Arts rights question was raised and discussed, later became a matter of record. One plan they contemplated was terminating their contract on Columbus Day, the theory being that because it was a holiday, Pacific Arts could not file for protection. The other plan was to contact all of my licensors, tell them that PBS was leaving, and encourage the licensors to leave with them.

The plans were deeply flawed, like most bad-faith actions are. First, Pacific Arts could file for bankruptcy protection at any time, holiday or not, so to keep Pacific Arts from filing they began a series of lies to cover their intent: intentional fraud, which is illegal. Second, trying to get the licensors to break their contracts with Pacific Arts would be illegal. Nonetheless, they conspired to steal the titles. When the idea came up in meetings that PBS would just have to "blow up" Pacific Arts to get the rights, it was written down in the minutes.

At the time I dove into the PBS deal, that type of thinking was foreign to me. I thought the idea was good enough and big enough for everyone to do well. The Pacific Arts staff, PBS, producers, and the rights holders to the titles all would be well served by the alliance.

But slowly, sadly, and surely Pacific Arts began to feel the bad faith of the PBS deal and it all came crashing down—or to put it as it had been recorded, Pacific Arts "blew up." And even after the crash, they sued me personally, so I had to sue them back in defense, and we were off to court. It took five years to get there, and it was a fight all the way.

But the most intense combat was the federal trial held in Los Angeles in front of a jury. PBS had orchestrated its malfeasance in a way that supposedly ensured that I would have no recourse to the facts, or the law, or even public scrutiny. So I had to put up a defense that was legally complicated and hard to understand. The main concept the jury needed to understand was that bankruptcy was designed to give an honest person a second chance, as well as provide protection, in some cases, from unscrupulous partners, malfeasance, or simple bad luck. They had to see that PBS's attempt to keep me from filing for protection was an illegal and unethical act.

The trial held me spellbound the entire time. Obviously, the stakes were enormous for me. If PBS prevailed, I would lose everything and be living in a trailer house on a vacant lot, and the specter of that was depressing. But as awful as that was, it was nothing compared to my interest in watching the process of jurisprudence at work.

My excellent team of two lawyers, Henry Gradstein and Bruce Van Dalsem, stopped regularly on the way to the courthouse in the mornings to give money to homeless people. They said it built up good karma. Trial lawyers create lots of theories about how to influence people, what to do or not do to get a jury to accept a particular story as the truth. I don't know whether PBS worried about karma, but one thing became quickly clear in the early days of the trial: they were out for blood. They wanted to personally ruin me and told me so. Why they wanted this I do not know. They said that when they won they were going to prosecute their remedies until I had nothing left, were going to take away everything they could from me: the copyrights of my songs, every royalty I had, every piece of property I owned, all the music, movies, videos, television shows—everything was going to go into their coffers and be chopped up and divided among their member stations and producers. They were going to see to it that I was left with nothing.

In the face of this ruthlessness, I resolved to stick to the truth, to never stray from it, even in a panic. My sophisticated friends told me this was naïve, and I suppose on some level it might have seemed that way, but in the end I really had no choice. I knew the facts as they happened, PBS knew the same facts, and those facts were against them. All I could do was trust that these facts would come to light. I had learned something about how lies work and perpetuate themselves; now it was time to understand how truth worked. However damning or misunderstood it would be, I resolved to depend on the truth.

On about the third day of the six-week trial, as I stood outside the courthouse waiting for Henry and Bruce, I started looking up closely at the impressive building. It was huge, with large columns, a big portico, and massive doors in the style of the public buildings of the 1930s and '40s. It occurred to me that the building had been built with a great purpose: to provide a safe space where people could find the truth, where accounts and disputes could be settled according to the truth. The truth had created the building; man's service to the truth was built into this edifice. It was nothing less than a temple of Truth, with a capital *T.* This calmed me. All worry fell away, and I went forward with a trust that held me throughout the trial.

⁂

Anecdotes and riffs are true things, even though they seem loose and unscientific. In music the definition of a riff is essentially broad. A riff is not necessarily a repeating phrase, like the guitar intro to "Paperback Writer," even though it may have started there. A riff by definition is not written or defined before it is played or sung or said. It is of the moment. It can be an added string of notes between a refrain and a verse, or a made-up phrase across the top of a series of chords, as in a jazz performance, but the critical distinction is that riffs are real-time, happening pre-thought in the moment, and many times a surprise. It might even be a wisecrack, if it's insightful enough.

A good riff can embody and express the essence of a song or melody in just a few notes, the same way a quick anecdote can frame an actual event, making its spirit clear even to those not present at the event. Truth works in this way—it is illuminated through the metaphor, the parable, the anecdote, and the riff. It is terse, clear, concise. The truth reveals the spiritual facts of life. A notable aspect of riffs and anecdotes is that they only happen once and never repeat. They are sui generis.

The ephemeral nature of a riff points, for some, to insubstantiality, but for others this is timelessness, an essential nature of the riff, the spontaneous and sudden appearing, then disappearing, of the genuine article, a quick wink that lets everyone know that the universe is watching out for us.

Riffs take readiness and practice, as does truth-telling. Silence is the gold standard because spaces in a riff count for just as much as what is spoken. When what is said is true, there is a ring to it that is like no other sound. It is a real sound, an actual sound, a sound that makes one turn their head, but its substance is spiritual, beyond the sense fences, the walls and clatter that hide so much.

⁂

When the advocates of the PBS position took the stand, there was an obvious difference between a practitioner of truth and a practitioner of lies. I watched the jury, and when someone on the stand told a lie, and there were several, there was a minute shift in the whole room. The jury recoiled by nanometers, essentially invisible to the eye. But in the temple of Truth, it was like a bad note in a song—only off by the slightest amount but sour and out of tune.

I watched this happen again and again in the trial, as the PBS staff and producers were divided by the jury into the authentic and the disingenuous. I knew who was lying because I was their victim and I had seen firsthand the crime, but it was amazing that the jury did too. The complex crimes—lies so expertly hidden that I despaired of anyone ever believing me—became apparent to them.

It had seemed impossible to me that a jury of people who had no notion of these subtleties could understand how it had happened. On the first day of the trial, after watching jury selection, I was even more frightened of getting pushed through a system without regard to the truth, or merely in regard to influence and manipulation. When PBS threatened me with awful outcomes and expressed their intent to destroy me personally, it was as if I were in the worst horror movie I could imagine. I was truly terrified. But as the trial unfolded, as testimonies defined the lies and the truths, the subtleties of convoluted laws and manipulations became clear, and I watched the jury behave like the audience they were, attentive, discerning, all with the same job of hearing and seeing the truth.

Every wrong note, every lie, caused a wince, and when the PBS witnesses took the stand, there was that awful squirming from the audience that goes on during a bad solo in a poor performance. The spirit of truth is palpable in these types of situations, and never more so than under the scrutiny of the plain and simple public eye.

The jurors in the PBS trial were for the most part from the

working class. As far as I know, none of them knew anything about the story they would hear or what the facts were. None of them were set up. I don't think any of them wanted to be there. But the hall of truth, as the court became, and the riffs and anecdotes that began to stitch together the picture of what happened, got their interest as time went on.

When the trial ended, the jury awarded me and Pacific Arts all our claims. Every accusation against me was judged as false, and I was found innocent. Every accusation against PBS was held as true, and they were found guilty. The jury awarded me $47.5 million in direct and punitive damages.

As the jury was leaving I made eye contact with a juror and said thank you. He shook his head and waved off the remark, needing no gratitude from me. It was just the way the facts were; the jury had just done its job, no thanks needed.

I loved winning. And I was thrilled with the money, and relieved. But the system was the satisfying thing to watch. We eventually settled for an amount I cannot reveal because it is sealed, but I wanted no more fight. The rights-holders were paid; many people came out OK; some people didn't. I personally had lost an enterprise that could not be recovered because it had been blown up—my video rights could not be easily reinstated.

I closed Pacific Arts as a video-distribution business. I still had my own works and copyrights, but the closure was a devastating loss to me, and I suffered with the sense of injustice and lack of recourse. I didn't whine or wail, keeping in mind my own counsel about not complaining about the air-conditioning on a private jet. I was learning that this kind of theft was attempted regularly in the halls of power.

⁂

Over the years I have become more comfortable with talking to myself. One of the benefits of talking to myself is that I always know when I am being ironic. Because irony depends on saying something you don't mean as if you mean it, or saying something that isn't true as if it is, and all the permutations of the above, it is a precise tool that can cut deep. When Victoria Kennedy came to meet me at a restaurant where I was having dinner, I got the feeling that she understood irony in a way that few did, and I instantly liked her, even if she used irony more like a knife than a spoon.

She was twenty-four years my junior, and when I met her she was nineteen. We were introduced by a mutual friend she knew from New York, where she was living. She had been one of the few people in the world who saw *Television Parts*, and when she found out that her friend knew me, she asked him if he would introduce us. The thing that caught her eye was the comedy video we made for Lois Bromfield's "Sorority Girls from Hell." Vic said she had never laughed so hard and knew right away she wanted to meet me if I was responsible. I knew from this that she was someone for whom funny was treasure.

I also saw that night in the restaurant a twinkle in her eye that I wanted to understand. She was a young international high-fashion model, stunningly pretty by anyone's standards. She was pretty, yes, but if she loved funny as much as I loved funny, if her sense of humor nourished her as much as mine did me, then there was a different and very real point of connection that I wanted to follow and get to know better. That was rare in my life.

Every one of my friends liked her, and every one of my friends cautioned me against getting involved with her. They reminded me over and over that May-December romances do not go well for the most part. They can work, but there are two different patterns to lives and they are greatly divided by age. It was hard not to be beguiled by her youth and beauty, but as we got to know each other over the next few months, there were many times we went to sleep happy and laughing—and woke happy and laughing—that ran much deeper than simple allure.

Our proper courtship occurred in Cannes during the 1988 film festival, and it was wonderfully romantic for me and, I think, her. I was there to buy and sell movies and titles for Pacific Arts, and she was in Rome doing a fashion shoot. She came to Cannes and we spent ten days together there, and for me the die was cast. I thought Vic was someone I could commit to. Again my friends cautioned me away from her because of the age disparity, and I was afraid of what might come because I knew they had a point. I was also hitting my midlife—depending, of course, on how long I stay on this manifest plane—so there were converging forces that needed reckoning and consideration.

At one point Vic offered the idea that we were different from most couples. I think she meant different from the couples she had been associating with. I responded laughingly that we were a cliché, a midlife producer and a young model traipsing about the festival, but deep down I knew what she meant and that she had a point. There was a difference.

We connected in important ways. I knew when she was just acting her age, and she knew when I was being ironic. Once, in New York, when I had gone to visit her and we were staying in a hotel, I stepped out on a Saturday morning to get something and realized I had forgotten my keys. I went back to the room, and as she opened the door I could see that she was watching cartoons on television. I looked at the TV, then she looked at the TV, and we both laughed. Me in resignation to the moment, she because the moment was funny.

Given this age gap, I knew I had to manage my own life's changing patterns as well as hers. If we stayed together, she would necessarily grow up in my care. I knew she did not need a parent. She said she was estranged from hers, but I didn't think that was entirely true. She was working in the upper echelons of the fashion industry, surrounded by professionals and artisans of sophistication far beyond her years, and she had developed an air of her own, mostly an insight into the distinctions between truth and artifice. She knew a good thing when she saw it, and for all the right reasons. Nonetheless, I tried to consider all that would happen over the course of a relationship between us. We would both age, and if we stayed together for years, then I would be an old man while she was still a young woman, right in the prime of her life.

One morning while she lay asleep and I was up and busy, I looked at her for a while, trying to imagine what she might look like as a natural woman of fifty and how that would make me feel—just how enraptured was I by her youth and beauty?—and for a moment I saw her as a mature and aging woman. Her face changed—the way the sun lit her hair had turned it almost white—and I clearly saw the lines of wisdom and growth that would someday be etched on her mortal frame.

In that moment, the lure of the beautiful woman vanished, and also in that moment, to my delight, I did not love her any less. As I gazed at her I could see that life was going to be very different. I had to come to terms with the fact that I could not commit to a beautiful young woman if that was all there was to it. My friends had been right about that at least. Whether she could commit to me remained to be seen, and that was a chance I had to take. Certainly it was a risk, that as I got older and as she hit her own midlife crisis she would fall away, drawn to the siren shores and trying to recapture failing youth as many of us do. I had to decide whether her sense of humor and my appreciation of her own good nature would win out over the sense of lost youth that the midlife crisis inculcates. For all her youthful antics, even the occasional mean-girl tricks of the beautiful, young, and cruel, I loved her sense of the true thing, since I knew that sense to be timeless and spiritual.

At that point I thought about how I might arrange my life with Vic as part of it, how I might handle her growing up while I was growing old. I had been separated from my wife Kathryn for a year at that point, and the divorce was coming final. I had deep ties of affection to someone else, but it was not a relationship that could last; it had begun to fray already.

One thing that changed in me when I met Vic was a new certainty that I was through with philandering and infidelity. I was disgusted with what it did to me as a man and how it had affected my life. I wanted to build a foundation of trust and love and fidelity in my relationship with all people. If Vic and I had that, then that was a start and would be more than enough reason for me to commit.

By that time, society had come to see marriage as a kind of second stage in long relationships, even childbearing ones, and Vic and I did not legally marry right away. The type of commitment we made was sincere and real, but it was not formal. There would be a time for "for better or worse, till death do us part," but this was not that time. I was sure I had fallen in love. I was less sure that she had, or even what that meant because of who we both were, age-wise and career-wise. Of all the women I had met, Vic had my heart in a way that was unique. I could commit to that, and take whatever time it took for us both to learn what we needed to learn.

My friends were all forty-five to fifty-plus, and they were all peering over the edge into the next stage of their lives. By contrast, my interest in peering over that edge was less than my interest in the present, the actual right-now present. What I could learn, and how I might learn, occupied my thoughts as much as anything. I wanted to learn about Vic, about metaphysics, about science and art and nature and the greater philosophical notions; I wanted to build and leave a legacy of something useful.

I thought I would start with the love I was in with Victoria and go from there, and I asked if this would be suitable to her, if she was ready to take a step like this as well. She said she had not thought of this kind of relationship happening so early in her life but that since it had appeared, she was happy and content with it like I was—so, yes, she would like that.

I offered to come live in New York, to get an apartment there for us and keep house as she was working, to write and to pay the bills. Her career had a certain momentum to it and I didn't want to interrupt that. I was also interested in what it would be like to stay home, to perhaps be part of New York society as Vic's partner, rather than she as mine. If she wanted to watch cartoons on Saturday, that would be fine. We could make a little home together and see how it fit.

Vic and I lived between New York and LA for a year. She seemed to tolerate the Northern California that I loved, but she did not love it as I did and always appeared happier leaving Carmel than going to it. Then, finally, we were both overtaken by New Mexico—specifically Santa Fe.

Patricia Hill, one of the Gihon board members, and her husband, a federal judge, had a home there, and Vic and I went one weekend for a board meeting. It was beguiling, as much as Santa Fe can be, and we started thinking that maybe instead of New York we could make a nice place for ourselves in New Mexico. Vic could perhaps base herself in LA, continue working, and come back and forth as needed. Vic liked the idea and so did I, and I started putting effort into finding a place in New

Mexico. Once, when landing at the Santa Fe airport, as Vic was looking out the window at the countryside and mesas and the Southwestern panorama, she said, "This feels like home." I felt the same way.

I finally found a place for Vic and me in a little settlement called Nambé, part of the Pojoaque reservation. It wasn't long before the Ranch, as we called it, took us both over. And when Pacific Arts "blew up" in 1994, we moved there full time.

Our first steps into Santa Fe were auspicious. The place I found was an enclave of sorts, and it appeared as if I could restore and repair a textbook adobe house along with some other buildings for Vic and me.

In addition, there was a large building with some offices attached that I could base the Gihon and McMurray Foundations in. The art conservator for the Gihon Foundation had told me that we couldn't keep traveling the art collection because it was slowly coming to pieces. Chalk was falling from the paper of a Mary Cassatt piece. A Grandma Moses painting had glitter dust falling from it. He told us that the entire collection was suffering and at some point would have to be permanently installed somewhere protected and safe; otherwise, we would lose it to wear and tear.

The large building in Nambé was perfect for setting up a gallery for the collection, although it was a bit remote. It would be open to the public, such as it was, but there weren't a lot of people around. Vic offered to help restore the small portable building that my mother had bought to start the Liquid Paper Corporation. This was the first building—outside of my childhood home, specifically the kitchen—that my mother had used for manufacturing and office space. It was a small storage building with windows and metal sides that sat in the backyard of our house in the very early years of the company. The building was now in storage, with piles of boxes, equipment, and early company archives stacked up inside it. Vic had it moved from its storage lot to the new property, had a concrete pad constructed for it, and then did an outstandingly beautiful and sensitive job of setting it up exactly as it had been in my old backyard, using pictures and snapshots and the collective memory of me and some of the early employees of Liquid Paper. It sat—carefully renovated and labeled, with portraits and placards—as something of a museum, just outside the building that now served as a gallery for the Gihon art.

We started spending more time at the Ranch, working on the various buildings and creating a nice space for the foundations and ourselves. Vic set up a new agent for herself in LA and started working there a bit, but our community revolved around Nambé, Santa Fe, and Los Alamos. More and more people started dropping in, visiting, becoming friends. It took Douglas Adams only one overnight visit to become thoroughly enchanted with the place.

I met Douglas through his agent. I had seen Douglas once before, in 1990, at the TED2 conference in Monterey, and while I liked his lecture, I did not meet him then. It wasn't until his agent told me that movie rights for *The Hitchhiker's Guide to the Galaxy* were available for sale that we finally met. I traveled to London to make the deal with Douglas, and we got on famously. But it was only after I was living in Nambé, after Douglas had become a good friend and regular houseguest, that I first heard of his encounter with the life-changing "Tuesday" cartoon. By that time we were close and comfortable friends, spending a lot of time together when we could. The Tuesday connection opened a whole new world between us and cemented our friendship as deep and abiding.

The *Hitchhiker's Guide* movie rights were sold and settled between us but never fully developed, although we spent a lot of time writing the screenplay together. Douglas rented Patricia

Hill's house in Tesuque, just up the road from the Nambé ranch, and moved in for the summer of 1997. We worked together daily. Once the PBS lawsuit seemed like it was headed to trial, I returned all the movie rights to Douglas and withdrew from the screenplay, telling him that I didn't want his movie rights to somehow become entangled in my ongoing troubles. The trial was still years away, and we were both disappointed, but in a way we drew closer and more like playmates than business partners, and this was when Douglas and I really had the best times together. Neither of us had an agenda except to play around and share toys and insights. He forged ahead with the screenplay alone, and the two of us forged ahead together with raucous dinner parties, nights of guacamole and margaritas, and days of magnificent mesas and the vibrating silver band on Douglas's wrist.

Our shared Tuesday held fast across great distances. Douglas was an avowed atheist and I was an avowed nonatheist. Douglas careened around his universe like he drove, changing the rules as he thought best for the joke. I tiptoed through my inner world looking for the rules that governed, being careful not to damage the tulips. We could easily spot the absurdity in the other's modus operandi, and that was the right time for ironic compliments among brothers and the magical peals of laughter, the Tuesday moments in which we understood the way we were both alike. When he died, it took years for me to recover from the sorrow—I don't think I will ever not miss him.

On our little back porch in Nambé, Victoria, Douglas, and I learned more and more about each other, our neighbors, the world, complexity, the arts and sciences. It was a happy, bucolic time.

But little by little, we also started to learn more than we wanted to know about the place we had gathered in, blissfully unaware of the dark.

13

For a while I lived with the idea that animals don't help each other, but the more firsthand experience I had with them, the more I realized I was wrong. I have actually seen—not on video but in real life, on my own roads—a group of squirrels physically assist an injured squirrel to safety. Carmel Beach is dog city, and it is not messy or rowdy or animal-against-animal. Dogs make friends quickly and easily, and either like each other or don't.

Douglas wrote a wonderful piece while he was staying in Santa Fe about two neighbor dogs that would wake him every morning with pleasant pleadings to go for a walk. When he would agree and go outside, they would instantly begin to ignore him and run ahead of him as he walked. Douglas said they were taking him "out on an ignore," which I thought was a funny way to look at it, a great riff in the classic Douglas style. I also knew he was wrong. I never said so, but when a dog appears to ignore a human, they are not unaware of the human. They are depending entirely on the human to be good and faithful, to feed them and walk behind them and protect them. They are not ignoring the human, they are taking the human for granted, which is the highest compliment a dog can pay us.

Carmel dog society is subtle and essentially hidden to the nonlocal, and even the locals without dogs don't understand it. Dog lovers do, and going to the beach with a dog is a lesson in manners—learned not from watching the humans but from watching the dogs.

Fritz, a lovely dog we had brought with us to New Mexico from LA, and Victoria's running mate through the arroyos of the Nambé ranch, at one point was diagnosed with cancer and shortly died. After he died, Vic was in a state of grief so deep that I suggested we take our other dog, Lily, to Carmel and walk on the beach. There, we could enjoy time with Lily and away from the loss of Fritz and the whole Santa Fe scene, could find some solace and perhaps healing.

Carmel allows dogs on the beach without a leash. They have to be controlled, but there is very little friction among them. Sometimes dogs on Carmel Beach hang out in pairs and trios. A group of four dogs starts to get pack-like, but without a belligerent and aggressive leader it will stay pretty sane and disperse quickly.

On the beach, the dogs run like the wind—a tired metaphor, but it is the one that is particularly apt for a dog on Carmel Beach. Running in their little bands, they all have an overdrive, like the wind, that hurls them in a gust faster than a human ever imagines they can go. These bursts are like dog riffs, because they end with the riffer trotting back to his friends, where they all dog-smile in admiration at the riffer's blinding speed.

But on the beach it's usually one dog and one human, and

an easygoing throw-something-go-get-it-then-bring-it-back-then-throw-it-again mindlessness. This is especially winsome when the dog participates.

Civil discourse has nothing much over canine discourse. Canines don't speak like humans, obviously, but they communicate in a rare and exquisite air of instant, clear understanding. Humans can learn a lot from dogs, and when Vic and I were in Carmel recovering from the untimely death of Fritz, it was the love of the dogs for each other that comforted and healed us.

We rented a little house in Carmel, and for the first time, I thought Vic started to understand what had so drawn me to that area. Because she had traveled extensively as a young girl, she had become immune to the seduction of beaches and fabulous towns, and to the beautiful homes photographers chose for their fashion shoots. New Mexico was the only place she ever said felt like home. But the trip to Carmel with Lily was restorative and soothing in its own way.

When we got back to the Ranch from that trip, I brought up the notion that we might buy a house in Carmel as a getaway. I said we could buy it easily, with no deep analysis, on the Internet. We could simply find a small, inexpensive house, listed by a friendly broker, and make the deal essentially sight unseen. Then we would have it for decompression and time away. It was a good plan. We had dug in deep in the decade we had been in Nambé, and if we were ever going to move permanently, it was going to take a while to pull it off.

In the meantime, I asked Vic to become a member of the board of the Gihon Foundation. After the art collection was installed permanently in the Nambé gallery, the board started thinking about the next steps for Gihon. We had closed the McMurray Foundation after having given away most of its money in grants, and so we were left with just the one—and that one without a clear mandate. Discussions among the board turned to possibilities for a new operating program for Gihon. We were, in essence, starting with a blank slate, and this opened a world of new opportunities.

Over the years I had met and shared experiences with people in many different disciplines. I was always happy to get a look at what they were doing, and they seemed interested in what I was doing, largely because our work was so different. These interactions gave both parties the opportunity to get deep into a different craft to see the world from a new perspective, at least momentarily.

The acquaintances I made shared their thoughts about their work in ways that helped and educated me. Usually, if a few of these friends came together, most knowing nothing about the others, little marriages would form—a poet with a scientist, a technician with a chef, a ballerina with a farmer—and leave a permanent mark on each.

I had seen similar sparks in John Brockman's Reality Club. Back in the sixties John had been the creative mind in charge of selling the movie *Head*. His idea for a poster was just a picture of a head staring at the camera, and I guess Bert and Bob couldn't think of anyone to pose, so Brockman himself became the head on the poster.

By the time we moved to Nambé, Brockman had been having Reality Club luncheons for a few years, in which good thinkers assembled and, as he described it, "asked each other the questions they were asking themselves" and listened to a short talk by a distinguished intellectual. They were ordinarily held in a comfortable meeting room in a good restaurant, and the few Reality Club meetings I had been at were impressive. I had invited John to use the Gihon Gallery in Nambé for one of these Reality Club meetings, and that meeting turned out to be stimulating as well as a lot of fun.

The Gihon board thought that perhaps formalizing this type

of event would work as a program for the foundation. It would be called the Council on Ideas. We would bring together a few people who might not ordinarily have met each other—no fewer than three, no more than five—making an effort to ensure that all were at the same level in their chosen field. We could seek out masters and experts and talented people who would share their points of view with one another over a weekend in Santa Fe, finding points of connection and revealing possible solutions to problems. The Gihon Foundation would facilitate this meeting—just get them all in a room and see how they fit. It might help, we thought, if each discipline represented had some shared quality with the other, if there was a natural harmony between them at the outset. *Like a band*, I thought.

"Like a bouquet," Murray Gell-Mann said as we talked over the idea at dinner. Murray had won the Nobel Prize in Physics and was famous for having discovered the quark. His license plate read QUARK. He and I had met through a mutual friend, and we enjoyed each other's company. We usually had a meal together once a week.

Murray thought *bouquet* was better than *band* as a metaphor for the Council on Ideas, since the participants would not all be playing the same song; they would all be coming from the same elevated level of thought, but with different opinions and observations.

After we selected the council's participants and assembled them there among the Gihon art, the task we gave them was to identify the most important question or issue of the time, discuss it, and come up with a statement about it that we could circulate to the general public. The meetings would be held over a three-day weekend, with everyone arriving on a Friday and leaving Sunday evening or Monday morning. All expenses would be paid, and we'd offer a nice honorarium for participating. Of course, it would be very important to have just the right arrangement of just the right flowers in just the right places. The first group of participants were all leaders in their respective fields: a professor of women's studies at a large state university; two Pulitzer winners, a playwright and a journalist; and the head of a national broadcast news service. They were all happy to get the invitation and were all happy to attend. I won't mention their names, though, because that first council became a fiasco.

The weekend started off with a casual reception at the hotel, but within minutes it had turned into a brawl. Not a literal fistfight, but two of the four members were obviously and strongly opposed to each other, and both were unabashed in stating their position and fighting for it. It was not civil discourse. It was insults and deprecations mixed with name-calling and shouting. The other two watched helplessly as the mental melee continued for the next two days. Finally, those two offered a paper that said, in essence, *Be nice to each other and do good work.*

One of the scrappers asked to have their name removed from the paper and the record of the meeting, a request we honored. We also decided not to publish the paper they presented to us.

I was crushed and a little horrified at what we had wrought. It was one of the worst fears a party-giver might have, topped only by the primal fear that no one will show. I thought we should withdraw the program or, more aptly, just run screaming from the room, but in their good sense and calm assessment, the other board members said we shouldn't give up just yet.

I could see that the problems with the first Council on Ideas were due more to carelessness in curation than anything to do with the character of the people who were there. I had read their respective CVs but had failed to do a personal interview so I could get to know them socially and politically. On their own, they were lovely people, with a lot to say. They were an intellectual fit, no doubt, but politically they were far apart. The foundation had to do more to ensure that this kind of thing didn't happen again.

All the board members, Patricia and Maryanne and Vic and I, now had some new ideas about whom to ask and how to set things up. We carefully selected compatible participants for the next council meeting, and this time it was a lovefest. The paper they developed over the weekend had some real substance to it.

Brockman's Reality Club meeting at the Gihon Gallery, having fostered to some degree the Council on Ideas, had also ignited our social life in a way I had hoped for. Vic and I found a new set of friends and acquaintances we likely never would have found on our own. Douglas became a regular houseguest and, for a while, our neighbor.

The movie *Men in Black* had just opened to a huge box office, the total reverse of a Friday Night Flight, and when I saw it, I thought the time had finally come for an outer-space science-fiction comedy movie. I called Douglas and told him to see the picture and to get his agent to start calling everyone about *Hitchhiker's Guide.* The Hollywood Mind is nothing if not impressionable, jumping on any and every bandwagon, so I was confident the HMers would see the potential. Douglas and his agent were able to sell the rights to a prominent producer connected to a big studio for millions of dollars. We were thrilled.

Vic, Douglas, and I usually ate at a restaurant called Gabriel's, or on the back porch of the Ranch, which was usually loaded with neighbors and friends, many of whom worked at the Santa Fe Institute. The SFI was home to a large collection of multidisciplinary thinkers doing studies in their respective fields—physicists, biologists, economists, architects, cosmologists, and mathematicians, all exchanging notes. Chaos theory and complexity had part of their origins there. The conversations of the SFI crowd did not touch on movies or television, but they covered the stuff that Douglas and I loved: physics, metaphysics, zoology, life-and-the-universe-and-everything, and Native American jewelry. Douglas could see very far in many directions of thought, so conversations with him usually traveled far, but they were always grounded in a certain science, or at least a near-field reality.

We were not empiricists so much as scientists having a good time playing with aesthetic possibilities. Mostly we connected on the humanities and social orders, discussing how cultures improved or even started.

This was where Douglas and I danced to distraction and exhaustion. He had much more focus than I, much more ability to absorb and evaluate ideas once he saw them. I was the one who pointed out the places where we could play and go exploring. And they were usually places Douglas had not thought of. He and I created a kind of vortex between us that we rode like the walls of a midway centrifuge ride when the bottom falls out. As soon as I would point out a curious connection, he would describe the connection in the context of comedy.

The combined vibrations coming out of Santa Fe were as wacky as they were real. Our next-door neighbor in Nambé would come over from time to time with a pitcher of martinis, and he and his wife would sit and drink it all. He was an engineer, and since Nambé sat halfway between Santa Fe and Los Alamos, I asked him if he had ever worked at the Los Alamos National Lab, where they designed and built the atomic bomb. He said he was a hydraulics engineer and had worked in Los Alamos on the water system there. He had been responsible for putting together a water system big enough for all the scientists and engineers that came together while they were building the bomb, but he had never worked on the bomb itself.

A few years later, however, he confessed to us one night, after he finished a pitcher of martinis, that he had, indeed, worked on the bomb. There was a pause, silence. I was fascinated and didn't want to break the pitcher-of-martinis (POM) spell. After enough time to decide there was nothing more coming unprompted, I asked, "What did you do?"

"I was the triggerman," he said.

Gulp. "What's a triggerman?" I asked.

He said, "I designed the triggers that set off the bombs, and then I set them off."

Huge gulp. Calmly I said, "Hiroshima?"

He said no. "Bikini Atoll, for the tests. I wasn't around too much of the war effort."

As POM conversations go, it was one of the more notable in my life, and particularly relevant and poetic because years earlier I had purchased the rights to *Radio Bikini*, a documentary about testing the atomic bomb at Bikini Atoll. It was a shocking documentary, showing sailors recreationally swimming in the ocean right after and right where they had just tested a nuke. Now the man sitting next to me was saying he had been the one who pulled the trigger.

It actually came as no surprise that he was up to his eyes in the lab; it seemed like everyone around there had been, on some level. Up in Los Alamos, if I pulled into a garage or service station to have my Harley worked on, it wouldn't take long to find out that the mechanic had a PhD hanging on the wall somewhere. The town was everything I had suspected, and my next-door neighbor was a triggerman. It was odd to think of him as an under-thirty military scientist with his hands on the trigger of a nuke.

All these sorts of people got wind of the Council on Ideas over time, so for every meeting we held, the crowd grew a bit. The Santa Fe Institute was well represented on the council itself, and we all became collegial. Although I was not in their league as scientists and engineers, they liked the pool at the Ranch, and the food. As guests came and went, it was nice to be included in their social circles. The Ranch was small by Southwestern ranch standards, but there was a field big enough for softball, and the pool was only four feet deep but very large, so it was good for standing in and chatting away the hours on a hot New Mexico afternoon. When the councils met, the members would at some point take a walk around the perimeter of the Ranch, sometimes alone, sometimes two by two. I could only imagine their conversations.

Some members of the council told me it had been an important time for them. Wendy Wasserstein told me it had changed her life. Wendy was a serious playwright and had won a Pulitzer for her play *The Heidi Chronicles*, so it was not a casual or flip remark. I liked her immensely and respected her even more, so when she said that, it stopped me cold. She was one of the smartest people I ever knew, and had an infectious Stoppard laugh that sent a clear signal that she knew what you were talking about in a way that went to the core of the idea, and she became an immediate partner in the discussion. She elaborated on having encountered ideas and having to focus in a way that was new to her and, she insisted again, life-changing. She said she had gone back home and written *The Sisters Rosensweig* in the afterglow of the meeting. When she told me that, I had the idea that the Council on Ideas might continue all my life.

Another member, the theoretical biologist Stuart Kauffman, wrote in a book about the council he was on and how meeting the poet N. Scott Momaday there had a big effect on him. This was another example for me of the solid worth of the foundation and the program. It was encouraging to get positive results after such a rocky start, and gave a particular boost to my understanding of philanthropy and of the currency of ideas.

Nevertheless, in time the program started to sag a bit. The meetings were starting to grow in recognition and attendance, but as more and more people came to the presentation of the position paper, the event started to look like a county fair. Toward the end of the 1990s, after the PBS lawsuit was settled, the meetings took on an air that was more like a party than a serious deliberation. I didn't know what to make of this. I asked the board what they thought, and we discussed it at meals and meetings while the Council on Ideas was going on. Vic and I talked at length about it, and the conversation never quite landed on what was wrong, only that something was. I didn't expect the position papers from the meetings to make headline news or be a part of legislative debate, but I did hope they would be taken seriously at face value. There were real words on those pages.

But the public discussion of the papers had taken on a bit of the shrill tone of 1970s talk radio or modern-day Internet comments, with people shouting over each other around a half-baked point of view. The fact that each position paper was generated over a period of time by careful thinkers who had given it their full attention and best analysis didn't have the weight I thought it would. Instead, as the crowd grew at each presentation, the questions became more confrontational. There were "just your opinion" polemics, even as the atmosphere became more high carnival with small talk. I actually put up signs at one of the position-paper presentations that said "No Small Talk."

What was happening was a kind of low-grade Celebrity Psychosis, but at an institutional level. I had assumed that large corporations, universities, and even nation-states were susceptible to CP, but I was seeing how even a mild case can transfer from an organization to its constituents and members. In its ability to distort reality, Celebrity Psychosis was stronger than I imagined. The more press and public attention the little councils got, the more they assumed their findings were important.

In the early 1990s, the PBS lawsuit hung over my head, like the sword of Damocles on a cobweb instead of a horse hair. From morning till night I fought hard to keep from getting depressed. The Council on Ideas and the friends I made in Santa Fe, at SFI, and at the Los Alamos National Lab had served to keep my spirits up, so watching the council getting tattered and tired was distressing.

The final Council on Ideas, in 1998, was more of a bacchanal than a meeting of great minds creating the world. By this time journalists were attending with intent to feast on ridicule, and we were low-hanging fruit. As word spread, the press would come either uninvited or in the company of distant invitees. The final council was one of a few portentous events that caused Vic and me to precipitously sell the Ranch and move to Monterey.

Three other orbital events were starting to exert a disturbing and distorting mass effect on one another, revealing more and more of the underbelly of the Nambé area. We learned about some of our unseen neighbors—what their activities were, what their lives were like, and even things about ourselves that we had not known.

Orbit A: I had chartered a helicopter to get from the Ranch to Albuquerque on an urgent errand. The only available charters were from the owners of a tiny Robinson helicopter trainer in ABQ. They could pick me up at the Ranch and get me back quick, but the copter was so small I couldn't take anyone else or any luggage, not even a briefcase. I only needed to act quickly. I didn't need to read; I would just sightsee for the duration of the short trip.

Unexpectedly, as we lifted off from the front field of the

Ranch, I saw for the first time who my neighbors were—and where they were. The terrain of New Mexico is full of caves and little canyons and arroyos, and it is hard to see what is tucked away until you are right next to it or high in the air above it. It makes for good outlaw territory, as it was in the 1800s. Hovering a few hundred feet over the Ranch, I realized that one of my neighbors had a junkyard full of cars that stretched over acres and acres of ground—stacks of rusted, wrecked, and rotting cars right next to each other. My little house and gallery sat on one end of the neighbor's ranch like the bump on a pickle.

We routinely heard gunshots coming from that junkyard area—and not only gunshots but gunfights, from all around our neighborhood. They were disturbing, to say the least, and frightening. The gunshots were distant, but something else—a smell—was nearby and ever-present. Sometimes it was strong, other times hardly noticeable, but I had not been able to tell what it was, since I had not yet had the experience of smelling methamphetamine preparation. It took years before I understood what the strange fumes were from.

Even the sounds of the night were of nature in turmoil and distress. Lying out under the stars of the clear New Mexico skies one night, I realized that the sounds of nature here were as loud as the sounds of downtown Manhattan; there were the howls and screams of predator on prey, distant echoes of anguish, packs of howling coyotes, urgent sirens, and of course the gunshots. Add the junkyard smell to this and I was starting to wonder just exactly where I had landed.

I knew there were reports of racial tensions here between Native Americans, Hispanics, and Caucasians, but I didn't realize how intense those tensions were until I had lived there for ten years. It might have been exacerbated by the locale. I was told by a local sheriff that the towns surrounding the reservations had some of the heaviest drug traffic in the US and were an intersection for unimaginable crime. All this was years before I saw *Breaking Bad*. When I first saw that show, I recall thinking about how much it reminded me of my junkyard neighbors.

Orbit B: Chris Langton, a friend and neighbor, lived just up the road a ways from me and was working on various projects at the Los Alamos National Lab, notably doing work on artificial life. He had written some impressive books on chaos theory and software based on the idea of swarms and simulations of cellular automata. He enjoyed playing blues harp and some slide guitar, and we would spend time together playing music in between discussions of a more complex order. Chris was keenly aware of the technology of the times and was a competent and practiced user of all of it. From him I learned a lot about programming and software in general, and about the society technology had created, and was creating, around itself.

Chris called me one day in the late 1990s to make me aware of a conference of leading-edge virtual world builders; it would be happening online, in a virtual world created by a little VR company named Active Worlds. I was fascinated and said that if he would help me, I would love to attend. He said it would take some powerful computing and the only way in was over the Internet.

We got a few computers and set them up with the proper software, and on the day of the conference we went in with several hundred other attendees from around the Internet. It was all virtual. Each of us had avatars as our in-world representatives. They were simple, almost stick figures, but they were in the right proportion to the virtual buildings; everything fit in size and perspective like a real-life conference hall. We walked the virtual halls and talked with other guests' avatars until the crowd got so large that the software crashed and the whole thing came to a stop.

This was long before the high-speed Internet and Moore's law–levels of storage had come into being, but in that little sample I thought I saw the future of the web. It was a simulator of the highest order, and in the right hands it could deliver a culture and society of colossal scale, with vast implications. The Virtual World Web. It was a toy at that time, but like a simple magnet, it possessed limitless potential connections in ways unimagined. If these predictions were true, it would be the foundation of a new medium.

In 1992, one of the council's position papers had said, "A world civilization is emerging. It will call forth our best. This culture, sustained by a transnational myth structure, must be generated with faith and imagination, not left to the slogans of advertising. We are being called to an enormous adventure. We are in the archaic stages of an historical integration that can lead to a new heroic age."

In these virtual worlds, I could imagine a network of unprecedented proportions facilitating the development of that "transnational myth structure" in ways the present 2-D flat-screen world could not. The virtual world created total immersion. Human activities—walking, dancing, sitting and talking—existed within a virtual space created to inspire, filled with beautiful architecture, sculpture, and renditions of nature herself. The potential for live events—storytelling, demonstrations, lectures and readings, forums and salons—was almost inconceivable, and I wanted to explore this new world in detail. I decided that if I wanted to be a part of, or a benefit to, this emerging "world civilization," I should build a virtual world on my own and start experimenting right away. I wondered how Gihon might be involved.

I built my first virtual world in late 1998, just before the PBS suit went to trial. I had so much to learn then, and still do, about what the culture and art of this new medium might be, but I wanted to open the technology to the use of not only gamers but people looking for connections and developing ideas—people who were starting something like the counterculture bands of past decades within this new cyberculture.

At the time, the web was crawling with anonymous, unwelcome opinions and overtures, and it felt like the unchecked actions of trolls and miscreants would get worse as the Internet got bigger. The useful and safe and curated environments would become a haven, a place to find friends and colleagues, collaborators, and audiences of like minds. Maybe even a better home for another Reality Club or Council on Ideas.

An artfully and benevolently crafted distributed network within virtual reality could open tremendous possibilities for unification, understanding, and cooperation among cultures. It would be not just another content carrier on Earth's own developing neural network; it would be interplanetary, a way not only to support the needs of a biological organism as we settled neighboring planets but to establish spirituality, humanity, and the fundamental sciences and arts of a sustainable culture.

Here indeed was another opportunity to assist women in this endeavor, right in line with the Gihon Foundation's mission to acknowledge the rights of women "morally, civilly, and socially."

I had written a novel some years earlier, in the mid-1990s, called *The Long Sandy Hair of Neftoon Zamora*, using HTML to create a text that had words, music, pictures, and video, all linked and cross-referenced around a story. It was the first long novel I wrote and the first time I tried intersecting forms around a simple single idea in such an extensive way. *The Prison* had mixed two media—text and music—years earlier, in 1974, and had given me enough insight into a mixed-media format that I was comfortable juggling ideas across multiple platforms. In 1994, I wrote *The Garden* around the same approach, listening to music and reading text, and had two parts of a trilogy.

But the virtual world moved me into another dimension and opened new possibilities. I set up an office/studio/warehouse in a small commercial district in Santa Fe, installed equipment and software, and went about building Videoranch, a website and virtual world.

There were a few hearty souls who visited Videoranch and started traveling around this new world, even though there wasn't much to do. The primary content was social. The virtual world—the chat rooms and avatars and streaming music and videos—held a kind of novel interest, but they quickly became background to the real content of social interaction, culture, and the arts. The shared experience was the value of the Virtual World Web. The medium was indeed the message.

I could understand why Walt Disney had built theme parks and why the Hollywood Mind followed him in. Amusement parks, as they were called, had been around for years, with food and rides, but Disney infused his art into his worlds and delivered entertaining content in a carefully created, well-maintained, and well-operated shared environment.

I could imagine Videoranch extending its virtual world into real places with real food and lodging, real stargazing and music, where people might meet and create a civilization and society from the shared experience they enjoyed in the virtual world.

Orbit C: The forest at Bandelier National Monument caught fire. The fire came up next to the Los Alamos National Lab, by some accounts very close to the weapons-grade plutonium stored there. Some scientists have said, and I have no reason to doubt them, that if plutonium catches fire, it is no big deal. But to my mind, there was something wrong with the recipe of a forest fire next to Los Alamos. I thought that whatever might happen if they mixed would be abnormally bad.

Vic and I could clearly see the town of Los Alamos and the lab from the Ranch, and we stood and watched the ground around it burn. At one point we saw a huge haze—it was more green than purple, but in any case, it was not smog—rise up and cover the city. It was of unimaginable size and of a color like nothing I had ever seen. Watching that jaw-dropping haze and light rise up over the entire city of Los Alamos, I suspected it was a glow radiating from something enormous.

I called Murray and asked if he might know what it was or where it was coming from and whether it was dangerous, and he said he didn't know. He thought it might be halation of the lights at the Los Alamos ballpark as they shone through the fog that sometimes hovered over the city. I responded that it looked like light of some kind, but I could not imagine it was from a ballpark. As any magician will tell you, the senses are not to be trusted, but something went off in my mind that said I needed to get out of there and take as many people with me as wanted to go. That haze was weirdly wrong, and it disturbed me. It might have been dangerous as well, but that wasn't as problematic for me as the simple presence of something so unnatural and abnormal—an unexplainable anomaly. It was the high-tech counterpart of the huge junkyard next to the simple little ranch that was my home.

These intersecting orbits had a dramatic effect on Vic and me, and I had the unobstructed thought that now was the time to leave Nambé particularly and New Mexico in general. Whatever was going on up the hill, I wanted no part of it, especially since not a word was being reported about it in local or national news coverage of the fire.

Los Alamos is in one of the most beautiful areas I have ever been in. Vic and I traveled through there many times on our motorcycles as we toured through Bandelier and on to places farther north. For a biker, that whole section of the US was dream riding in the summer, with long, gently curving, traffic-free roads and magnificent views of gorgeous countryside in all directions. But Los Alamos itself had a dark underpinning due to the weapons research that went on there, and more specifically, due to the *types* of weapons they were exploring.

Driving through Los Alamos, my first impression was that it was like the town in David Lynch's *Blue Velvet*: beautiful people in a beautiful place, along with something decidedly dangerous. I wondered many times after talking to my triggerman neighbor *how* world-destroying technology could be secured—or *if* it could be secured at all. I imagined that policing such risk might be beyond the reach of ordinary processes. Living nearby—driving through town, shopping there—started to confirm this notion.

Now, with the sky on fire, I had an almost panicked sense that Vic and I and the dogs needed to leave immediately. We could come back for our stuff. I called a charter company and arranged for a flight out of the regional Santa Fe airport for me, Vic, our new dog, Roy, and our longtime dog, Lily.

It was a small, out-of-the-way airport with a runway big enough for most jets, and the fixed-base-operator building, the airport offices, and the terminal were crammed with firefighters, air support, and news media. As a pair of weary firefighters came in from a water-bombing run, I asked them how it was going up there. At that moment the TV in the terminal lounge reported that the Bandelier fire had been brought under control and all was well. The two of them looked at each other and then at me, then rolled their eyes and walked away without a word. As we lifted off we could see the Bandelier fire and the huge plumes of black smoke rising from the mesas.

Three hours later, Vic and I were in Carmel-by-the-Sea. The house we had bought on the Internet, to the consternation of my real-estate-agent friend, was in poor shape and would need lots of work, but it was habitable, and a perfect rescue stop. Sort of. The first rainstorm revealed that the roof was essentially nonexistent. Water poured through as if from a showerhead. But I have to say that I loved it. The whole house was made of clear-heart redwood with quarreled windows and an old shake roof, a small, traditional house only blocks away from the city center and only four blocks from the Carmel dog beach. The city had arms that enfolded us protectively. I was happy to be back. Vic seemed satisfied as well.

I set up a little studio in the garden toolshed in the backyard of the house and started trying to write some music, but it was slow going. The extensive setup in Santa Fe and Nambé would take some time to unwind. The ranch house and the foundation office had expanded and were dug in deep. Videoranch had to go on hold as well, as far as any real artistic exploration or development was concerned, until we got settled more permanently in Carmel.

Working on the Carmel house with Vic was a pleasure. She was grown up by now, and there was harmony in the household. Douglas came to visit often, but he couldn't stay with us since there was no room, and by this time he had a house just down the highway in Santa Barbara. The tremors of the New Mexico ranch receded into an empty calm, as we spent less and less time there, returning only a few times to gather things, move out, and list it for sale.

In the Carmel environs I started to notice a difference in the way I was treated. There had been a slow disassembly of the CP helmet, and soon I realized I was not only invisible to the general public, but I was also categorized as an old man as I went about my day. It was a new world for me. I liked it in one way because as the personal recognition factor diminished to zero, the CP went with it to a large extent—at least now it wasn't fostering self-delusion, and only the infrequent unexpected glance came my way from a stranger. For the most part I was invisible, except for the prejudice that greets an old man, and that was easy to live with in a community of other old men. Not only was I invisible, I was also able to do a lot of my work in secret. I carried my own little old-white-man room with me wherever I went, and I hid out in there. My own interesting (to me) internal colloquy never stopped, and in order to keep from coming across as crazy, all I had to do was keep my mouth shut.

The transition of Videoranch from the physical plant in Santa Fe to Monterey went smoothly. We set up shop at a commercial business park and installed the computers and data links we needed to fire up the new Videoranch 3D—VR3D. The original members of Videoranch saw no difference, of course, since it was all virtual, but I kept feeling the need to solve the problem of an "empty room." A virtual world was mildly interesting to most people, but with nothing to do inside it, most of them lost interest quickly. Gameplay was the quick fix, but I worried that the virtual world would disappear into the mechanics of the game.

I was more interested in culture building. I set my sights on trying to embed live events into the world seamlessly, where the virtual world would essentially disappear at the same time that live performances actually appeared in-world. These performances could be the cultural hearth fires that people need to gather around to share and communicate.

I fashioned a technique and process for embedding this real-time live-streaming into the virtual world and started hosting live shows every weekend. It was simple enough and required very little coding, mostly simple HTML and some off-the-shelf computer and video equipment. The first performer in there was Jason, one of my sons, and then I hired a local blues band from Santa Cruz, who took the name Ranch Dressing and started playing every weekend in the studio lab; from there they were piped out over the Internet and into all the world.

At one of the shows, an acquaintance who was in the high-tech sector said that I should apply for a patent on the technology and the process. I had no idea about how that might work or if the process was even patentable, but I took the advice and started checking around. I was steered toward a patent lawyer named Lee Van Pelt, and I asked him to take a look. Vic and I drove up to his office, and I showed him the site and waved my arms and talked about the future, and after a little thought he said, "I think you may have a patent or two here. Maybe even a general patent. But be prepared, the journey is arduous and expensive."

It was daunting, to say the least. I had never tackled anything like this, but the notion felt solid enough, and Lee seemed to be offering good counsel. He cautioned me several more times that the road was hard and expensive, and that more patent applications were denied than accepted. Duly warned, and after giving it some thought, I told him to go ahead.

Then there was an ominous moment, and though it was confusing and slight, it registered a feeling of dread in me that I could not explain. When Lee asked how we wished to list the patent, I said jointly, with me and Victoria. But Victoria said, "No, just in Michael's name." This was unexpected and so unusual that for a moment I was afraid something was terribly wrong. I looked at Vic, but she waved my concern away. Lee did as Vic instructed. This was early 2007.

Vic and I continued to work on Videoranch and the programming. One of her many duties was booking the acts for the concerts, and we tried sundry types of live events, but there was a struggle with the technology. This sector of the tech world was moving fast, and while the VR3D content idea had merit, my sails were not cast in the winds of the latest technology, and the VR3D virtual world began to lag behind developments in the software, particularly gaming. I thought I needed to push hard to find the right path through this tech jungle and knew it would take my full attention. The crowds were growing steadily and seemed to want more, and the idea of the Virtual World Web was clarifying in my head as a more and more realizable way for people to connect and enjoy each other.

The Gihon Foundation was still awaiting opportunity. The decision to stop the Council on Ideas left room to start another new program from a clean sheet of paper. My life and the lives of others seemed enriched by social connectivity, and any event that promulgated that was a candidate.

I remembered well my Jimi Hendrix Experience and the mark that performance made on me. Watching the gift of a pure idea live and in real time had no equal; nothing could compare to it. A program for the performing arts seemed like the next step for Gihon, so we set that up, even though it was early to set the precise guidelines. To bring people together around ideas, feed them, and help them feed each other with such a program seemed out of reach, but it felt like an idea waiting to happen. A few more pieces needed to fall in place, and we needed a few more flowers in the bouquet. I could give it some time to grow in thought.

There was, alas, an alien plant that had begun to grow in that garden, and it was, unknown to me, slowly taking everything over.

14

In March 2007, I came into Vic's home office to find a note taped to her computer informing me that she had left me. It was only a couple of lines, but anyone who has lived this moment knows how the destruction sets in like a slow-motion airplane crash. I was inundated with all the usual emotions we go through if we ever hit this whitewater. She had left for a man she met on the net—in Videoranch.

She came back for a visit, but not for long. In 2010, she was gone for good. Videoranch, the home fires, and my whole life slowed, a boat with sails luffing in the middle of a stark and windless ocean, desolate with loneliness and desertion. Within this dark hour, the cloud of being an old man lost any of its comfort and occluded any light that might have been left.

It was not a good time to do anything but sit and wait—on what, I did not know. Friends told me time would heal this pain. I knew it would, but that was little help. I was confused. I had committed unconditionally to Vic, never lied to her nor betrayed her. Nothing was further from my mind than the philandering and lies of my earlier days. I had been certain my reformation would lift me out of my disastrous past-life faults. It had occurred to me that she might be the unfaithful one, but I had loved her to a fault.

As the days and months dragged on, and the enormity of the infidelity became more apparent, there was a collapse of finances as well as the home. In the wake of the 2008 financial crisis, the financial markets had pulled way back, decimating the value of my portfolio, and the housing market had fallen as home equity and mortgages turned completely upside down because of the subprime mortgage fiascoes. With Victoria gone, I was now alone and having to face problems and situations—solo, and squarely—that I had always had someone to talk to about. This was entirely new for me.

I began to reach out further than I ever had in my thought, looking for an order to life. I was searching in waters I had never sailed in, looking for any landing I might find, thinking, praying, cogitating, ruminating, meditating, and sometimes almost drowning in the waters of High Lonesome. I vowed to search my own thought and seek the part of the relationship that I had failed at, to take full responsibility for it. I refused to involve myself in ongoing self-pity, to fall into recriminations, to seek retributions, or to entertain the ideas of fault-finding or blame. I could see that Vic had hit a very bad streak herself, that she must have been unhappy, and I felt a deep compassion for her. I knew it must be a hard time for her too. I would not allow condemnation to take me over, either for Vic or myself. I would not complain and I would stay away from rough waters and hold on until life got easier, but the next stage came without a warning, and events were obviously going to get worse *before* they got better.

In a perfect rendition of Job, my sight began to rapidly degrade and I lost my sight to cataracts, and at the same time lost my flexibility to an undiagnosed condition that crippled me, making it difficult and painful to walk. I was essentially helpless, a captive in my home. After a few months I knew I had to make some effort to remedy the situation, and while I knew that doctors could not heal a broken heart, I thought maybe they could heal a blind cripple, which is what I had become.

There is a common and widespread misunderstanding about the teachings of Science that adherents are not allowed to go to a doctor or take their children to a doctor. This is false. Christian Scientists can do whatever their conscience dictates, just like any other scientist. Going to a doctor violates no church rule and is not even censured. Many Christian Scientists use doctors for various reasons. The *Manual of the Mother Church* mentions in the bylaws only that Christian Scientists should obey the laws of the land, and it specifically states that if the law requires they seek medical help, or if it requires that their children are examined, treated, or vaccinated by doctors, then the Christian Scientist should comply.

This misunderstanding about Science and doctors comes from many sources, but it is never less than false. Seeking a doctor's help does not lessen the effectiveness or truth of the teaching or render it ineffective. I called an ophthalmologist and he removed the cataracts, dropped a pair of intraocular lenses into my eyes, and I see perfectly now. It was a relief, and I was grateful for the timing, because even though I couldn't walk, at least I could see.

The crippled part was weirder and more complicated. I went to several specialists, many of whom had differing opinions about what was causing me to lose the use of my left hand and to drag my right foot. Both conditions were painful in the extreme and did not seem to be improving, but all the doctors offered were pain pills. These were somewhat effective, and I thankfully got a few nights' sleep, but I knew the condition was not improving and the pills weren't putting me on the path to health or being cured. At best the pain pills were a kind of dreadful maintenance. The various doctors all had different prognoses, some of them dire. I had little reason to hope, but I did not accept that this was a condition I would continue to live with. I did not know how or why, but I had an abiding sense that all of these trials would pass somehow.

In these difficult moments I remembered a time with a doctor friend of mine whom I knew socially in New Mexico and liked very much. She traveled around the reservations giving free medical aid and treatment to the Native Americans. One evening over a long dinner with her and her husband, she told a story about something that had upset her during that day's work. A family brought in a grandmother who was in the last stages of a disease. My friend—let's call her April—said it was heartbreaking to tell this family that the disease their grandmother had was incurable and that the grandmother would shortly die.

I said, "But, April, why did you say that?"

"Because it was true, and I thought they deserved the truth," she said.

"No it isn't. The truth is that you didn't know how to cure what she had. Not that it is incurable. There is a big difference."

She pondered this and agreed. "Yes. That is what I should have said—that I don't know how to cure it."

Each doctor I went to had diagnoses that were variations of this same story. While they did not think it was fatal in the near term, because they didn't really know what it was, they thought it might be incurable. Some thought there was a chance the condition might self-heal, which I assumed was their term of art for "go away by itself," but most of them disagreed on what the condition was.

On advice from a friend, I headed up to Stanford Medical Center and asked one of the doctor-teachers there to take a look. He seemed smart and somewhat acquainted with the symptoms, but had not encountered this before. He said he thought it was something to do with my immune system. He said he would prescribe treatment if I would allow his students to come and study the condition on one or two of my visits. If it was what he thought it might be, then the only treatment he knew of was to shut the immune system down with a particular, and very expensive, drug and let the immune system restore itself in a kind of reboot. He thought that might cure the condition but was unsure.

I was working and praying mentally every day as I had been taught, but with no change in my condition, so I agreed to put myself in his care, take the medicine, and see where it went. He prescribed a drug, gave me a regimen for taking it, and told me not to stray from the plan.

One rule that Christian Scientist practitioners are taught is not to treat a medical condition that a doctor is treating. The two treatments are antithetical, and while CS treatment may be the higher way for some, a kind and caring doctor should be left alone to provide the care they think is best. To apply the science of mental healing at the same time a physician is using *materia medica* is at least unethical and potentially dangerous, like mixing two different drugs from two different doctors, neither of whom knows of the other's presence, prescriptions, or practice.

In agreeing to take the medicine, I had to agree with myself to abandon my practice of Science for healing and lean on the good intentions of the doctor and his immune-system reboot. I took the week's worth of pills, but after taking them and waiting the prescribed time, the only change in my condition was that I felt a little worse. There was certainly no physical improvement or even any hope, so I told the doctor that I didn't want to continue with his treatment. He was very unhappy about it, prescribed me some pain pills that he said would help if things got bad, and told me to come back if I changed my mind. I didn't tell him I intended to depend on metaphysics and its science, because I didn't think it would have been helpful to him or me.

I stayed in bed for several weeks, doing the best I could on my own, calling various Christian Science practitioners and getting nowhere, and finally I gave up. I had practical, and very touching, emotional help from friends, who brought me food, drove me around, and watched over me. I had some increasing movement, and the pain lessened, and it seemed like my body might be healing naturally, like a paper cut or a scraped elbow heals.

I had left the Videoranch pilot light burning but stopped all the concerts, and the visitors shrank to only a few diehards who liked having their own private chat room. I tried to think about the business and finance, about art and music and the foundation, but as anyone who has hit these health bumps knows, everything stops until things get better. And, somewhat to my surprise, things actually started to improve. I spent hours daily in painless study and prayer and contemplation.

Slowly I saw some normalcy return, and as I got my movement back in my hand, I was also able to get up and get around. I recalled during these long days of mental work another event in my life regarding health and science.

A musician who connected with me after a concert during the Kathryn years had become a good friend of mine. He was highly educated in music, trained in the classics and well traveled, working with large orchestras. We had a couple of lunches and some social time together in the days following that concert, and after a while I invited him to our house in the Carmel Highlands.

He was a gourmand and a great cook and offered to cook a meal for us, so we happily accepted, offering to assist. Our initial conversations had revolved around the high arts and metaphysics, and I told him something of my history with Science and some of the Eastern teachings. He was an Orthodox Jew, as was his wife, and had deep family ties to Israel and regularly practiced his faith. He was a genuine seeker of truth and was curious to learn wherever he could. After our talks, he bought a copy of the Christian Science textbook and began reading it. He was well into the book and said, while he was cooking, that he wanted to pursue learning as much as he could about it. He wanted to practice it if he could.

As he was talking, he produced several large bottles and began setting out all his pills in carefully ordered rows on the kitchen counter. There were a dozen or more of varying shapes and colors, and I jokingly said something like "At least you'll save a lot of money on pills." I was amazed when he paused, looked at the pills that were set out, gathered all of them up, and then threw the entire setup and all the bottles into the trash. "I'll just start now," he said, and we both laughed, but I was uneasy. It was a dramatic act for sure, and I silently hoped he hadn't done something he would regret.

He told me later that he had come to dinner that night having come from the doctor, who had diagnosed the large lump on his ankle as malignant and spreading. I told him I had no recollection of this.

He said, "You told me to throw away the pills. Those were all chemotherapy medicine. I threw them away, and the lump fell away shortly and it never recurred. Surely you remember the large lump on my ankle?"

I did remember that. But the remark I made about the pills was meant lightheartedly, as an encouraging remark. "I never knew you were diagnosed with cancer," I told him.

"Oh, yes," he said, "a painful malignant tumor. Don't you remember how I limped? Cancer."

This event had rolled around in my head over the years, and was coupled with Babaji's instruction to the mother of the sick child. But I could not shake the feeling that in all the instances of healing I experienced or witnessed I had made no active effort. Where healing was going on, it was going on without my personally knowing about it, or how to do it. Yet I had no doubt that there was a healing and restorative power operating. That much was obvious.

I felt confident it wasn't supernatural in any sense, just natural good taking care of her own, replacing the beliefs of a mortal with the facts and forces of the supremely natural world. It was a world that, to some very small degree, I had come to understand was infinite. It was spiritual, and my access to it was through the spirit of Science, through arts and culture.

In this infinite, continuous nature, existence could reconcile the Standard Model of particle physics to a greater infinite whole, the way mathematics reconciles definite integers to Infinite Number, or the way definite colors are reconciled to Infinite Light, or definite tones to Infinite Sound. I could understand this plurality even though to my struggling and sometimes pain-filled human body and mind it seemed far-fetched—and at times irrelevant. Nevertheless, I was certain something was going on that kept my thought active in the direction of infinite good, that perhaps the omnipresence of life was bringing something to light in my local experience that was healing me and those around me. The past became a finitude. The future became a fiction. Here and now, the living, infinite mind and soul became truth to me and opened the door to freedom.

Over the next several weeks, my health returned to normal, and I also began to recover by degrees from the terribly broken heart I had been nursing. I was grateful to feel the physical comfort and lively presence of real good.

I could walk. I could see. I could play. I could sing. As well as I ever could. I put together a little tour of my solo work to exercise this burgeoning health and to avail myself of the idea that the devil has no access to the singing man.

It was time to move into the next phase of my life: More study. More prayer and meditation. More mathematics, more research and development. More performing. More playing.

It was also important to spend focused time on restarting Videoranch and getting the site back up to standards and in sync with the times, the media, and technology. To create an operating structure for it that would make it available to humankind, wherever they might land. There was a good reason to do this now. A new day had dawned for Videoranch and VR3D. New technology was available and I could see a way for Gihon to benefit the endeavor, to point to new directions and models of business building and development.

Even with this bright horizon my spirits were flagging. There was a nagging sense of something amiss about the last few years, especially coming as they did so soon after I felt such progress toward understanding an infinite existence. It would seem that two of the more dire and painful events in my life had just occurred, and they had been particularly intense because they were so unexpected. All of the progress I felt was wrapped in the shadow of doubt.

At length there came a moment of recognition that lifted me out of the despair completely and pointed me to the ever-presence of good, to life just at hand that was infinite and perfect, however obscure it might be to the physical sense. In that moment, I was poised on the point of one question: How had these awful and painful things happened to me while I was right in the deepest part of my dedication and practice? The answer came quickly, and aligned perfectly to my need: I had hit these hard times precisely *because* of my dedication and loyalty to this life-giving truth of existence.

It was a strange and powerful recognition that the suffering I experienced was the first fulfillment of the continuous desire to know more of the living truth and the science of healing. It was as if the thing I was praying for was hidden by the effort I was making. I needed stern guidance and strong encouragement to make me let go of that which was hiding it. I understood that I would not have made such a change in my efforts had the lessons been any less painful or dramatic. Considered in the range of human sufferings, mine were trivial, but the answer to my cries for relief was perfectly aligned to my need.

That was not quite all of it. There was a closer component of this struggle that had revealed itself, which I could now appreciate and see as part of the new direction of my life as the panorama of it unfolded: It was a simple truth that came from a deep wellspring. Often, at times closest to total collapse, we are conformed to a fitness to receive.

A few years after Victoria left, I came into the Videoranch studios one morning to set up for some visitors who were stopping by. It was a few days after Christmas, and the studio was cold and a little gloomy in the early-morning fog. The room had a good green-screen stage I had installed for VR3D, and we had produced over two hundred concerts there when we were testing the basic technology to make everything work. But the stage was mostly unused now. In the years of sadness and illness, I had shut the whole enterprise down to a pilot light, a trickle of activity.

I knew the early-morning coastal fog would burn off in a

few hours, and it was forecast to be a sunny day. I started the coffee and turned on the lights, and my assistant, Jessica, came in. I had met her when she was eighteen and living with her mother in Santa Fe. She came to work shortly after that and stayed with me, helping Vic and me while we set the studio up. Now she had a husband and a daughter, so she only worked part time to help me keep things in order. Thankfully, she had also become a dear friend and part of my extended family. Jess went upstairs to her office and returned a few minutes later with the mail, a stack of letters.

I flipped through them quickly and saw one with a return address from the patent office. My heart sank. The patent lawyer, Van Pelt, had not been wrong about how hard it would be to secure a patent for my VR3D technology; I had gotten five rejections so far on this trail, each one with a new challenge to the ideas and process. They were tough letters to get, and all had required arduous work by Van Pelt's office to meet each challenge, cost many thousands of dollars, and took many months to process. It was now more than five years since the original application, and as I held the envelope in my hand, I felt sure I had reached the dead end of the road.

But this letter was different. It said the United States Patent Office had awarded me the patent and issued patent number US8339418 to me for the embedding of real-time video into a virtual environment. I was wild with joy, so happy that the strength of my reaction surprised me. The patent validated the work in just the way I'd hoped, but the effect was immense. It was the only patent I had ever gotten, the only one I had tried for, and while other inventors have hundreds or thousands of them this one award gave me a sense of accomplishment like no other. "Holy smokes!" I said to Jessica, and she and I laughed the hallelujah laugh—the laugh beyond all delight.

Some time later I gave the patent to the Gihon Foundation.

It was a great way for me to pick up where my mother had left off, a way to give the patent the wings of the infinite and a way to give the patent to the artists who used it as a performance medium. The whole process, I came to realize, had been a gift.

Even the letter from the patent office had contained a clue. When I reread it a few hours later to make sure it wasn't a mistake, I noticed that the patent had been awarded on Christmas Day. I had no idea the patent office was even open then—much less issuing patents. But there it was, right at the top: December 25, 2012.

A Tuesday.

acknowledgments

This book would not be here but for the inestimable help and support of Rob Horning, John Brockman, Kevin Doughten, Jessica Kent, and P. J. O'Rourke, for which I am deepy grateful.

—MN

photo credits

Page 3: *Reproduced with permission of Punch Ltd., www.punch.co.uk*

Page 23: Me and Jimi sitting on a bed in Micky's hotel room, probably somewhere in the US after a concert. Mick took the picture with a little Kodak Instamatic. *Photo: © Micky Dolenz*

Page 40: Richard Cullen Adair—my great-uncle Chick by marriage to my great-aunt Aida, my mother's aunt. *Photo: Courtesy of the author*

Page 55: Phyllis Barbour and I on our wedding day in San Antonio, six months before our first child, Christian, was born. *Photo: Courtesy of the author*

Page 71: Me and the guys—Davy, Micky, and Peter—probably in RCA Studio in Hollywood. The man behind Davy is likely Hank Cicalo, the engineer. *Photo: © Henry Diltz*

Page 98: Me and Jack backstage—maybe Salt Lake City or maybe Cow Palace in San Francisco—maybe Mars. Who knew? *Photo: © Henry Diltz*

Page 122: The First National Band—Red Rhodes, left, then John London, John Ware, and me. In some dirt lot, next to a truck. *Photo: © Henry Diltz*

PHOTO CREDITS

Page 140: Baba Hari Das. I called him Babaji, he called me Michaelji—although not out loud. I don't know where or when this was taken. Probably before I met him. Maybe not. *Photo: Pradeepwb—the author's camera, CC BY-SA 3.0., https://en.wikipedia.org/w/index.php?curid=43640608*

Page 166: A still from the "Rio" shoot. One would have to watch my instructional video "World of Colour" to know what color Nancy Gregory's dress is. She's on my left. *Photo: © Henry Diltz*

Page 200: My mother, Bette, and I in Houston. I think I was around five or six years old here. *Photo: Courtesy of the author*

Page 225: Me and Garry Shandling deciding what to do next, on the set of *Television Parts,* doing the car mechanic comedy video. *Photo: © Henry Diltz*

Page 242: Me and Skippy-the-Plane outside my Santa Monica Airport hangar in a pilot-plane embrace. *Photo: Courtesy of the author*

Page 267: Me and Douglas Adams outside the Tesuque Village Market on a cold, snowy day in New Mexico. Douglas is on the left. TVM was a breakfast place not far from my little ranch in Nambé. D. and I ate breakfast there regularly. *Photo: Courtesy of the author*

Page 290: A giant rock on Carmel Beach that was staring at me, so I stared back. Nice, friendly rock. Reminded me of the Pietà. *Photo: © Tony Kent*

about the author

Michael Nesmith's creative innovations have touched nearly every corner of the arts. His career in music and television took him from starring in *The Monkees* to a celebrated run of albums as a solo artist and in the First National Band. He won the first ever Grammy Award given for a music video and created the TV show *PopClips*, a forerunner of what would become MTV. He produced the films *Repo Man* and *Tapeheads* and was among the first to realize the potential for home video. He was the president of the Gihon Foundation, which has organized programs such as the Council on Ideas and promoted women in the arts and STEM fields. He was the author of two novels and the founder of the Pacific Arts Corporation, which produces projects in the worlds of audio, video, and virtual reality, including Videoranch3D. Michael Nesmith died in 2021.

Printed in the United States
by Baker & Taylor Publisher Services